"Although these types of retreats are not heretical per se, Janssen clearly demonstrates the semi-Pelagian nature of these 'spiritual' retreats which he argues is incompatible with the Reformed Biblical doctrine of Luther and Calvin.

"Janssen's work is a loud wake-up call to the church and should be read by every pastor, elder, youth pastor and lay leader alike. Janssen's challenge is for the church of Jesus Christ to move beyond psychologized religion and back to the Biblical means of true Christ-centered worship which through God's Holy Spirit is the only source of real and lasting transformation."

Dr. Daniel F.A Hitchcock
Associate Professor of Psychology
Department of Psychology, Counseling, & Human Services
Geneva College
Beaver Falls, Pennsylvania

"I welcome this much needed exposé of a truly deceptive and harmful movement done in the name of Christ. I have witnessed first hand the damage done to individuals and congregations by Cursillo and TEC. Christ has ordained that His people be sanctified by His Word of truth (John 17:17) but Cursillo is able to transcend all denominational divisions and distinctives by jettisoning instruction in the Word and relying on secular, physiological techniques to produce an emotional high which is then said to be the work of the Spirit. The high cannot be maintained without continued dependence on manipulative methods. Reverend Janssen gives a well documented analysis of the psychological techniques and harmful effects of the Cursillo methodology. Church leaders need this book. All Christians should heed its warnings."

Reverend Ralph A. Pontier, Pastor
Emmanuel Reformed Church
Neerlandia, Alberta

"Warning: The secrets and surprises of Cursillo are revealed in this book! However, when movements which claim to be 'Christian' in their emphasis need to use secrecy and emotion to bring their candidates to 'catharsis', then what place is left for the Word of God? Indeed, what place is there in such movements for followers of Jesus Christ?"

Rev. Mark Verbruggen, Pastor
First Christian Reformed Church
Sioux Center, Iowa

"I was trained as a stage hypnotist and stage illusionist before going into the ministry. Later I was trained as a clinical hypnotherapist. Between these two events I attended a Protestant version of Cursillo as a Protestant Chaplain. The event was a long, thinly veiled-over religious trance induction designed to solicit a desired response. Dr. Janssen demonstrates for the reader, on several levels, why this is directly opposed to the Gospel of Jesus Christ. In a postmodern culture experience is the 'thing.' Dr. Janssen demonstrates why 'decisions for Christ' at these events do not last because they are not commensurate with the personality of the participant. The short term is hypnosis. We are shown how Cursillo imitates the Spirit of God and despite superficial 'renewal or changes' it is not the Spirit…but a spirit of this age that imitates God. Dr. Janssen shows us that Revivalists haven't exited the hypnotic stage… they simply changed their names. This is a valuable resource for anyone who has endured a Cursillo or associated Protestant event, or thinking of attending one, and will proved a profitable resource to point you back to Christ."

Dr. Christopher Faria, D.Min, Ph.D.
Senior Pastor Westminster Presbyterian Fellowship
Adjunct Faculty New Geneva Seminary
Colorado Springs, Colorado

"Scripture is quite clear: personal and church conversion, revival, renewal, and reformation come through the proclaimed word in the power of the Holy Spirit. As both Gijsbert Voetius and John Paul II knew well: the gospel does not coerce, it persuades. This has not stopped merchants and technicians of renewal from trying to short-circuit the Holy Spirit and manipulate people. Cursillo, according to the author of this well-researched and thorough study, is such a questionable technique. He tells a cautionary tale but also—rightly!—calls the church to pay attention to its unpaid bills."

John Bolt
Professor of Systematic Theology
Calvin Theological Seminary
Grand Rapids, Michigan

"They would utilize our campus up to four times a year. As a recently hired Youth Leader, I was repeatedly told by the pastor, 'They are a Christian Renewal Group.' And yet, I would witness the 'advance team' preparing for their weekend retreat: windows being blacked-out, small sleeping cubicles erected, Kleenex boxes everywhere, and a kitchen filled with snacks and sweets. As our congregation exited the Sunday morning service, these groups would emerge from the Youth Building, singing 'campy songs' to our congregation on their guitars. They seemed 'renewed;' but it also seemed awkward.

"This is why this book is extremely important! With thorough research and documentation Brian V. Janssen unveils the history, philosophy, theology, psychology, and the predictable 'clinical' results of the Cursillo weekend. Christian churches, or those invited to these weekends, MUST BE INFORMED about the techniques implemented by Cursillo, which sadly manufactures spiritual experiences that, '…have the appearance of godliness, but deny its power.' – 2 Timothy 3:5

"Does a Cursillo weekend really have the 'power' of conversion? Those attending claim that they have changed! However, *Cursillo: Little Courses in Catharsis* also has the power to convince the church what the Scriptures teach: God's grace is a gift received by simple means. To manufacture anything else apart from this cheapens the authentic renewal of God's grace by His word and Spirit."

Rev. Kent Moorlach
Communion Presbyterian Church (ARP)
Irvine, California

"Brian Janssen has not only written a fine introduction to and faithfully Reformed critique of the Cursillo movement, but also—and more importantly—in doing so has issued a well-needed challenge for Christians to think about how we, together with our culture, value experience over truth and thus increasingly write off the means of grace that God has given us. We would do well to sit down with this book and read it so that we might rightly despair of human methods and instead put our confidence in the Word and sacraments that God has provided for our faith."

Rev. Nicholas Davelaar
First Christian Reformed Church
Hospers, Iowa

"This is an important – and much needed – book. Dr. Janssen correctly analyzes the social psychological techniques used by Cursillo and other like-minded organizations that seek to promote their beliefs by manipulating their participants. The Gospel has always been about what God the Father has done through the sinless life of obedience and sacrificial death of Jesus Christ for His people. No man-made techniques, however pragmatically 'successful', will ever replace the right preaching of God's Word by those competently trained to understand and communicate it. Instead of training church members on how to get their friends and family to attend a Cursillo weekend, the church should be teaching and training its members to accurately understand the Holy Bible. Dr. Janssen has done a great service for the church of God."

David A. Wilcox, Ph.D., M.Div., LMHC
Associate Professor for Graduate Counseling Psychology
Palm Beach Atlantic University
West Palm Beach, Florida

"Through careful and thorough scholarship, and interviews with leaders and former participants Janssen provides the first and only attempt I am aware of that effectively de-mystifies the secretive 'Cursillo' type spiritual retreat movement that has swept much of the evangelical Christian church in America. He rightly classifies the methods used as psychological manipulation which creates a cathartic experience often misinterpreted as a manifestation of the Holy Spirit. Janssen correctly and convincingly dismantles the underlying philosophical and theological assumptions of this movement and reveals the naked truth that the predictable emotional responses attained are most likely a mere human phenomenon.

CURSILLO
Little Courses in *Catharsis*

CURSILLO
Little Courses in *Catharsis*

*A Critique of Cursillo,
Walk to Emmaus, Via de Cristo, Tres Dias,
De Colores, Teens Encounter Christ (TEC),
Chrysalis, Kairos, Great Banquet, Dias con
Cristo, Celebration, Challenge, Vocare,
Tirosh, Chayah, Unidos en Cristo, Chrysalis,
Alarga, The Journey, Faith Walk, Vida
Nueva, Aventura, Awakening, Camino,
Credo Recovery, Diaspora, Discipleship
Walk, Footsteps, Happening, Jubilee
Journey, Keryx, Koinonia, New Beginnings,
Paseo con Cristo, Pilgrimmage,
and other Cursillo-like Movements*

Brian V. Janssen

RESOURCE *Publications* • Eugene, Oregon

CURSILLO: LITTLE COURSES IN CATHARSIS

Copyright © 2010 Brian V. Janssen. All rights reserved. Except for brief quotations in critical publications or reviews, no part of this book may be reproduced in any manner without prior written permission from the publisher. Write: Permissions, Wipf and Stock, 199 W. 8th Ave., Eugene, OR 97401.

ISBN 13: 978-1-60608-775-6

www.wipfandstock.com

Manufactured in the U.S.A.

Unless otherwise noted, Scriptures quotations are from The Holy Bible, English Standard Version, copyright © 2001 by Crossway Bibles, a division of Good News Publishers. Used by permission. All rights reserved.

TABLE OF CONTENTS

Introduction	*The Concern About Cursillo*	1
Chapter One	*The Quest for Emotional Experience*	9
Chapter Two	*Is Cursillo a Cult?*	20
Chapter Three	*The Methodology of Mind Control*	29
Chapter Four	*The Origins of the Cursillo Method*	54
Chapter Five	*The Theology of the Cursillo Method*	62
Chapter Six	*The Techniques of the Cursillo Method*	87
Chapter Seven	*The Effects of the Cursillo Method*	106
Chapter Eight	*Other Forms of Cathartic Experiences*	120
Chapter Nine	*In Their Own Words: Sharing Cursillo Stories*	148
Chapter Ten	*Thinking Through the Stories*	179
Chapter Eleven	*The Unpaid Bills of the Church*	186
Chapter Twelve	*After the Weekend is Over*	200
Appendix A	*The Perspective of Post-Calvin Reformed Confessions and Catechisms*	212
Appendix B	*A History of Confusing Psychology with Religion*	239
Bibliography		264

Preface

Not long before this book went to press, a local Cursillo leader announced to a group of college students that he no longer attended church. He explained that he had grown beyond church, that he no longer needed what the church had to offer, and so for him the church was unnecessary. Yet in his own mind this man remained a Christian of the highest rank.

This, of course, was not surprising. Those who attend a Cursillo weekend are assured that they are now (after seventy-two hours of "training") instant Christian leaders, the true backbone of the Christian community. They have had the authentic encounter with Christ (which their local church had somehow failed to provide), and they now have a covert mission: to target especially the powerful and influential, enlisting them likewise to undergo the Cursillo initiation, and so to build up the Cursillo community.

The Cursillo community? Most Christians would be surprised to find that there is an organized, stealth movement in their midst, a movement which is no longer loyal to church, creed, or denomination, but which seeks to transcend all of these through loyalty to a technique, a method, and in the end, a powerful, pleasurable experience. "It was the greatest time of my life." "You have to attend one of these weekends." "I can't explain it to you; you just have to experience it." And so it goes.

But what of this transforming technique, this magical method that has become the new center of so many people's lives? Is it psychologically sound? Is it true spirituality? What are the lingering, unintended side-effects? Where did it come from, and what is its purpose? And most importantly, is there any biblical warrant for creating a Cursillo community apart from, and in many cases opposed to and in competition with the church?

I must pause to give thanks. I have appreciated the courtesy and Christian charity of local Cursillo leaders who patiently answered my questions and gave me some inside access into the workings of the movement in our area. I wish to thank also the fine staff and faculty of the Doctor of Ministry program at Covenant Theological Seminary for patiently reading and critiquing earlier drafts of portions of this work. Thanks and love to the faithful congregation of the Hospers Presbyterian Church which has challenged and supported me for over twenty-three years. And thanks to many (too numerous to name) colleagues and friends who have listened and questioned, read and reflected. Thanks to my three children, David, Kristin, and Jonathan, who have been forced to endure my relentless musings and orations about the Cursillo movement (and have added some astonishing insights of their own). And my deepest gratitude belongs to my loving wife and faithful friend, Susanne, who has demonstrated the truest "long-suffering" as we have been wrestling together with Cursillo for the past decade and more.

Finally, I owe a large debt of gratitude to three high school students who were honest enough to ask an important question: *"Is this for real?"*

INTRODUCTION:
The Concern About Cursillo

Cursillo. De colores. Palanca. Ultreya. Clausura.
These are key terms in a new vocabulary that accompanies an entirely new way of life for many Christians. But consulting a Spanish-English dictionary will help little in understanding this growing phenomenon among Roman Catholics and, more recently, Protestants of several denominational affiliations, including Episcopalians, Methodists, Lutherans, Presbyterians, Baptists, and Dutch Reformed.

The terms do, however, signal the Spanish roots of the Cursillo (pronounced "cur-SEE-yoh") de Cristiandad, literally "little courses in Christianity." The methods and techniques of the Cursillo were developed in the 1940s by a team of Spanish laymen, chief of whom was Eduardo Bonnin, a psychologist. The Cursillo was recognized as a powerful tool for church renewal by the local bishop, Juan Hervas, who energetically promoted and propelled the Cursillo into a worldwide movement.

The Amazing Scope of Cursillo

It is hard to overestimate the impact of the Cursillo. The statistics are one measure of its success. In the early 1980s it was estimated that over two million Roman Catholics were members of Cursillo.[1] According to the National

---

[1] Marcene Marcoux, *Cursillo: Anatomy of a Movement: The Experience of Spiritual Renewal* (New York: Lambeth Press, 1982), 26.

Cursillo Center in Dallas, Texas, "as of 1981, almost all of the 160 dioceses in the United States had introduced the Cursillo Movement." This was well over two decades ago when the Cursillo had been in existence a bare thirty years. In the twenty-eight years since, it has grown among Roman Catholics. What's more, it is truly global:

> Today it is a worldwide movement with centers in nearly all South and Central American countries, the United States, Canada, Mexico, Portugal, Puerto Rico, Great Britain, Ireland, France, Germany, Austria, Italy, Yugoslavia, Australia, Japan, Korea, Taiwan, the Philippines, Sri Lanka and in several African countries.[2]

The National Cursillo Center claims that the Cursillo movement has at least the unofficial endorsement of the Catholic Church in both the United States and Rome:

> The Cursillo Movement in the United States was organized on a national basis in 1965. At this meeting a National Secretariat was organized, and a National Cursillo Office (currently in Dallas, Texas) was established. Furthermore, it is linked to the National Conference of Catholic Bishops....The movement is a member of the International Catholic Organizations of the Pontifical Council for the Laity in Rome. [3]

Another measure of the success of the Cursillo is that it has made remarkable inroads into Protestant groups as well. The Methodists, for example, have adapted their own version of the Cursillo called "Walk to Emmaus," which is used internationally and boasts one million U.S. participants to date, and has a youth version called "Chrysalis," patterned after the Roman Catholic "Teens Encounter Christ"[4] in which 150,000 youth have participated to date. An organization called the National Presbyterian Cursillo has secured a license from the Roman Catholic Church to use the name "Cursillo" in the weekends hosted among Presbyterians; the group has local chapters in twelve states. The Episcopalian Church has its own Cursillo which has chapters in over twenty dioceses nationwide and internationally. The Evangelical Lutheran Church in America calls its version of Cursillo "Via de Cristo" (Way of Christ). It originated in Florida and Iowa in 1972. Via de Cristo has held events in

---

[2] The National Secretariat of the Cursillo Movement, *The Cursillo Movement: What is It?* (Dallas: National Cursillo Center), 13.
[3] Ibid.
[4] Robert Wood, *An Early History of the Walk to Emmaus* (Nashville: Upper Room Books, 2002), 28-29.

Introduction: The Concern About Cursillo

twenty-five states and some foreign countries, with 84,000 U.S. participants to date in 44 centers. Cursillo is becoming increasingly popular among the Dutch Reformed (RCA & CRC) of Northwest and Central Iowa, Southwest Minnesota, Southeast South Dakota, and Western Michigan, with youth and young adult versions of each. According to the Reformed Church in America's website, the Cursillo appears to have denominational endorsement.[5]

There is a prison ministries version of the Cursillo sponsored by Kairos Ministries. It currently operates in 270 prisons in 33 states, as well as England, Australia, South Africa, Costa Rica, and Canada. According to its website, "More than 170,000 incarcerated men and women have been introduced to Kairos, since its inception. The current number of volunteers exceeds 20,000 per year."[6] Tres Dias is an interdenominational, Protestant version of the Cursillo which began in Newburgh, New York in 1972 and became international in 1985, spreading to Germany and Korea. According to its website Tres Dias operates internationally through 63 centers and has served "tens of thousands of people."[7] A Canadian Cursillo website (cursillos.ca) declares that "The Cursillo Movement has spread in more than 60 countries and across the religious spectrum." It offers links to 1,550 Cursillo-related websites and to 81 Catholic and Protestant movements based on the Cursillo.[8] The same source indicates that the pace of Cursillo weekends continues. During the week of February 19-22, 2009, for example, 40 Catholic and Protestant Cursillo weekends worldwide were held, including 29 in the U.S. alone. This was no anomaly, since the next week, February 26-March 1, 2009 reported 36 Catholic and Protestant Cursillo weekends, including 26 in the U.S.

But the impact of the Cursillo can be seen more clearly in the impression the Cursillo initiation weekend makes on "candidates" (those attending the initiation, seeking to "make Cursillo" and become "cursillistas"). One Roman Catholic cursillista reports a typical response:

---

[5] www.rca.org/NETCOMMUNITY/Page.aspx?&pid=1614&srcid=2058 and www.rca.org/NETCOMMUNITY/Page.aspx?&pid=1291&srcid=1701
[6] http://www.kairosprisonministry.org
[7] http://www.tresdias.org/hp.htm
[8] http://cursillos.ca/en/liens.htm Names for Protestant versions of Cursillo are also listed: EPISCOPALIAN/ANGLICAN: Episcopal Cursillo, Happening, New Beginnings, Dias con Cristo, Anglican Cursillo, Challenge, Vocare, TEC; LUTHERAN: Via de Cristo, Lutheran Cursillo, Happening, TEC, Tirosh, Chayah, My Father's House; METHODIST: Walk to Emmaus, Methodist Cursillo, Unidos en Cristo, Chrysalis, Alarga, The Journey, Search for Christian Maturity; PRESBYTERIAN, BAPTIST AND OTHER DENOMIATIONAL: Presbyterian Cursillo, Presbyterian Pilgrimmage, Koinonia, Celebration, Faith Walk, The Way of Christ, Vida Nueva, United Church Cursillo; NON-DENOMINATIONAL: Aventura, Awakening, Camino, Credo Recovery, DeColores EnChristo, DeColores Ministries, Deco-Tec, Diaspora, Discipleship Walk, Ecco-I, Epiphany Ministry, Footsteps, Great Banquet, Happening Ecumenical, Journey though Faith, Jubilee Journey, Kairos, Kairos Outside, Kairos Torch, Keryx, Koinonia, Paseo con Cristo, Residents Encounter Christ, Tres Dias, UTEC.

> I was born again. The night of the cursillo, it was somber. At night I took out the cross and held it in my hand and I looked at it; I was changed. Something happened to me that can't be explained. I was filled with love, and I knew that God loved me, but I didn't know it by reason or intellect, but it was in me. I started to cry and knew that something very unusual had happened. I knew why I was put here and that I had a purpose. I was born again. I realized that I am tied to others and have a sense of awareness.
>
> My old self died, and my new self is to see the lovable in each person and to see the unlovable as lovable. To see people as He sees them and not as I see the surface.[9]

Another cursillista offers high praise. "It was an overpowering, beautiful experience. Peaceful, deeply moving, it touched my whole being. There was an overwhelming peacefulness."[10] As another phrased it: "It became an integrative experience. It deepened my faith and made it more personal. It became a way of life. My faith became my priority."[11]

The Protestant version can be just as powerful and transforming, according to the positive reports of many who attend. A retired Reformed Church in America pastor, deeply involved in the local Cursillo movement, asserts that Cursillo has succeeded where the church has failed:

> Dear Brother, you speak of how the call to unity and oneness has failed in communism and socialism and democracy, in the world. You could also add the church, the kingdom of God to that list! I feel that is more where you and I, as we exercise the gift of prophecy, need to be doing the talking!
>
> I just came home from a four day retreat (Cursillo) in which, judging by the testimony time Sunday night, about 30 guys who were turned off to God or who were stuck with a head knowledge of the Lord got there [*sic*] spiritual hearts started, and five or six guys who were ignorant of the Lord got reborn and plugged in to the fellowship of believers.
>
> I talked with several of the other staff members about how this king of revival and miracles and movement of the Holy Spirit ought to be happening in the hometowns and churches from which we all come! I found a common agreement that one reason it happens an [*sic*] Cursillo and is so scarce in our home congregations is that at

---

[9] Marcoux, *Cursillo, Anatomy of a Movement: The Experience of Spiritual Renewal*, 91.
[10] Ibid., 92.
[11] Ibid.

Introduction: The Concern About Cursillo

Cursillo, there are no walls, do [*sic*] denominational and congregational divisions-we are, at Cursillo united, of one mind and purpose and spirit-and that is of Christ![12]

Similarly, the following testimonials appeared on a brochure advertising the TEC (Teens Encounter Christ) Weekend, the youth version of the Reformed Cursillo:

(Male) T.E.C. was one of the funniest and best events I have ever been to. To me T.E.C. was more than just a spiritual high. It was spiritual <u>growth</u>. I just wish everyone would go through T.E.C. so they can experience the love of God like I did. (emphasis original)

(Male) This T.E.C. weekend I went to was one of the best weekends of my whole life! I learned many new and awesome things. The #1 thing I learned is that Jesus is my best friend in the whole world and that he cares for me a lot. I used to think God hated me and he didn't care what I did and who I hurt. But now I realize my past mistakes and pray to Him every day and night to forgive me and to give me the strength to carry on. I also met a lot of special people that I now call my best friends. That means a lot, because I've never had people this close to me and I think it kicks butt. All in all, I hope I can work a T.E.C or 2 so I can have Jesus work though [*sic*] me to help kids with problems similar to the ones I had. This was a really great weekend!

(Female) T.E.C. was awesome! Everyone there was so accepting and supporting and just glowed with Jesus' love. It was the first time I actually realized there are people who really do love me. I made all kinds of new friends and had the time of my life!

(Female) T.E.C. has been an experience I will never forget. So much strength is found not only in going through but working. Team unity is so awesome & great friendships are made. God is love. Let go and let God.

These reports are certainly compelling. To put them into perspective, though, you should know that these TEC testimonials were secured at the close of the weekend, while the graduates were still basking in its glow, before the effects had begun to wear off. One of the above participants attended several

---

[12] E-mail to author, 24 February 2003.

more weekend events as a leader, giving talks describing his troubled past and the wonderful transformation resulting from his initial TEC weekend. In a short time, however, he began using drugs and eventually dropped out of church.

The Concern about Cursillo

Still the experience of Cursillo is undeniably potent for many. Words like "overwhelming," "great," "powerful," and "best experience of my life" are not uncommon. Such high praise should not be taken lightly because it is so typical and universal in the Cursillo experience. When members of our congregation attended such weekends and began actively to promote such weekends, as a pastor, as a shepherd responsible for the spiritual care of God's people, I became convinced that this phenomenon required further scrutiny.

But here I came to a near dead end. A quick search of available literature yielded almost no information which examined Cursillo from a critical or objective perspective. My questions posed to colleagues in ministry and to local religion and psychology professors at Reformed colleges in the area confirmed what I found (or did not find) in the literature. To the question, "What do you know about Cursillo?" the most frequent response among ministers or professors was "not much." Most had heard of it and knew people who had attended. Many had been urged to attend themselves. Some were able to refer me to people who were in leadership of these events.

And even my contacts with local Cursillo leaders proved disappointing. It turned out that through my limited reading, I knew more about the history of Cursillo than they did. None had ever heard of Eduardo Bonnin or Bishop Juan Hervas. What they did know with great precision was the format and methods of the Cursillo weekend, the powerful techniques that produce the glowing effects reported by so many of the Cursillo graduates.

Apparently the format, methods, and techniques are the defining ingredients of the Cursillo movement. Philosophical and theological matters are given little attention. For example, when I asked the National Outreach Coordinator of the National Presbyterian Cursillo via email what modifications had to be made in the Roman Catholic Cursillo to make it more Presbyterian and Reformed, the response was revealing:

> I am honestly not familiar with the actual Catholic Cursillo, so I don't know exactly what things may be in the Presbyterian weekend that may be different from the Catholic weekend....
>
> I am very familiar with the Presbyterian Cursillo weekend though, and if you have specific questions about our weekend, please ask me

Introduction: The Concern About Cursillo

and I would be glad to answer to the best of my ability.[13]

The coordinator's lack of information dismayed me.

Please understand the gravity of this concern. This is a quiet, one could rightly say "secretive," global movement among Christians, originally among Roman Catholics, but increasingly promoted among Protestants. It is for many, by their own report: "the best experience of my life," one that "touched my whole being," "in which I was born again." And yet of this phenomenon, there has been little inquiry or critique in print from a Reformed pastoral or theological perspective. As members of my congregation went deeper into the movement and openly recruited others, I became concerned. What is Cursillo? Why is it so secretive and controversial? If it really does produce all the purported benefits, why has the whole church not embraced it?

This monograph is my attempt to answer those questions, to begin to fill the gaping hole of silence and lack of inquiry on this subject. Because the experience of Cursillo is admittedly so powerful, a simple answer would not suffice. Hopefully, this will not be the last word on Cursillo from a Reformed perspective.

The Conclusion About Cursillo

At the end of many hours of study, I can now confidently offer up front my conclusion about Cursillo and related phenomena: Cursillo is really "Little Courses in *Catharsis*." Or stated more fully,

> **These weekend "high" experiences are largely dependent on universally applicable, manipulative, somewhat deceptive and not uniquely Christian psychological and physiological techniques designed to wear down resistance and produce an emotional high/ cathartic experience, which is then interpreted as religious experience. While the short-term effects may be pleasant and desirable, the long-term consequences are mostly negative. And since these weekends have no biblical warrant, they should be avoided.**

The various aspects of this conclusion will be thoroughly explained in the following pages.

As members of my church began to describe the details of the Cursillo-type weekend they attended (something they had been forbidden to do by the event's leadership), parts of the weekend began to sound quite familiar. It

---

[13] E-mail to author, 1 April 2001.

seemed very similar to numerous weekend renewal events I had attended and even led in previous years. At this point it would be helpful for me to back up and explain a part of my own past, a personal quest for emotional experience.

1. *The Quest for Emotional Experience*

THE QUEST BEGINS

It was late spring 1973. I was a teenager and had already been a believer for several years. I attended with my family a fair-sized, Presbyterian, country church, a lively, evangelical church which took the Bible seriously and taught the Westminster Shorter Catechism. As a congregation we had been praying about a weekend event that was to take place in our church in cooperation with the Methodist Church in our community. What caught my attention was that everybody seemed to be talking about it, anticipating its arrival. We had preparatory prayer meetings in peoples' homes, something I had never experienced before. As a youth group, we also had special meetings in which all we did was pray. They were unlike anything I had known. It was remarkable to sit with other youth and pray for anything we could think of, but especially about this weekend that was coming to our church. We prayed for thirty minutes, and the time seemed to fly by. This was truly noteworthy and unprecedented. It created a tremendous curiosity about this upcoming "weekend."

And then the weekend came. In all candor I cannot remember many of the details. As one who has attended over twenty similar weekend experiences and has coordinated a weekend exactly like this for an entire congregation, I now know in depth precisely what took place. But let me try to piece together the recollections of a thirteen-year-old.

There were a lot of new faces in our church that weekend. These people were invited guests who had taken their own time and paid their own way to travel and stay with us. They had come on a mission to help us. And many of these new people were young, about my age or a little older. They smiled and laughed a lot and seemed to be so happy. Some of them brought guitars and taught us new songs that were not hymns but sounded like songs we heard on the radio. The boys had long hair and wore in-style, up-to-date clothing. My impression as a young teenager was that these people were cool, and I was immediately attracted to them.

But they did more than laugh and sing. They also told incredible stories about their lives. And even the way they were chosen to speak was remarkable. The youth team leader selected witnesses to speak without any prior notice or warning. It was as though God was directing the whole thing. And before they spoke, each witness asked a friend to pray for him or her, to ask God to speak through them. The witnesses said they had not thought ahead of time what they were going to say, and didn't even know what they were going to say. When they spoke, it was as though God himself was speaking. And they told extraordinary stories. Some of them had lived scandalous lives. A few had tried drugs, which seemed quite shocking to me. But all of them had had an encounter with Jesus Christ, and He meant everything to them. They also told us they loved us and hoped that we would have an encounter with Christ as well.

Again, I don't really recall a lot of the details of the weekend, mostly impressions. I remember that something powerful happened on Saturday night, with a lot of deeply-felt emotion and crying. The next morning everyone was so happy in Sunday School, which was led by the witnesses. One girl about my age cried because she had skipped the rest of the weekend. She could tell that something had happened to all of us and that she had missed it. I remember going into a packed church service. The pastor didn't preach that morning, in fact, he sat with the rest of us while the witnesses led the service. The leader of these witnesses talked for a while and then told us he needed to rededicate his life to Christ that very morning. He invited us all to do the same, and then went and knelt down in front of church. His wife joined him as did several of the witnesses. Soon others from our congregation joined them. I felt a powerful urge to do the same. I asked a friend if he wanted to go forward too, and we went together. When it was done, the front of the church was crowded with kneeling people, most of them weeping.

That noon we had a potluck meal. Some of the teenaged witnesses went barefoot in the fellowship hall, which was a little shocking. Then they said their "good-byes" and went home.

And that evening the church gathered in a wrap-up service. Again, the sanctuary was packed with excited people. There was a little singing of choruses at the beginning, but no preaching or teaching. Instead, any and all were invited to come to the front and tell what the weekend meant to them. It was incredible and unprecedented in all my brief experience. Ordinary people were talking in front of church and were describing what Jesus meant to them. But I only recall one specific comment that was made. A respected man in the church asked a question: "Would we all feel and act this way in six weeks? Sure, we all call each other 'brother' and 'sister' now, but what about in six

Chapter 1: The Quest for Emotional Experience

weeks?" As I recall, someone made a little joke about it. Everybody laughed, and we moved on. And I remember thinking, "This will last forever. This kind of feeling will never fade away."

Following this weekend, our church was different, and I was different. Summer vacation soon hit, and I had lots of time on my hands. Living on a farm, I had the wide open spaces to roam as well. And I was sure I was right and the respected man's concern was unfounded. I remember waking up happy and going to bed happy. I would walk around the farm, off to the pasture to fetch the milk cows, or all alone down the gravel road, and I would sing all the verses of all the hymns I could think of at the top of my voice. I was so happy and carefree. I prayed all the time and was constantly filled with joy.

And, it seemed that the respected man's concern was groundless with respect to our church as well. Church was different. People were excited now. This excitement was celebrated through various special meetings in homes and in the church. Adults talked with me and made sense. They treated me almost as an equal. There was such a feeling of unity and love in our congregation.

But…in time…the respected man's concerns proved to be prophetic. It all began to wear off. People in the church stopped calling one another "brother" and "sister." School began again, and my church friends seemed no different than they had been before the weekend renewal experience. I had less time to walk and sing and pray, and the feelings went away. Instead, I felt a great sense of sadness, disappointment, and disillusionment. But I kept on going to church. Though the feelings left, I did not lose my faith, which I had already before the weekend renewal experience.

A Renewal of the Experience

And then came what seemed to be the solution to it all. I got invited to be on a team of witnesses! We would travel to another church and help them experience the same kind of weekend we'd had. At the conclusion of the weekend at our church we had all been asked if we would be willing to go to other churches and serve as witnesses there. I vaguely remembered signing up to become a witness. And now it was becoming a reality. I could help others find the joy and happiness I had found. But I could also recapture the joy that had dissipated from my own life. I was sure I had found the real thing. I was going to become like one of those people I admired. It was a dream come true!

And it was! I still recall the great anxiety of traveling to this new church with people I had never met before. The team of witnesses was different for every weekend. While I knew a few of the people on the team, most were strangers to me. And there was great apprehension when the youth team leader said, "Now I think we should hear from a couple of witnesses." We honestly did not know who he would choose. And I honestly did not prepare anything for my witness. We were instructed not to. And in a moment we could be called on to share something, even though we had no idea what it was going to be! I remember ducking, hoping I would not be called on, terrified and feeling great relief when someone else was chosen. And what incredible stories they told, again of getting into trouble, of using drugs and sleeping with girlfriends. There wasn't a dry eye in the place when that witness finished, including mine.

The weekend was very much like the one in my home church. There was singing and sharing and laughing. On Saturday morning, we sang at a nursing home. It was shocking and unsettling to see the older people, some of them senile, calling to us, grabbing at us. We tried to sing songs to them and to talk with them. It was deeply moving. Then we had a fun activity: bowling. We all laughed a lot. There were a few hours in the afternoon for a break, but then we were back to the church for supper, for lots of laughter and fun. Then we sang together for a time. We broke into small groups and were asked to write a "spiritual graph," to share our own faith journey. People were excused from talking if they felt uncomfortable, but most joined in.

Then we were all brought back into the large group. The youth coordinator spoke some more, we sang some more slow and serious songs. I think some witnesses spoke, and I might have been one of them. And then we all moved to a different room, a smaller room. It was dark and there was a single candle burning in the center of the room. We could barely make out faces, so we felt more anonymous to the group. The youth coordinator introduced the pastor who set out the elements for communion and then left. We were invited to come to the center of the room and take communion if we wanted to, or to come with a special friend or two and share communion together. After all were finished, one of the guitarists sang a slow song in a minor key. It was already late at night. We were all tired from the late night before. I remember being emotionally wrung out because of the sadness of the nursing home, but also the silliness and giddiness of our other activities that day. The other witnesses had expressed so much love for everyone. We had been through so much together as a group, that I already felt a tremendous bond toward everyone. The guitarist continued to play minor-keyed chords on his instrument.

And then someone began to cry. It started as a sniffle, but quickly erupted into deep and wracking sobs. Soon the people close by hugged her, and they began to sob as well. In a short time, all of us were crying, some gently, some with the same, uncontrollable sobbing. The room became quite noisy as all were weeping together. The most stony-faced high school boys became teary, even those who had come only to this part of the weekend and just to be with their girlfriends.

After the sobbing began to subside, the youth coordinator changed the mood. He said, "We don't have to cry; we have joy in Jesus!" Immediately, the guitarist broke into an upbeat song we all knew, and we sang at the top of our voices. After singing and laughing and more crying and lots of hugging, we tore ourselves away. We went home, emotionally released and fell into a peaceful, though short night's sleep.

And in the morning, there was a different spirit in that church. There was warmth, excitement, joy, unity, and love for all to go around. The same Sunday morning procedure was followed in this church that had been used in my home church. The pastor sat in the back, the witnesses spoke, the adult coordinator invited the people to rededicate their lives to Christ, and he told us he needed to rededicate himself to Christ that morning. He kneeled down first, followed by several witnesses, and in a short while the front of the church was jammed with people on their knees. We had the potluck together, said our tearful "good-bye's," and after more hugging, we went home.

I was happy, though absolutely exhausted. But when I arrived home, brimming with renewed joy, I was stunned to find that my family did not share my enthusiasm. I had been away and now brought home a suitcase of dirty laundry. I had neglected my chores and still had homework to complete. What's worse, I had no one with whom to share this weekend experience. Nobody from my school or even church had been there. When I tried to speak of it in my youth group or Sunday School class, there was only modest "that's-nice-we're-happy-for-you" interest expressed. My "wonderful weekend world" unhappily collided with my "regular world," and my glowing joy was indeed short-lived.

This was utterly disappointing. But there was a remedy. I got an invitation to be a witness at another weekend, which I eagerly accepted. Maybe the second one was a fluke. Maybe the third would have more permanent results. But it didn't. This is not to say that it was not a re-charging experience. It definitely was that, though the effect was less potent. Again, I had recaptured it, and again, it had worn off.

Deeper Involvement

About this time I moved to a nearby town and attended a different school. I continued to attend my home church, but also joined a large youth group in the new town. And it felt like home. The leaders of this new youth group liked the weekend renewal experiences as much as I did. They invited a team of youth witnesses to come and lead their youth group in a retreat weekend on more than one occasion. Now it seemed my problems were solved! I could receive regular re-charges, but so would my friends. We would all experience it together, so we could all continue to share it together.

All the necessary components of the weekend renewal experience were employed on these weekend retreats. The first night, Friday night, began with eating, singing, sharing by witnesses, small groups in which everyone was invited to speak. But it didn't end there. The meeting broke at 11:00 p.m. And then we went for pizza! Most of us did not get home until quite late, so we were very tired the next day. But the morning began bright and early with donuts and juice and singing and sharing. In the mid-morning we went to visit a nursing home where we saw very sad things: confused people desperately calling out for help. We sang songs to them, but had to choke back our tears.

After lunch together, we went bowling, all the while laughing and being silly together. Saturday night ran much the same as on church weekend experiences complete with candle, communion, sad songs, witnesses, crying, hugging, joyful praises, and lingering until we had to go home. The next morning was the same as usual, with great joy, unity, and sharing. As I recall, the youth provided special music in the worship service that day. After a meal, we said our "good-bye's" and the witnesses went home.

Though I cannot recall all of the details, I know my life began to revolve around these "weekend renewal experiences." They took several forms. I continued to serve as a witness on the youth team of weekend Lay-Witness missions at churches around the area, driving as much as three or more hours to get there. I had learned to play guitar, and so became an even more valuable member of the team. I also attended the community youth group, led by those who liked weekend renewal experiences. They held more retreat weekends, and shorter overnights called "lock-ins" which always ended up in a darkened room with a candle, communion, and crying. I began to share leadership in some of these events. But I also traveled with some of my friends to other types of retreats. I continued into this my first two years of college since I lived at home and attended a community college nearby. In all, I suppose I have attended or led 20-30 weekend renewal experiences of this sort.

A Growing Awareness

But I began to notice some things. First, I observed that for a weekend to be successful, that is, for the weekend to achieve this deeply-felt joy and bonding, it had to follow a predictable pattern and had to incorporate certain elements. For example, shorter overnight experiences like "lock-ins" had much less dependable and shorter-lived results. On the other hand, if these methods were used well, I have never personally known them to fail. They regularly produced the desired effects.

The other thing I noticed was that the effect of the weekends on me continued to diminish to the point that they no longer had any effect at all. I began to feel deep sadness when, on Saturday night after Saturday night on weekend after weekend, while others were swinging from sobbing to singing like clockwork, I felt nothing at all except a sense of disappointment and loss.

Something else should be noted. I used these methods on two different youth groups I led, and one church I served as pastor. The results were completely predictable, though the settings were different. The first youth group upon whom I used these techniques was of the church where I served as intern pastor. I had been their youth leader for about six months when I invited a couple of friends to the church who had helped lead these weekend experiences with me before. We used precisely the same methods I had seen and used many times before, and we achieved precisely the same results: the Saturday night sobbing, singing, and bonding, and the Sunday morning euphoria and tearful "good-byes."

The second youth group experience was a bit different. I had accompanied the youth group on a work trip to inner-city Chicago as their devotional leader. Toward the close of the long, exhausting week, one night after a small group Bible study, I turned out the lights and lit a candle. I talked a long time in a quiet voice about our need to commit our lives to Jesus. Then I sang a slow, sad song. I told them I was going to rededicate my life to Christ. I knelt at the front of the room near the candle. In moments I was surrounded by nearly the whole group, most of whom were crying. I then said, "We don't have to cry; we can have joy in Jesus!" I struck up an upbeat praise song, and we all sang at the top of our voices.

"Is This for Real?"

But one other incident happened that night that surprised me, that turned my thoughts in an entirely new direction. I had been sound asleep in my sleeping bag when I was awakened by three of the young people. They had been talking into the wee hours, and they had a question for me: "Is this for real?"

In my groggy condition, I remember that I could not think very clearly, and I was a bit annoyed at the question. As I recall, I answered with something like, "Of course this is real. You were there. It happened. You were invited to rededicate your life to Christ. You felt the Holy Spirit's power and responded. Yes, it was real!" I then prayed with them and went back to sleep. But the question continued to haunt me: "Was this for real?" Somehow they had sensed that it was not. And I began to wonder myself: "Is this for real?" As it would turn out, that simple question has become one of the great turning points of my life. But let me tell of the experience of another man I know.

ANOTHER QUEST FOR EMOTIONAL EXPERIENCE

Alan (not his real name) was a few years older than me, in my brother's grade in school. He was active in his local church and other Christian groups. It was 1974, and after he graduated from high school, Alan was snagged by the wanderlust. He said he had been driving in his Jeep one day and heard a song on the radio. One line in the song captivated him: *"Me and you and a dog named Boo, travelin' and a-livin' off the land."* Alan thought this might be God's way of telling him he should take some time off after high school and see the country, and that maybe God had something big for him to do.

So he loaded up his Jeep, took all the money he had, and began to tour the country. As I heard Alan tell his story, he didn't focus much on his travels, so I cannot relate any of the incidents along the way. But eventually he found himself in California, at Fisherman's Wharf, well-known sightseer's location in San Francisco, looking very much like a tourist who was far from home.

He was approached by an attractive young lady with a radiant smile, a hint of a glowing, inward joy. As they talked, she seemed genuinely interested in him. In the midst of their conversation, she invited him to spend an afternoon and evening with her at a spiritual group meeting. Since Alan was already a Christian, since he was alone, and since the girl seemed to like him, he gladly agreed to go. He wondered if this was maybe the reason he felt the desire to travel. Perhaps this was the "great thing" that God had for him to do. So Alan tagged along.

The afternoon and evening surpassed all his expectations. After a large community meal, the leaders led some mixer-games. It was a relaxing time of singing and sharing, and the girl who had first invited him stayed with him the whole evening. Since he was admittedly quite lonely, and since he'd had little human contact, he greatly enjoyed the evening and felt a strong attraction to the group. So it was only natural that he agreed to go with them when he was invited to a weekend retreat.

He traveled with her and others to an isolated location near Booneville, California, several miles north of San Francisco. The retreat center was a set of dormitory-type buildings in a secluded location. There he found a large group of people about his age, many of whom he had met at the evening of fellowship. Again, the girl who first met him stayed close by him the whole weekend, though there was no romantic contact. He felt strongly attracted to her. The weekend retreat was billed as a relaxing, getaway time with no worries or cares.

This he found to be true. They played group games, enjoyed lengthy small group sharing in which all were encouraged to talk freely about themselves. There was singing and "fellowship." Alan said it took him back to his days of youth or childhood, a carefree time with no responsibilities. He remembered that everybody seemed so interested in him: he was the "center of attention," a celebrity to the group. He now suspects these "interested people" were not merely retreat goers, but members of the group who were instructed to shower him with attention and affection. He now observes that during the weekend, newcomers like him were greatly outnumbered by members of the group who clearly overwhelmed them. He also noted that everyone on the weekend was paired up in a male-female relationship. Except for restroom breaks and sleeping, he was constantly accompanied by his attractive, female companion. She would often hold his hand as they walked and talked together. There was some teaching during the weekend, and he noted that the attitude was a bit of irreverence toward the traditional. They made fun of out-of-date rules and practices, pointing out many of the failings of the organized church.

Alan was deeply drawn to this group of people. He remembered feeling incredible love from them, unconditional love like he had seldom experienced before. He felt an immediate and powerful bond with the whole group. For a young man far from home, it felt as though he had found a true, spiritual family, and he was deeply saddened when the weekend drew to a close.

But maybe it didn't have to end! The retreat leaders extended another invitation. Alan was being invited to stay at the retreat center for a whole week. In exchange for some chores, he, along with other young newcomers would be offered room and board. Best of all, he could live in community with these loving people. They really could be one close and committed family. Surely this must be God's will for him. This was why he was prompted to travel halfway across a continent. He was home, where he was loved, where he belonged, with this joyful group of spiritual people.

Alan accepted the invitation eagerly. And he joined in with all the activities just as eagerly. He and all his new brothers and sisters were up early, hard at work at manual labor, raising vegetables and doing other chores on the retreat center grounds. He didn't mind the work. He felt good about doing his part, and nobody else seemed to mind either. The meals were not much to brag about: a completely vegetarian diet. But he was happy to make the sacrifice: anything to stay with his new-found family of Christians. And the long days were composed of eating, three teachings interspersed throughout the day and a couple of blocks of work, morning and afternoon.

Each day ended in singing and sharing and testimonies. Often the testimonies went late into the night, but it was so meaningful that he didn't mind the late hours. The testimonies consisted of a person of the group sharing their story, how they came to this retreat center, how they'd had their doubts about the group, how they may have heard negative reports about the group, but each testimony ended with the person having overcome their doubts and offering a ringing endorsement of the group and its beliefs. At the conclusion of each testimony, the new convert was heartily applauded and given numerous hugs. Alan said that each testimony was offered as though the decision had just been made, as though this was the first time the testimony was given. He now believes that most of the testimonies had been rehearsed and were actually given by members who had joined the group long before.

And during the week he found himself and everybody else paired up again, and always in male-female couples, except that this time it was a new girl since the first girl could not stay for the week. His new "friend" was surprisingly well-suited to his interests and personality. Alan believes that one of the reasons the members were so interested in him during the first weekend retreat was so that they would be able to select a suitable new companion for him for the week.

Alan found that the combination of the early mornings, the physical labor, the inadequate, vegetarian diet, and late nights of singing and testimonies began to wear him down. He found himself quite weary at the end of the day. The teachers were interesting to listen to, though they always spoke in a quiet, even tone. Once in a while, they said some things that seemed a bit unusual, but since they were Christians like he was, and since he had felt the genuineness of their love, he was sure they must be right.

But the teaching became more and more bizarre. He was certain that he had never heard many of their beliefs in his home church or in Sunday School; but then he was young and inexperienced. Maybe he had not listened very well in church. Besides, they kept quoting Scripture verses, especially from the Old Testament in support of their teaching. And, in truth, he had little energy or desire to resist them. Every question was quickly answered, though it seemed that questions were not very welcome. Others in the group acted impatient at questions, and eventually they were asked with less and less frequency. But Alan did not want to resist. He did not want to be a contrary voice or spoil all the love and unity he felt within the group. And even if he would have wanted to, he was so tired and undernourished that he did not have the power to resist. Alan said he felt himself being worn down, physically, emotionally, and spiritually.

Alan continued to stay with his new "family" for the week. The second weekend he was there, he was informed that he was doing so well that he was to be moved into the advanced group. This group left the retreat center and went up into the hills for intensive training. During the first week, Alan had heard three teachings a day for five days. During this advanced training, he got five days worth of lectures in two days. Alan described this as a "bombardment." Physically and emotionally he was completely worn out. He began to suspect that something was amiss, but he had little time to think, little strength to resist. At the end of this time, he was taken aside and told that the source of this teaching was from the Rev. Sun Myung Moon. Rev. Moon was held up as the only hope of mankind's salvation, and he was urged to join them in serving Rev. Moon's glorious vision.

Alan said that it was at this point that he made the decision to leave the group. He was already a Christian and realized that this was a deceptive and destructive cult. He had decided to stand up to the group and warn the other newcomers who had similarly fallen under their influence. He had to leave this new "family."

But in the mean time his "old" family, his parents, became alarmed at what was happening to Alan. They contacted an anti-cult organization and learned that if Alan had been there a week, it would be very difficult for him to leave of his own will.

In desperation, his parents resorted to a ruse. His father called with an emergency message: "Alan's mother had been in a serious car accident and was in a life-threatening condition." Sympathetic hospital officials agreed to cooperate. The California Highway Patrol delivered the message to the group's leadership, who were suspicious and refused to tell Alan the news for a couple of days. The group's leadership even called the hospital where Alan's mom was supposedly being treated. The hospital staff confirmed that Alan's mother was in critical condition following a car accident. After warning him that it may be a trick by his parents, they finally gave him the message. Alan was allowed to leave the retreat center. But even as he left he was accompanied by a group leader who warned him of "Satan's attempts" to draw him away from the "truth." He was given a toll-free telephone number to call should he ever desire to come back. Even after he was home, Alan reports that members of the group watched his house for several months. Alan had just escaped from the Moonies.

Why do I relate this story? Am I equating Lay-Witness and other weekend renewal experiences like Cursillo with a cult? Certainly not! Alan's involvement with the Moonies was very different from Lay-Witness or other Christian weekend experiences for the simple fact that the Unification Church is a non-Christian cult, while the other movements professes the historic Christian faith. But there are striking similarities in the methods they each employ.

2. *Is Cursillo a Cult?*

I have been asked this question several times. Let me state my answer plainly: ***"No! Cursillo is not a cult."*** Even though we will make some comparisons between the techniques used by a destructive cult like the Moonies and by the Cursillo, it is important that we avoid placing the Cursillo in the same category. Such accusations are inflammatory and unfounded. However, if we find that the Cursillo employs some of the same questionable methods as destructive cults, this should raise serious questions.

What is a cult? There are various definitions. Theologically-speaking, a cult is a group which purports to be Christian, but whose beliefs are so divergent from the historic Christian faith that it has ceased to be Christian. Cult scholar, Walter R. Martin observes:

> From a theological viewpoint, the cults contain not a few major deviations from historic Christianity. Yet paradoxically, they continue to insist that they are entitled to be classified as Christians. [14]

Included in this category would be the Mormons, Jehovah's Witnesses, Christian Science and the Unification Church, to name a few. By this definition, the Cursillo would clearly not be a cult.

More broadly, a cult may be an offshoot of some other, non-Christian religion, or some quasi-scientific group such as the Hare Krishnas, the Bahai Faith, Zen Buddhism, Spiritism, Scientology, the New Age Movement, or the Rajneesh cult. Again, by this definition, the Cursillo would definitely not be a cult.

But there is another way of defining a cult, and this not so much related to the content of its beliefs, but the conduct of its leadership. Robert Jay Lifton, medical doctor and long-time researcher in the psychological aspect of cultic groups writes: "Cults can be identified by three characteristics: a charismatic leader who increasingly becomes an object of worship as the general

---

[14] Walter R. Martin, *The Kingdom of the Cults* (Minneapolis: Bethany House, 1982).

principles that may have originally sustained the group lose their power; a process I call coercive persuasion or thought reform; economic, sexual, and other exploitation of group members by the leader and the ruling coterie."[15]

One thinks of Jonestown, Guyana and the 912 people who perished in 1978 having trusted and followed to the end the charismatic leader, Jim Jones. Or of Waco, Texas and the seventy-four followers of David Koresh who similarly died in the spring of 1993 in the inferno that was formerly called the Branch Davidian compound. Or of the thirty-nine Heaven's Gate cult members who in March of 1997 followed leader Marshall H. Applewhite in committing mass suicide, expecting to regroup on a space ship hidden in the tail of the Hale-Bopp Comet.

These are what could be termed "destructive cults," not merely groups holding beliefs outside of the mainstream, but those which seek to control and exploit for the benefit of the leaders. While these examples are extreme and vastly different from the Cursillo weekend, the techniques employed by both are remarkably similar (these techniques are detailed in Chapter 3 and 6).

Fundamentals of Cult Dynamics

University of California at Berkley psychology professor Margaret Singer has devoted most of her life to the scholarly analysis of cults. According to her estimate, and depending on the definition, there are somewhere between three thousand and five thousand cults operating in the United States. In the past two decades "as many as twenty million people have been involved for varying periods of time in one or another of these groups." [16]

Her definition of a cult is not unlike that of Lifton's above: "For our purposes, the label *cult* refers to three factors:

1. The origin of the group and role of the leader
2. The power structure, or relationship between the leader (or leaders) and the followers
3. The use of a coordinated program of persuasion (which is called thought reform, or, more commonly, brainwashing)."[17]

She goes on to expand on each of these three elements. [18]

---

[15] Robert Jay Lifton, *The Harvard Mental Health Letter*, Vol. 7, Number 8 February 1981.
[16] Margaret Thaler Singer with Janja Lalich, *Cults in Our Midst: the Hidden Menace in Our Everyday Lives*, (San Francisco: Jossey-Bass Publishers, 1995), 5.
[17] Ibid., 7.
[18] The following expansion is found in Ibid., 8-10.

1. The Origin of the Group and the Role of the Leader.

First, "Cult leaders are self-appointed, persuasive persons who claim to have a special mission in life or to have special knowledge." Somehow these leaders have come up with special insight and understanding which their followers need to be complete, and with whom they will share these secrets.

Second, "Cult leaders tend to be determined and domineering and are often described as charismatic." They have enough personal charm or persuasive power to get others to follow them, even to the point of great personal sacrifice.

Third, "Cult leaders center veneration on themselves." Rather than God, the teachings or the sacred books, the focus of adoration and attention is on the leader. Followers often must separate from other loved ones in order to prove loyalty to the leader.

In the experience I have had with the Cursillo, there is often affection and admiration for the leaders. But certainly nothing close to this level of devotion is either required or offered.

2. Structure: Relationship Between Leader and Follower.

First, "Cults are authoritarian in structure." The cult leader is the recognized authority from which there can be no appeal and no disagreement. The leader may delegate authority to others, yet this is only on a limited basis, and is strictly regulated.

Second, "Cults appear to be innovative and exclusive." Cult leaders may claim they have discovered the only truth that all other religions were striving to achieve, and that they alone possess the answers for life's problems. This exclusivity extends to their followers whom the leaders claim to be "chosen" or "special." To leave the group, one will have to surrender their special status.

Third, "Cults tend to have a double set of ethics." Within the group, strict discipline, absolute honesty and purity must be maintained to the point that one is continually confessing contrary thoughts and deeds. But toward nonmembers, "the ends justify the means," and deception, trickery and manipulation are all used and even encouraged.

The Cursillo does evidence some of these traits. The leaders clearly are in control of every minute aspect of the weekend, and authority is delineated according to specific titles such as "rector," "spiritual director," "table leader," and speakers called "rollistas" or "professors." What's more, the Cursillo offers something innovative and exclusive. There is a clear distinction drawn between those who have "made Cursillo" and are therefore "Cursillistas" and those who are mere candidates or the uninitiated. This exclusivity is heightened by the secrets or "surprises" which the insiders know about, but are restricted from divulging to others (in order not to "ruin the surprises"). And there is a clear pragmatism evidenced in the Cursillo. In conversation with Cursillo leaders, some expressed reservation and admitted that the techniques might be too intense, but the bottom line is that they "worked," and "if it works, don't fix it."

3. A Coordinated Program of Persuasion.

Cults tend to employ "specific techniques of exploitative persuasion....in order to induce people to join, stay, and obey." These techniques are examined at length in chapters 3 and 6, but Singer offers the following generalizations:

First, "Cults tend to be totalistic, or all-encompassing, in controlling their members' behavior and also idealistically totalistic, exhibiting zealotry and extremism in their worldview." In destructive cults, members are expected to surrender more and more of their lives to the group, and allow the leaders to have complete and unquestioned domination.

Second, "Cults tend to require members to undergo a major disruption or change in life-style." While I would argue that any genuine commitment to Christ requires the same, this is not what Dr. Singer is talking about. Cult groups increasingly require separation from family, friends and job in order to become completely immersed in the group's mission. The result is isolation which results in an enforced dependency.

And the Cursillo has elements of this as well. Christians who truly embrace the Cursillo believe strongly in its methods and results. They will staunchly defend it and will find themselves withdrawing more and more from their local churches in order to devote more time to planning and working at Cursillos, attending Cursillo group reunions and ultreyas and sponsoring new candidates. They will find themselves drawn to fellow Cursillistas (those who have "made Cursillo" or graduated successfully from the weekend). Consequently, they tend naturally to be drawn away from former friends and family members who are not involved in the Cursillo.

Again, let me stress that the Cursillo is not a cult, which is to say that we should not adopt a reactionary stance. Even though it may employ some cult-like features, it does not require nor receive the unthinking loyalty as do the destructive cults. Still, those cult-like features need to be recognized and repudiated.

An Example of a Cult Recruitment

Steven Hassan is a former cult member who now works to expose the tactics of destructive cults. In his book, *Combatting Cult Mind Control*, he describes his own initiation into the Unification Church and his nearly two and one half years of involvement with them in key positions of leadership.[19]

College student Steven Hassan was at a vulnerable point in his life, having just broken up with his girlfriend. He was confused about the future direction of his life, but felt a strong pressure to make some kind of significant contribution with his life. One day he was approached at the student union cafeteria by three attractive women of Japanese background and an Italian-American man, all dressed like students and carrying books. They engaged him in conversation for three hours, at the conclusion of which they invited him to an informal meeting. The four assured him that they were not part of a religious group but were members of something they called the One World Crusade, a community of young people from all over the world, seeking to solve the very problems he had been thinking about. Since he wanted to make new friends, he agreed to go.

The meeting was quite enjoyable. He was attracted to these young people who seemed so happy with their lives, and who related as brothers and sisters in a loving family. He was invited to attend another night, which involved a lecture by a woman from Holland. The lecture was "vague and a bit simplistic, but pleasing." Hassan felt he could agree with everything that was said. But this lecture did not explain why everyone in the group was so happy. He began to wonder if something was wrong with him, or if there was something extraordinary about them. He was intrigued. He attended another meeting, and this time the lecture had clearly religious overtones. He didn't notice at this point that his questions were never answered. But he was confused and announced he would not be coming back.

This seemed to set off a silent alarm among the group. As he walked out to leave, a dozen members rushed out after him and surrounded his car, stocking-footed in the February cold. They refused to let him leave unless he promised to come back the next night. He finally relented.

The next night he describes as "love bombing." He became the center of attention and was constantly told how good, smart, and dynamic he was. Also, he was invited over thirty times to a relaxing weekend retreat. By rare coincidence he had the very next weekend off. He took this as a possible sign that he was to go.

As the van pulled up to the lavish estate of the retreat center, he was told that this weekend would be a joint workshop with the Unification Church. Hassan was stunned. He was unaware that the retreat was really a "workshop" and that some "church" was going to be involved. He requested to leave, but because the site was isolated and nobody was returning to the city that night, he

---

[19] The following is summarized from Steven Hassan, *Combatting Cult Mind Control* (Rochester, VT: Park Street Press, 1988), 12-34.

Chapter 2: Is Cursillo a Cult?

was coaxed into staying.

The weekend began by the group being divided up into small groups and seated on the floor. Oddly, they were given paper and crayons and asked to draw common objects: a house, tree, mountain, river, the sun, a snake. Nobody objected; all simply obeyed. Then they took turns introducing themselves and were led in folk singing. Hassan says he was "embarrassed by the childishness of it all, but no one else seemed to mind." He said it brought back warm memories of summer camp. That night the men and women were segregated to sleep in crowded bunkhouses complete with two loud snorers, making for a poor night's sleep.

In the morning, he was taken aside by "an intense young man from the group house" who urged him to "not have a closed mind" but to "hear the whole thing." After calisthenics and breakfast, they were seated on the floor and sang folk songs together. Then "a charismatic young man with ice-blue eyes and a penetrating voice introduced himself." He was the workshop director, and gave the ground rules for the weekend. "We were told we had to spend all of our time together in the small groups to which we were assigned. There was to be no walking around the estate alone. Questions were to be asked only after a lecture was over, when we were back in our small group."

The lecturer was introduced: "an American in his late twenties, dressed in a blue suit, white shirt, and red tie." He "exuded the charm and confidence of a family doctor." As the lengthy lecture droned on and on, Hassan became uncomfortable. The strangeness of the situation suddenly struck him. He liked the people, but disliked the rigid structure, the childish atmosphere and the deceptiveness of the purpose of the weekend. He was told to keep his questions for the small group, and in the small group he was told that his questions would be answered by the next lecture.

Every moment of the weekend was completely structured, allowing no free time. He estimates that the newcomers were outnumbered by members three-to-one, and they effectively kept newcomers from talking to one another. Before the day ended, the newcomers were asked to fill out "reflection sheets," what they were thinking and feeling. These, of course, were analyzed by the leaders. The day concluded with another fitful night's sleep.

The second full day, Sunday, followed the same format as the day before. But Hassan was by now disoriented and confused. He seemed to be the only one questioning the weekend. Perhaps there was something wrong with him? Perhaps he was not intelligent or spiritual enough to grasp it? He began to listen with greater earnestness.

Sunday evening, he was faced with another "surprise." He was anxious to get home, but the "weekend" included another day! Since nobody would be returning to the city until the next night, he was stuck. And he was urged to stay with the promise that "it will all come together" on the last day. Hassan admits that part of him "was really curious to hear the whole thing." He was hooked.

And on the third full day, Monday, Hassan says, "we were lifted up to an unprecedented emotional high." The lecture was especially impassioned and came to an astounding conclusion, a supposedly "scientific" conclusion: that God had sent his second Messiah into the world between 1917 and 1930! With this ringing in his ears, Hassan, completely exhausted, was loaded in the van and taken back to the city, but he was not yet allowed to go home. First he was taken aside by a leader and read a brief biography of Rev. Sun Moon, of his life of suffering in the battle to proclaim God's truth and to fight Satan and communism. He was urged to pray about what he had heard and to think deeply about the serious responsibility of bearing the truth he had now received. He was assured that if he walked away now, "he would never forgive himself."

Confusion best describes Hassan's state of mind. He felt strongly the need to get away from these people and to think for himself, but he also felt guilty about his rudeness toward them. When he returned home, his parents thought he had been drugged. They were alarmed when he told them that he had been with members of the Unification Church and that they told him to sever all contact with them. He says he struggled with the decision for several days and engaged in "earnest prayer." Eventually he felt (at the time) he received a sign that he should return to them. As soon as he did, he was "whisked off to another three-day workshop."

The second workshop was nearly identical to the first, even in content. But Hassan decided he had been "too cynical" the first weekend, and this time he took it all in. He writes:

> By the end of those three days the Steve Hassan who had walked into the first workshop was gone, replaced by a new "Steve Hassan." I was elated at the thought that I was "chosen" by God and that my life's path was now on the only "true track." I experienced a wide range of other feelings too: I was shocked and honored that I had been singled out for leadership, scared at how much responsibility rested on my shoulders, and emotionally high on the thought that God was actively working to bring about the Garden of Eden. No more war, no more poverty, no more ecological destruction. Just love, truth, beauty, and goodness. Still, a muffled voice deep within was telling me to watch out, to keep questioning everything. [20]

The rest of Hassan's story, how his "new identity was constantly reinforced while his old identity was suppressed and denied," how he moved up in the ranks of the organization, and how he recruited others and how he

---

[20] Ibid., 19.

Chapter 2: Is Cursillo a Cult?

eventually left the cult is truly fascinating.

Part of his return to his former self was reading psychiatrist Robert Jay Lifton's book *Thought Reform and the Psychology of Totalism*. From this he learned the shocking revelation that the Chinese Communists used the same mind control tactics that he had been using (and had been used on him) in recruiting new members. To Rev. Moon, the Chinese Communists were "Satan." Hassan was forced to ask himself, "Does God have to use the same tactics as Satan in order to make an ideal world?" [21]

This led to other, similar questions of a moral nature: "Does the God I believe in need to use deception and mind control? Do the ends truly justify the means? I had to ask myself whether the means determine the ends."[22] He learned that Lifton had identified "eight basic elements of the process of mind control as practiced by the Chinese Communists."[23] His exit counselors showed him that "no matter how wonderful the cause, or how attractive the members, if any group employed all eight of Robert Jay Lifton's elements, then it was operating as a mind control environment."[24]

Hassan then makes this observation:

> Since leaving the group, I have come to believe that millions of people have actually been subjected to a mind control regimen but don't even know it. Hardly a week goes by that I don't talk with several people who are still experiencing negative side effects from their experience of mind control. Often, it is a great relief for them to hear that they are not alone and that their problems stem from their involvement with such a group.[25]

(Chapters 3 and 6 detail ways in which participants at Cursillo and other weekend renewal experiences are exposed to many of these mind control techniques.)

It is important to stress again that the Cursillo should not be equated with a cult, even though similar tactics are employed. The main reason why the Cursillo should not be considered a cult is because it is missing certain crucial elements common to destructive cults. One is the lack of the nearly-divine leader who is idolized and given complete authority. The Cursillo leaders I have spoken with are sincere, humble and ordinary Christians whose clear goal is to help others and not to promote themselves. Another missing element is the excessiveness with which these mind control techniques are used in destructive

---

[21] Ibid., 28.
[22] Ibid., 54.
[23] Ibid., 53.
[24] Ibid. For an evaluation of Cursillo with respect to Lifton's "eight basic elements" see chapter 7.
[25] Ibid., 54.

cults. While the intensity of the Cursillo weekends can be high (so high that a local Young Adults Together Encounter Christ (YATEC) leader confessed to me he would not be sending his teenaged children to a Teens Encounter Christ (TEC) Weekend), still they do not reach the extremes seen in destructive cults. And the other element common to cults but missing in the Cursillo is the physical, sexual or financial exploitation of the membership. I have never heard of any allegations to this effect in the Cursillo or related weekends.

And yet we should understand that when mind control techniques are employed, the potential for a movement to spawn a destructive cult is quite real. In his book *Churches That Abuse*,[26] Westmont College sociology professor Ronald M. Enroth describes dozens of Christian fringe groups and churches, most of them quite small, which, usually with initially good intentions, have become excessively authoritarian, manipulative, and intimidating. Each of these is a tragedy that could have been prevented. Being aware of the mind control techniques and refusing to use them is the surest way to avert similar problems in the future.

---

[26] Ronald M. Enroth, *Churches That Abuse* (Grand Rapids: Zondervan, 1992).

3. *The Methodology of Mind Control*

Mind Control?

Why are Cursillistas restricted from revealing too many of the details of the Cursillo weekend? The usual answer is in order not to "ruin" it by taking away the "surprises." "Surprise" implies something akin to a pleasant, unexpected birthday party. But these "surprises" are much more. The Cursillo surprises are in reality powerful techniques of psychological persuasion. These techniques are alternately called "psychological coercion," "coercive persuasion," "thought reform," "mind control," and (unhelpfully) "brainwashing."

The latter term, "brainwashing," is so completely negative and controversial that it is best not used. Former cult member and author Steven Hassan draws a significant distinction between "brainwashing" and what the destructive cults do. The term he prefers is "mind control." "Brainwashing" is a term devised in 1951 by Edward Hunter, a journalist. He noticed how during the Korean War captured American servicemen suddenly changed their beliefs and loyalties and admitted to completely fictional war crimes. The process of effecting this change Hunter called "brainwashing."

But there is a real difference. In brainwashing, the subject knows he is in the hands of the enemy, in a life-threatening situation. And the means of bringing about the change is often severe abuse and even torture. Obviously, nothing like this takes place on Cursillo weekends, and even the vast majority of destructive cults never use torture to achieve their ends.

The mind control used by destructive cults, however, is much more subtle.

Mind control, also called "thought reform" is more subtle and sophisticated. Its perpetrators are regarded as friends or peers, so the person is much less defensive. He unwittingly participates by cooperating with this controllers and giving them private information that he does not know will be used against him. The new belief system is internalized into a new identity structure.

Mind control involves little or no overt physical abuse. Instead, *hypnotic processes* are combined with *group dynamics* to create a potent indoctrination effect. The individual is deceived and manipulated—not directly threatened—into making the prescribed choices. On the whole, he responds positively to what is done to him.[27]

What's interesting about the Cursillo weekend is that while parts of it become quite intense and emotionally uncomfortable at times (a symptom that mind control techniques are being used), what is usually remembered is that it was a "good experience."

Hassan describes mind control as: "a system of influences that disrupts an individual's identity (beliefs, behavior, thinking, and emotions) and replaces it with a new identity. In most cases, that new identity is one that the original identity would strongly object to if it knew in advance what was in store."[28]

But how are these changes effected? What techniques are used? The specific psychological techniques used in Cursillo will be described at length in Chapter 6. Here, we consider the stages of mind control, the steps in the process, and the conditions for mind control.

Three Stages of Mind Control

The process of gaining control of the mind follows a predictable three-stage pattern. These have been described by Edgar Schein in his book *Coercive Persuasion*.[29]

The first stage Schein calls "Unfreezing." To prepare a person for radical change, first his or her reality must be shaken up: the subject must be disoriented. His or her common way of understanding or interpreting their world must be disrupted. Various techniques can accomplish this, and the effect can be most powerful when the techniques are combined. Sleep deprivation, new diet and eating schedules, isolation in unfamiliar surroundings, removal from regular support systems, sensory or emotional overload, rapid exposure to new and conflicting even irrational information, guided meditations, vigorous calisthenics, even group singing can help to disorient the person and create anxiety.

A further goal in the unfreezing stage is to undermine self-confidence, to "break you down so they can build you back up." The subject is bombarded

---

[27] Steven Hassan, *Combatting Cult Mind Control*, 56, emphasis original.
[28] Ibid., 7.
[29] Edgar H. Schein, *Coercive Persuasion* (New York: W. W. Norton, 1971).

with the idea that they are badly flawed. Personal inadequacies, sins, failures, as well as past disappointments are greatly exaggerated to the point that the person is left in an anxious and incomplete state. The result is a heightened suggestibility and openness to whatever the group may be presenting.

The second stage in mind control is "Changing." Once the subject is sufficiently disoriented and made to feel incomplete and inadequate, the solution offered by the group is more easily accepted. The group's answer is now stated repeatedly by group leaders. This is reinforced by the testimonies of those who may pretend to have been reluctant, but now are making the desired commitment. And this is even more subtly reinforced by members of the group posing as new recruits who act interested and continually direct the real recruit's attention to the solution offered by the leader.

Understandably, this process can be quite emotional for the subject. Because of the disorientation in the first stage, the anxiety can be pronounced. The person often draws into this anxiety painful memories from the past, perpetual struggles with personal failures, sad and shameful recollections, and deep-seated fears. Together, these frequently produce an overwhelming tension which seeks release. This release often comes in a dramatic catharsis, a let down of emotion, followed by an immediate attraction to the group and affinity for its teachings. In the euphoria that follows, the teaching of the group is quickly imbibed with little critical inspection. After all, it is reasoned, anything that can produce an experience this good must be the real thing.

The third stage is called "Refreezing." Here the new identity is solidified and reinforced. A system of rewards is offered for conformity while punishments are meted out for non-compliance. "Most of the modern-day thought-reform groups seek to produce smiling, non-resistant, hardworking persons who do not complain about the group practices and do not question the authority of the guru, leader or trainer."[30] One of the strongest ways to refreeze the subject into the new identity is to have him or her recruit others into the group. If one can successfully bring others into the group, it only reinforces that the group and their teaching must be right and true. Dr. Singer observes that "cults only have two basic purposes: recruiting new members and fund-raising."[31]

Again, one can draw remarkable parallels to the processes used in the Cursillo initiation weekend. The first night is spent in uncomfortable and somber silence, the purpose of which is to "awaken the moral consciences of the participants, beginning with an analysis of their own lives and causing them to desire to encounter God."[32] Clearly this is a description of "unfreezing."

---

[30] Singer, *Cults in Our Midst*, 77.
[31] Ibid., 11.
[32] From *"What is Cursillo?"* a publication by the National Cursillo Center, PO Box 210226, Dallas, TX 75211.

The Friday and Saturday of the Cursillo weekend are devoted to understanding yourself and what motivates you and your relationship with God, through various presentations or talks which are then discussed and analyzed at table groups (with complete strangers). This is the inculcation of the new identity, the "changing."

And Sunday is devoted to learning how we can help God in fulfilling His will. This is the beginning of the "refreezing." At the conclusion of the Sunday events, the participant is welcomed into the Cursillo community. Ideally the new Cursillista ever after participates in a weekly Cursillo small group reunion where the new ideas are reinforced, and a monthly large group gathering called the ultreya, where the new ideas are celebrated. And the new Cursillista begins to sponsor new candidates (new recruits), also a key feature in the "refreezing" process.

It is interesting that the local leaders of Young Adults Together Encounter Christ (YATEC) are not so subtle in their descriptions of the weekend. The first day is "die day" where your old self dies (unfreezing), the second day is "resurrection day" where your new self is reborn (changing), and the third day is "go out and serve/take it back home day" (refreezing).

Six Conditions for Mind Control

Cult researcher and psychology professor Margaret Thaler Singer describes six conditions necessary to create the atmosphere for mind control to take place.

1. Keep the person unaware that there is an agenda to control or change the person.
2. Control time and physical environment (contacts, information)
3. Create a sense of powerlessness, fear and dependency.
4. Suppress old behavior and attitudes
5. Instill new behavior and attitudes
6. Put forth a closed system of logic[33]

1. A first prerequisite is to *keep the person unaware of what is going on and how she or he is being changed a step at a time.* As a person being influenced,

> you are kept unaware of the orchestration of psychological and social forces meant to change your thinking and your behavior. The cult leaders make it seem as though what is going on is normal, that everything is the way it's supposed to be. This atmosphere is

---

[33] Singer, *Cults in Our Midst,* 64. She expands on each of these in the following pages.

Chapter 3: The Methodology of Mind Control

reinforced by peer pressure and peer-modeled behavior, so that you adapt to the environment without even realizing it.[34]

If the hidden agenda were announced ahead of time, few people would volunteer to participate. So what will actually take place is only described in general and vague terms, and the leadership invariably does not distribute a weekend schedule which is a common complaint of those who dislike the Cursillo weekend. The weekend itself is simply called a "pleasant spiritual getaway" or "a refreshing time of fellowship." The few Cursillo brochures which are available are remarkable for their lack of information. And each table group contains a couple of leaders (one or both may be incognito) who model the proper, compliant behavior.

2. A second prerequisite is to *control the person's social and/or physical environment; especially control the person's time.* The Cursillo weekend is hosted at a distant location where the entire schedule is controlled by the leaders. Participants are often driven to the location and so have no personal means of escape. They are urged to surrender their wristwatches so they lose track of time. Outside phone calls and other "distractions" are discouraged.

3. A third prerequisite to create the proper atmosphere for mind control is to *systematically create a sense of powerlessness in the person.* "Cults create this sense of powerlessness by stripping you of your support system and your ability to act independently."[35] Cults will take away friendship and family networks. Another way to achieve this is to take away the subject's main occupation and source of income. Students are routinely instructed to drop out of school.

This obviously creates a sense of dependency on the group. A TEC leader told me that students are carefully selected for table groups ahead of time so that there will be nobody sitting at their table whom they knew before the weekend, not even someone from their same school. The rationale offered was so that the teen could "make new friends" and "discover the large Christian community that is out there" and to "establish relationships that last a long time, someone to turn to when you need help." But this practice would in reality inhibit the maintenance of such relationships since none of these people are from your home town, your home church, or your pre-TEC world. Rather, the real reason for the separation is to effectively remove the subject (at least for the weekend) from his or her usual support system and create a dependency on the new group.

4. A fourth prerequisite is to *manipulate a system of rewards, punishments, and experiences in such a way as to inhibit behavior that reflects the person's former social identity.* The values and beliefs of the person prior to entering the group are

---

[34] Ibid., 64-65.
[35] Ibid., 65.

routinely discouraged and suppressed. Old ways are defined as irrelevant, unnecessary, and unworthy.

    5. A fifth prerequisite, similarly, is to *manipulate a system of rewards, punishments, and experiences in order to promote learning of the group's ideology or belief system and group-approved behaviors.* Several features of the Cursillo weekend combine to create this system of rewards and punishments. When candidates give reports they receive applause regardless of the quality of their performance. Table leaders are always present in order to model correct behavior and reward proper responses. And one feature of the Cursillo weekend is called "unconditional love" (a reward for being on the weekend). Any kind of "sharing" by candidates is encouraged and approved (rewarded), but especially the responses that contribute to the movement and ideals of the weekend.

    6. A sixth prerequisite is to *put forth a closed system of logic and an authoritarian structure that permits no feedback and refuses to be modified except by leadership approval.* Questions or contrary views expressed during the weekend are not exactly punished as much as ignored. When I made Cursillo, I found that the pace of the weekend was so rapid and crowded that critical evaluation was inhibited. There was simply no time allowed to explore views other than those being expressed by the leadership. And my questions and objections to local Cursillo leaders were regularly dismissed from a pragmatic perspective: "Cursillo works, so don't try to fix it."

    It should be disconcerting to discover that all of these six conditions for mind control are purposely built into the Cursillo weekend to some degree or another.[36]

TECHNIQUES USED IN WEEKEND RENEWAL EXPERIENCES

    In order to host a successful weekend renewal experience like Cursillo, or weekend youth retreat of this variety, you must combine several techniques in a pattern and flow that builds toward the climax of an emotional catharsis. An emotional momentum must be initiated and sustained if the weekend is to "work" and people are to experience the catharsis and bonding. When these methods are skillfully employed, I have never known them to fail. The number of these techniques used and their combination and order differs somewhat according to the type of weekend experience: Cursillo, TEC, Lay Witness Mission, youth retreat, Large Group Awareness Training, etc. But the techniques are indispensable to achieve the desired effect.

---

[36] Psychologist Robert J. Lifton identifies eight psychological themes which are central to totalistic environments. Singer (*Cults in Our Midst*, 69-74) discusses these themes. Application of some of these is discussed in chapter 7 of this book.

These techniques can be divided into two categories: 1) psychological, pertaining to the mind and perception, especially the emotions, and 2) physiological, producing physical changes that lead to an alteration in one's state of consciousness.

The psychological techniques include anticipation and unburdening, emotional washing, "love bombing," peer pressure and the desire to fit in and belong, the fear of missing "it," the appearance of the miraculous or the mysterious, and the unburdening and regression to childhood. The physiological techniques include sleep deprivation, withdrawal from the familiar, loss of time consciousness, sensory stimulation including touch, lighting and music, hyperventilation, repetitive motion, and dietary changes. Not all of these must be used every time, but enough of them must be skillfully combined to create the momentum and achieve the desired effect. What follows is a brief description of each.

The Psychological Techniques

These methods are used create emotional changes in the participant with a view to preparing him or her for the emotional climax and catharsis experience.

1. Anticipation.

The participants are told usually long ahead of time that something wonderful is going to happen to them on the weekend. This is often in the form of a testimonial in which the leader or veteran tells about the powerful, life-changing experience they personally underwent along with the lasting benefits. And yet few details are supplied. This creates not only a sense of anticipation, but a sense of mystery. Something incredible is promised, but it is left unspecified.

For Alan, the anticipation was somewhat self-created by his wanderlust and feeling that "God had something big for him to do." Of course this was piqued by an attractive young woman smiling at him, appearing to be interested in him, and inviting him away for a weekend with her at a "spiritual" retreat. It would be safe to say that Alan had high expectations for the weekend.

The anticipation for the Lay Witness Mission is created in part by the extensive preparations. Numerous committees are formed and everybody's help is employed, often in mere busy work. But the increased activity creates a "buzz" of anticipation before the event itself begins. This is often enhanced by the knowledge that "people are coming to visit us," and yet there is a continuing sense of mystery as to why they are coming, or what will be happening.

In some of the weekend retreat experiences like the Cursillo, the potential participant must be personally invited, even "sponsored" by a past attendee, creating a sense of privilege and special status. Participants are often referred to as "candidates," implying that they are "wanna be's" hoping for a potential full admission if they successfully complete the "short course" and "make Cursillo." And past attendees are forbidden to tell others what really happens during the weekend. This creates a mystique that only heightens curiosity and anticipation. I have spoken with people preparing to attend YATEC who expressed fear about the approaching initiation, already in a heightened emotional state before the weekend began. This anticipation is critical to create the expectation that something remarkable and mysterious is going to transpire. And this tension finds its release in the cathartic effects of the climax.

2. Emotional "washing."

A wide range of emotions are expressed, encouraged, and modeled by the leadership and speakers during the weekend. The goal is to spark the same emotions in the participants: everything from boisterous, giddy laughter to deep, wistful sadness to attraction and affection to regret and shame.

I can still remember clearly when I caught on to this technique of emotional washing, thought it was not in the context of a weekend renewal experience. It was during orientation at the Christian college I attended. Somebody from the drama department had written a play about dorm life. It was extremely funny, and I remember laughing until the tears flowed and my sides ached. And then suddenly, in a matter of seconds, the mood shifted to seriousness, to unbelievable grief and sadness—one of the dorm buddies said his brother had died shortly before college began. I remember feeling the abrupt shifting of emotional gears and how it captivated my attention. It was absolutely silent in the auditorium, and every eye was riveted to the scene unfolding before us. And I distinctly remember noticing that this sudden shift of emotions was very captivating.

But I also noted that the same was true of television melodramas and films. In the completely controlled and contrived environment of the television sound stage and the movie set, the screenwriter is free to create and manipulate emotions of any variety: humor, poignant drama, moral outrage, hatred and vengeance, lust, despair, or hopelessness. Shortly after the dormitory drama I watched on campus a sappy melodramatic film called *The Champ*, about a boxer and his son. The boxer dies at the end (sorry to spoil it for you). I was deeply moved. I was emotionally washed. Many movies aspire to create this kind of emotional washing, and millions attend faithfully in order to be so washed.

Alan was particularly moved by the joy shown by the Moonies, the heartfelt singing, the warmth and acceptance he felt from them all, the "testimonies" by those who professed to be new believers. He felt a strong emotional tug to stay with the group and to become like these caring and committed people.

In Lay Witness Missions, the speakers who are chosen usually are able

Chapter 3: The Methodology of Mind Control

to express their emotions freely, vividly confessing a sinful and sordid past or describing heart-wrenching tragedies or struggles. They can quickly shift back and forth from crying to laughing. Playful attitudes during meals, recreation times, and "ice breakers" create a sense of childlike (childish) silliness that elicits deep laughter, as participants "let down their hair." In a matter of minutes, someone will then be sharing the pain of their divorce or of a child's death, running participants through the emotional wringer.

In some cases, such as TEC and YATEC, graphic drama is employed to help participants "see" and especially "feel" the pain of Christ's death on the cross or the joy of the resurrection in the stations of the cross. And the effect is to "wash" the participant in emotion so that their own emotions, which may have lain dormant, are reawakened and engaged. This emotional washing is vital in breaking down the participant's defenses. This, in turn, will enable him or her to achieving the cathartic effects of the emotional climax.

The sudden shift of emotions is seen clearly during the Roman Catholic Cursillo in the abrupt and dramatic change from the somberness of Thursday which is then "punctured by a tone of happiness" on Friday morning. "Unprepared for this transition, many are startled and confused...." As one participant observed:

> I came out of Mass in a deeply meditative state of mind. The same attitude could be observed among the others. *Then the silence which had been reigning since the previous evening was broken by a song which is very popular in Spain.*...I did not like that. I was not in the habit of singing at the top of my voice on coming out of church. Then the members of the directing team began to laugh and joke. One could see that they were sincerely happy and joyful, but their laughter seemed to me out of place after the deeply serious moments we had just experienced in chapel.
>
> In this way, talking, singing, joking, we then made our way towards the dining room. I noticed that, like myself, many people found the overflowing joy of the directing team out of place.[37]

Cursillistas who give rollos (talks) at the Roman Catholic Cursillo are strongly urged to include abundant emotional self-disclosure in their messages.

It is the giving of words, spoken not only from an objective, intellectual position, *but also from the depths of their emotional, private selves.* Each rollo, then, is a witness to the power of religion in their lives and the offering a *personal disclosure that strikes many* because of its honest

---

[37] Marcoux, *Cursillo: Anatomy of a Movement*, 70-71, emphasis original.

revelation, the gift of words that come from the self, not easily, but with difficulty *and the shyness of revealing what generally is marked by a guardedness.* Especially in a society where religion is considered private and spiritual feelings remain undisclosed, the rollos break this norm, *and the shock of personal revelation overwhelms many candidates.*

In this way, each rollo is a witness to being a Christian. The talk not only explains an idea, it implicitly exhibits it in the presentation. For without doubt, *the cursillo understands the power of disclosure, of revealing feelings in the process of communication."*[38]

Expressing emotion as a means of stimulating emotion in others is a well-known psychological technique suggested, for example, by Carl Rogers in his Client-Centered Therapy approach. "Therapists who speak genuinely out of their own strong feelings tend to evoke and liberate clients to release and express their own emotional experiences."[39] Remarkably, critics of Rogers' approach charge that "the self-expressing therapist *actually creates emotional experiences in clients* through such transactions rather than releasing some feelings that are implicitly existing within the client."[40]

3. "Love bombing."

During the church weekend experience, "unconditional love" is offered freely and in great abundance. This is crucial to develop the unity and family feeling essential to a successful weekend. For many reasons, our culture produces lonely people. Marital breakups, impersonal workplaces, busy lives, passive forms of entertainment, as well as the general self-centeredness of contemporary life combine to produce people starving for affection and care. In such weekends, these are offered in great measure.

This was quite evident in Alan's case. He was a red-blooded, young man, far from home, not having had close, friendly contact with anyone for some time. The smiling, attractive, "Christian" girl who belonged to this loving "family" of caring young people, who showed acceptance and affection with such ease and abundance combined to strike him at his most vulnerable point.

On Lay Witness Missions and other weekend renewal experiences, people are often told they are loved unconditionally. At several points during the weekend, everyone is instructed to shake someone's hand and say, "God loves you, and so do I." Participants' comments are heard to with interest. In the small group sharing there are "no wrong answers." Everyone is accepted and valued for the weekend, creating a powerful bonding effect. In Lay Witness

---

[38] Ibid., 76-77, emphasis added.
[39] James O. Prochaska, *Systems of Psychotherapy: A Transtheoretical Approach* (Homewood, Illinois: Dorsey Press, 1979), 123.
[40] Ibid., emphasis added.

Chapter 3: The Methodology of Mind Control

Missions, if someone expresses a need during a small group session, the witnesses or leaders will often pause the meeting and pray for the hurting person, sometimes laying hands on them, demonstrating their genuine concern.

At the conclusion of such weekends, participants often feel a reluctance to leave, and a desire to hold "reunions" is common. At the end of one YATEC weekend, participants were given a T-shirt with the words "One Body" on the front. Veterans of these events often report feeling closer to fellow participants than they do to members of their own churches or even family members, so powerful is this bonding effect. And the goal is to make the participant feel "safe," to break down resistance and defenses.

A similar technique of "love bombing" is found in the giving of gifts, called "palanca" in Cursillo or "wheat" in TEC and YATEC. In the Roman Catholic Cursillo, the gifts are intended to have a dramatic effect.

> This ritual *purposefully catches the candidates off-guard* as they receive letters, cards, posters, and a variety of objects. Palanca are symbolic offerings to candidates implying some sacrifice by the giver and handed to the candidate as *a public statement of caring*. These gifts of caring are from individuals the candidates are acquainted with and those who are strangers.[41]

The effect of these gifts is profound. "The candidates realize, simply yet directly, that someone outside the sphere of initiation is thinking about them and will continue to keep them in mind until Sunday evening."[42] So not only is the candidate showered with "unconditional love" by the team members, but he or she is the recipient of love from home, and even from complete strangers.

What's more, the palanca, the love notes from home, are reminiscent of the psychological technique known as an "intervention." An intervention is used as shock therapy to a substance-abuser in denial. The person addicted to alcohol or drugs will often deny their problem. If a loved one attempts to confront the addict, he or she is easily disregarded. In an intervention, most or all of the significant people in the addict's life (spouse, children, parents, friends, boss, co-workers, pastor, etc.) are gathered and the addicted person is brought to the meeting unaware. The combination of the surprise of the meeting and the unified voice of all family and friends together becomes a powerful emotional motivator aimed at overwhelming the abuser, breaking down defenses and initiating change. This is similar to the effect of the palanca. Long-time Roman Catholic Cursillo observer Marcene Marcoux notes:

---

[41] Marcoux, *Cursillo: Anatomy of a Movement*, 80-81, emphasis added.
[42] Ibid., 81.

> The palanca catch the initiates by surprise with an overflow of Christian love and concern. Some, overwhelmed with the palanca, begin to cry as individuals at their table comfort them and share in the intensity of this experience [note—the beginning, the flash point of the cathartic experience, ed.]. Others take the impact less emotionally, but even among these, many are dramatically affected by the sacrifices. And this is exactly the aim of the palanca.[43]

Marcoux then quotes Cursillo leaders in an incredible admission: "...the cursillista is brought up short and made to realize that *he is going to have to respond in a way that he probably never did before.*"[44] She explains:

> The team aims at shocking the candidates to alter their everyday consciousness....For the cursillistas, the shock or "breaking" as it is called within the movement, is the necessary rupture with a traditional perspective on the self, the church, and society, preparing the initiate for a transition into a different religious model of social reality–a realm with contrasting religious emphases and distinctive social consequences. The cursillo initiation is consciously structured to produce a break with the things that are taken for granted, and *each aspect of initiation: the Thursday retreat, the rollos, and these palanca, are designed to achieve this dramatic outcome.*[45]

As is the case in the psychological "intervention" technique,

> ...the palanca which affect people most are those offered by someone they know. The fact that a spouse, one's children, friends, sponsors, and neighbors are sacrificing for them provides the most overwhelming impact, with responses ranging from being impressed to being speechless, from smiles to tears of joy.[46]

The cumulative effect of the "unconditional love" felt from the group and these "love notes from home" is powerful. Now the participant feels added "pressure from home" to respond positively during the weekend: "We love you, we're praying for you, we wish the best for you (and we want something wonderful to happen to you this weekend)." This anticipates the next technique.

---

[43] Ibid., 85.
[44] Ibid., emphasis added.
[45] Ibid., 86, emphasis added.
[46] Ibid., 88.

4. Peer pressure and a desire for acceptance and belonging.

Participants will find that there is a "condition" to the "unconditional love" offered. The participant will feel a tremendous need to "respond" when everyone else responds. A "group" feeling often arises early in the process. It will seem to participants that everybody else is going along with the group: laughing at the silly jokes and songs, crying when others cry. This attitude is led by the team of leaders, all of whom know the routine and participate with energy and enthusiasm.

Alan noticed all of the followers of Rev. Moon smiling, seeming to enjoy themselves and being happy. They all showed love and acceptance warmly (as they were instructed) and listened attentively to the speakers, nodding in agreement. They wanted to be there. They seemed to have found something Alan had missed, and he wanted it as well. And the only way he could get it was to stay with the group and become like them. What's more, the seemingly "spontaneous testimonies" by those who were purportedly just now deciding to join the group were undoubtedly well-rehearsed and calculated for maximum effect: "I too had my doubts, but I overcame them, and am now joining the group, and won't you do the same?"

The Lay Witnesses also know the weekend routine quite well. They know when to laugh at the leader's jokes and when to cry at the sad stories. They eagerly go around shaking hands and saying, "God loves you and so do I." They join in the motions of the songs or clap along with enthusiasm. They offer hugs to all, but especially to other team members, creating the "in group" and "out group" feeling (and don't you want to be a part of the "in group"?). This creates a desire to fit in with everyone else, a peer pressure and a desire for acceptance and belonging.

Remarkably, in Cursillo and its imitators, leaders are interspersed into the crowd. Often at least two are seated at each table group *incognito*! They pretend merely to be candidates like the rest. From this vantage point, they can guide the group into proper responses. In a surprise move, these leaders only reveal themselves when they rise to give their rollos or talks.

This kind of infiltration means that critical questions and contrary voices will seldom arise, and if they do, they can be quickly dealt with and dispatched. And this is critical to the success of the event. The weekend experience is like a locomotive that starts out slowly and must reach a certain speed and intensity in order for the cathartic climax to occur. Questions, criticism, or failure fully to participate must be dealt with and overcome early in the weekend.

If a strong-willed participant were to refuse to perform childish motions to the silly songs or refused to tell someone "God loves you, and so do I," it might affect others adversely, and the momentum for the weekend would be lost. The "high" would never be hit, and the weekend would be a failure.

Alan discovered that questions were not all that welcome, and in fact, that dissension or disobedience was met with the ultimate threat: the disapproval of or even expulsion from the group. That's why it was so difficult for Alan to keep in contact with his parents, or even for him to come to his mother's bedside when he was convinced she could be dying. If his new "family" did not approve, he could risk the loss of their acceptance and love which he could not bear.

The promise held out by the weekend experience leaders is: "You can become like us if you will only go through the same experience we've had." And, in fact, that is precisely what happens. Participants can immediately become like their new heroes and are invited to sign-up to become Lay Witnesses, or to "work a Cursillo" some time in the near future. Those who are most effective, that is, who have had a rich experience and are able to talk about it freely and emotionally would be invited back again and again.

But if someone were to stand during the post-cathartic climax sharing time and ask, "Is this for real?" the response would be something less than "unconditional love." And if at that time someone were to say, "I felt emotionally used and manipulated by this weekend," then the "there are no wrong answers" rule would suddenly cease to apply. The person would be pitied and/or prayed for as an "outsider," but the substance of their concerns would not be addressed, and that person would feel very much withdrawn from the group.

And even the person who attends the entire weekend but who, for some reason or another does not have the cathartic experience, that person is made to feel distant to the group, to feel that something must be wrong with him or her or to feel that their spirituality must be less than genuine. Or if, as in my case, after repeated weekend renewal experiences, the cathartic high can no longer be attained by the burned-out veteran, that person is left in a pitiable condition. It is interesting that some weekend renewal experience leaders refuse to allow people to repeat the experience. Veterans of the Cursillo weekend experience may return to work at a Cursillo, to serve on the teams of leaders. But they may not go through the initiation experience itself again. Perhaps the leaders instinctively know that repeated exposure will dull the effects.

5. Fear of missing the high.

The centerpiece of the weekend experience is the emotional high that follows the catharsis, often taking place on the second night of the weekend. If the momentum has been building properly using the techniques described here, the result is a growing emotional tension that seeks opportunity for release. It should be noted that not only events from the weekend, but other emotional situations, unique to the individual, are drawn into this mounting tension. So the pain of a divorce, the shame of an extra-marital affair, feelings of personal inadequacy, the grief at the loss of a loved one, anger at an enemy, the fear of the future, the turmoil of an unresolved decision, sadness at a friendship gone

Chapter 3: The Methodology of Mind Control

sour, the turbulent confusion of adolescence, any and all of these, unique to each participant get drawn into this emotional tension. And if the defenses are sufficiently broken down, in the darkened room, with the catalyst of other people's emotions flowing freely, the release usually comes. Psychologists speak of this as "catharsis," a purifying or cleansing of the emotions, a technique used in psychoanalysis for relieving tension and anxiety by bringing repressed material to consciousness.

This emotional release is often very satisfying. From firsthand, repeated experience I know it to be powerful, even intoxicating. At the time, it seems to be the perfect solution to all your troubles. You just feel better. And who does not deeply desire to feel better? Once you have had this experience your troubles, fears, anxieties, and inadequacies are of little consequence. With the tension released, the result is a heady euphoria and a quiet contentedness.

Speakers at weekend renewal experiences will often describe how this happened to them on a similar weekend. They will say something like, "It was the greatest experience of my life. I hope it happens to you. I don't know if it will or not. I hope it will, but if it doesn't that's all right." And as they speak they will often re-live the joy of when it happened to them. The participant will feel that the speaker has experienced something wonderful, and this experience is dangled before the participant. And yet, as the tension mounts, there is the nagging fear that "It might not happen to me! I might be left alone with my problems. My tension might not be resolved." This becomes a powerful stimulus to participate with diligence so that "what happened to them might happen to me."

6. The appearance of the miraculous/mysterious.

The psychological techniques often include the appearance that something miraculous, or at least mysterious, is taking place, proof that God is real, that this experience is genuine, and that something truly remarkable is taking place this weekend.

For Lay Witness Missions, this miracle/mystery is supplied by the practice of having the leader call someone to witness without prior notification, by the practice of having one witness pray for another witness just before that witness speaks "that God would speak through them," and by the practice of the witnesses not planning ahead of time what they are going to say. A loose biblical support is sometimes offered for this "off the cuff" manner of speaking by referring to Luke 12:11-12: "And when they bring you before the synagogues and the rulers and the authorities, do not be anxious about how you should defend yourself or what you should say, for the Holy Spirit will teach you in that very hour what you ought to say." Though this is obviously taken out of context, to the naive it may appear that the witness is speaking a message directly from God, "just like it says in the Bible," i.e., a miracle.

In other contexts, a speaker may relate how they almost were not able to make it to the weekend experience due to some misfortune or conflict, but at the last minute the problem was cleared up. The implication is that a miracle took place, and this whole weekend experience is more special because miracles have made it possible.

I have heard leaders of Cursillo weekends talk about "miracles" happening all weekend. These "miracles" were of the variety of people feeling better about themselves, or confessing a sin, or making a profession of faith, or forgiving someone, or of promising to try harder at a marriage. To call such events "miracles" only lends to the mystique of the weekend, proof that this indeed is "for real." The presence of "miracles" or mysterious happenings serves to heighten the anticipation and suggestibility of the participants.

7. The unburdening and regression to childhood.

The seventy-two hours of the weekend renewal experience include a nearly complete releasing of adult responsibilities, of worries and cares. While observing at a YATEC weekend, I commented on the abundance of snacks that were constantly available. I was told that "we don't want anyone distracted by hunger." It was intended to be a pampered weekend where one is listened to and waited on around the clock. This leads to a releasing of anxiety, and a refocusing on the subject at hand. When my wife and I had small children, I would often long for a weekend without the kids. But this creates an escapist, regressive mindset, back to a simpler time, back to a time before adult worries and cares, back to childhood.[47]

Alan said the carefree life of the Moonie retreat center led him back to feelings of childhood. He loved it and wanted to stay. He felt like he was a celebrity. One can see how a participant on a church renewal weekend would enjoy the three free and easy days of the pampered life. This is designed to break down defenses and lead to a closer bonding and affinity for both the group and the weekend experience, as well as to allow the cathartic release of emotional tension, since children are more readily allowed to show their emotions (such as crying) than are adults. And children are more pliable; they quickly recognize their need for others to lead them and more compliantly take direction.

The Physiological Techniques

While some techniques are used to affect the emotions, others are aimed at the body, creating an altered state of consciousness.

---

[47] Cursillo table groups are instructed to make posters depicting a previous talk. What should not be overlooked, though, is that adults then find themselves sitting in groups at tables and using crayons to color pictures, as they once did long ago in elementary school *when they were children*.

Chapter 3: The Methodology of Mind Control

1. Sleep deprivation.

The chief of these physiological techniques is the interruption of sleep patterns. When a person does not get proper rest, the result is often changes in their mental state, sometimes serious changes. In fact, anxiety and depression are often exacerbated by insomnia, and the usual remedy is to prescribe tranquilizers or "sleeping" pills. Severe sleep deprivation can cause hallucinations, altered moods, and heightened suggestibility. Who as a youth has not had the experience of staying up too late and getting "punch drunk": feeling silly and giddy, laughing at anything, or feeling wistful, mournful, or melancholy, and this simply as the result of missing sleep?[48]

Alan found himself exhausted living and working at the Moonie retreat center. Consequently, when he heard teaching that seemed odd, he was too tired to oppose or even resist it. It became easier for him simply to accept it, and, for a time, he believed it all, even though it was false.

Every participant would agree that weekend renewal experiences are not very restful. Even the nights leading up to the weekend tend to be restless, as preparations must be made to be gone for the weekend, and as anticipation may cause sleeplessness. But most weekend renewal experiences themselves in which I have participated were very short on rest. I can remember feeling tired, even exhausted at every one of the weekend renewal experiences I attended.

One participant in a Cursillo weekend reported that she had gotten a total of six hours of sleep in the entire seventy-two hour weekend. In many of the weekend renewal experiences, the participants stay on the grounds, often in a church building. This involves sleeping in uncomfortable circumstances, in sleeping bags on the floor: not a very restful night. The lack of sleep has a wearing-down effect which breaks down the defenses and creates the heightened suggestibility.

The leaders of the Roman Catholic Cursillo admit to the rigorous physical demands of the weekend. For this reason, they will only accept candidates meeting certain age requirements and in good physical health:

> Candidates must be in good health, with an absence of major physical problems. Although minor ailments and sicknesses are not deterrents, individuals with a past history of severe physical problems are discouraged from attending. *The four days of initiation, with long hours and an exhaustive schedule of events, can create a strain.* To prevent detrimental effects, those with questionable health are discouraged, or in some cases, excluded from joining.[49]

---

[48] Cult experts Steven Hassan (*Combatting Mind Control*, 102) and Margaret Singer (*Cults in Our Midst*, 132-135) both cite the use of sleep deprivation as a common tool of mind control among destructive cults.

[49] Marcoux, *Cursillo: Anatomy of a Movement*, 39-40, emphasis added.

2. Withdrawal from the familiar.

The weekend renewal experience often takes place in an unfamiliar setting. The participant is removed from familiar sights and sounds of home and workplace. After all, they are called "retreats." The usual patterns and familiar routines from which we draw strength are completely disrupted. It is as though one has entered another world. Again, this change of physical circumstances creates a breaking down of defenses.

And regular channels of information are removed: newspapers, radio and television. It is as though the whole world has shut down and all that matters is the weekend experience. This withdrawal from the familiar produces an intense focus on the present, again, breaking down defenses and precipitating a crisis experience.

Far away from home, Alan was completely removed from the outside world to the retreat center, which became his "world" for the time that he was there. And every aspect of his life was controlled: his routine, his diet, the people who talked to him, his female "companion," what he heard. Virtually all contact with the outside world was severed. Alan was under the complete control of others.

The Thursday experience in the Roman Catholic Cursillo is purposely designed to disorient the candidate.

> Clearly, *Thursday is structured to effect a disorientation of the candidates, that is, to plunge them into a shocking state of self-awakening.* The individuals must handle this shock in isolation since they are prohibited from speaking with other candidates and must maintain silence. They are segregated from others and left without any supportive group to share their frustrations and anxieties. *Candidates listen to words that may upset them and that are designed to do exactly that.* The images and examples are purposefully selected to instil [sic] aloneness and helplessness.[50]

The withdrawal from the familiar is a common element in the Emotional Flooding Therapy known as Primal Therapy, pioneered by Arthur Janov. The aim of Primal Therapy is to help patients regress into profoundly cathartic experiences in which the repressed pain of childhood trauma is released. Therapy begins when the patient gives up

> everyday defenses against tension and pain. Cigarettes, tranquilizers, alcohol, TV, sex and socializing are avoided as the client is isolated in a hotel room during the first week of therapy. *Not only does such sensory deprivation weaken defenses*, but it also removes external distractions and

---

[50] Ibid., 69, emphasis added.

allows internal stimulation to emerge into the center of attention.[51]

Interestingly, the "sensory deprivation" of familiar comforts and supports is the starting point that culminates in the primal catharsis.

3. Loss of time consciousness.

Routine is not only interrupted by the physical location, but by the artificial schedule. Often participants are urged to take off their watches and forget about the time so they can simply take in all that God has for them. But the effect is to keep up a "what's coming next?" frame of mind. Observing a YATEC experience I noticed the windows were blocked off with paper to remove any sense of night or day.

In the Roman Catholic Cursillo, this unexpectedness is essential:

> One factor which marks the first evening, as well as the entire initiation, is *the sense of unpredictability*. The candidates find themselves in an unfamiliar setting with few clues as to what to expect. They cannot easily prepare themselves to react since they are unaware of what is to come. The tenet of secrecy, even when modified, assures that *they will be uninformed and possessing few ways to guard against the forthcoming events*. Many, then, will be unprepared for handling the unexpected.[52]

This physically disorienting technique keeps the participant off-balance and wears down the defenses, thus enabling the growing momentum of the mounting emotional tension which then culminates in the cathartic release.

4. Sensory over-stimulation and manipulation.

A consistent feature of all weekend renewal experiences is tactile over-stimulation, usually in the form of hugging. Touching has an undeniably powerful influence. Psychologists often describe the physiological changes that take place as a result of physical touch.

As a result of the breakdown of the family in our society, many people live alone. They long for physical contact. With all the hand-shaking, back-rubbing, and hugging, these weekend renewal experiences can meet this felt need, but they can also produce an overload of tactile stimulation. On the other hand, for most people there is a "personal space" that must be maintained. You've felt this space violated if ever a stranger stood too closely to you or you

---

[51] Prochaska, *Systems of Psychotherapy: A Transtheoretical Approach*, 282, emphasis added. The similarity of the techniques used in the Cursillo and Primal Therapy is discussed in chapter 8 of this book.
[52] Marcoux, *Cursillo: Anatomy of a Movement*, 70, emphasis added.

were forced to sit close to a stranger in the cramped quarters of an airplane or crowded taxi. And yet, on these weekend renewal experiences, the leaders encourage the violation of this personal space. At various times, team members will give an unsolicited hug or, while standing in a circle, everyone will be instructed to "turn to the left and give a back rub to the person next to you." And then you turn to the right and do the same, and you have instant physical contact with a stranger. This repeated violation of personal space tends to break down taboos and resistance. It tends to join the group together prematurely and synthetically, creating artificial feelings of closeness and oneness.

But it does more. Except in some Cursillo weekends where men and women are completely segregated, this tactile over-stimulation can easily create a sexual tension as well. Let me state the obvious: adolescent boys and young men often enjoy giving back rubs to and receiving warm, lingering hugs from attractive girls and young women. And this is undoubtedly true in the opposite direction as well. Part of the dynamic of the weekend is a growing sexual tension that needs to find release as well.

Alan admitted that a significant part of his attraction to the group was a physical attraction to the young ladies with whom he was paired off. Walking together, holding hands, and "brotherly-sisterly" hugs created a strong sexual attraction which became hard to walk away from. As I recall, romance tended to bloom freely on Lay Witness Missions and especially on youth retreats. I am aware of one engaged couple who met during a coed Cursillo weekend. Not surprisingly, when their romance began to cool, they headed back to work a Cursillo together.

Senses other than touch can be manipulated as well through mood music and mood lighting. A consistent feature of the weekend renewal experience is candlelight in the darkened room. The candle and the dark room often enable the cathartic climax for at least three reasons.

The first is anonymity. The candidate is almost hidden by the near darkness. In the dark, it is easier to confess sins or profess commitment. And in the dark it is not so awkward to begin crying, essential to the emotional release. But the flickering flame in the darkness also creates an eerie, mysterious feeling. The surrealistic shadows and shrouded faces produce a mood that hints toward the suspenseful and supernatural. From childhood most people have felt a little spooky in the dark. This uncanny ambiance heightens suggestibility. And the darkness contributes to the dark and doleful mood of the occasion. In order to cry, one usually must feel sadness, be it the sadness of a touching story told by a witness, the sadness of personal troubles, or the sadness of the death of Christ. But the all-important spark that ignites the release of emotion is the first flowing tears. A candle in the darkness creates the somber mood that starts the tears falling.

And the technique of mood music hardly needs explanation. If you doubt this, just watch a dramatic movie and pay special attention to the music. It will invariably be coordinated to produce the appropriate feeling at precisely the right moment. In fact, a change in the music is often a signal that something is new about to happen. Dissonant music can create tension and suspense, somber, minor-keyed music can create solemnity and sadness, light, fast-paced music can create feelings of joy and peace and so forth.

Of course "mood music" is a large part of the effectiveness of building the emotional tension, but it is especially critical at the point of cathartic climax. As a guitarist, I can recall numerous instances where, in the "darkened room with the candle in the middle" the leader would whisper, "Play some music." We knew what to do: play some quiet, sad chords, but usually not a recognizable melody. It was mood music. And usually at this point someone would sing a sad song, and then the crying would commence. After an appropriate amount of crying, the leader would change the mood of the group, and the vehicle of change was the tempo of the music. A brisk song of praise would turn the tears to giddy laughter. With the emotions fully spent, the result is a sense of relief and inner tranquility. The catharsis has served its purpose and achieved its effect.

5. Hyperventilation.

> Hyperventilation is an overall label for the effects caused by overbreathing and repetitive sighing. The condition is easily induced by having people do continuous loud shouting and chanting….Overbreathing can also be produced through intense heavy expelling of air in more private, quiet ritualized chants.[53]

The medical effect of such overbreathing is to cause a drop in the level of carbon dioxide in the blood, creating a temporary feeling of light-headedness or dizziness. The result is that people feel "high," but also experience a loss of critical thinking and judgment. Unscrupulous religious and cult leaders will often direct people to chant or breathe deeply and reinterpret the resultant effects of hyperventilation as a mystical experience.

Psychologist Margaret Singer registers surprise that otherwise well-informed people could by duped by such an obvious trick.

> I have observed several groups that have members sit on the floor in a darkened room and rapidly and repeatedly yell such phrases as "fear, fear, fear" or "out Satan out." After a number of minutes, when the leaders assess that many in the room feel giddy and tingling,

---

[53] Singer, *Cults in Our Midst*, 128.

> the leaders turn up the lights and reframe the physical condition: "See, as we told you, you are going to be transformed!" Although many in the room appear to be educated, no one spoke about recognizing the effects of hyperventilation, effects most of us have heard about in high school or college science courses. Because of peer pressure and social constraints built in by group procedures, no one asked, "Are you sure this isn't really the effect of hyperventilation rather than out-of-this-world ecstacy [sic] and enlightenment?"[54]

Spirited singing, enthusiastic chanting, deep breathing, and vigorous activity can all quicken the respiratory rate and produce hyperventilation, and most or all of these are present in the program of weekend experiences. If this trick is used with regularity by the unscrupulous, how is its use justified by the leadership of weekend religious experiences?

6. Repetitive motion.

> Constant swaying motions, clapping added to chanting, or almost any repeated motion helps to alter a person's general state of awareness. Often the repetitive movements are combined with forms of chanting to blend the effects of hyperventilation and dizziness. Dizziness can be produced by simple spinning or spin dancing (in which the person also whirls around and around), prolonged swaying, and trance dancing (often done kneeling and rocking from side to side and backward and forward, with rhythmic repetitive drumming and background music). Again, the effects of these motions are relabeled by group leaders as ecstacy [sic] or new levels of awareness.[55]

It should be noted that rhythmic motions such as swaying and clapping are regular features in the weekend experience. By themselves, they may seem innocuous, but combined with the other psychological and physiological factors, they contribute to the altered state of awareness.

7. Dietary modifications/sugar high.

Perhaps the most shameless and obvious physiological technique used to create an altered state of awareness is the sugar high. I remember two high school boys telling me that their usual Friday night routine included a couple of two-liters of Mountain Dew and HBO. They would stay up all night. What a blast! It felt so good, and then they could crash the next day. I recall my own

---

[54] Ibid., 130.
[55] Ibid., 131.

small children running round and round, jabbering uncontrollably after drinking sugary sodas. That was until the sugar wore off, and they then collapsed into a weary heap. The leaders of destructive cults have likewise noticed this effect.

> Many groups have also hit upon sugar buzzing, that is, loading a person with lots of sugar, a technique that helps overcome low feelings and makes people temporarily feel energized. One former cult member said that, in her particular temple, she was to buy two and a half pounds of sugar per member per week to mix into various mushes, milk drinks, and desserts. During long sessions in one of the political cults, leaders would often give someone twenty-five or fifty dollars to go out and buy an armload of candy bars to bring back to the members at the meeting to keep everyone going.[56]

A participant at TEC reported that candy, caffeinated soda, and other junk foods were readily available at all times, creating the sugar high. I was told at a YATEC event that abundant snacks were provided at all times because they "didn't want candidates feeling any physical needs." Physiological changes as a result of a high sugar diet lead to a greater excitability, an altered state of consciousness, a "high" experience. Emotional results are nearly guaranteed. But it is also interesting that Alan specifically noted the "wearing down" effects of the vegetarian diet. He was broken physically, emotionally, and spiritually, and what he ate had direct bearing on his ability to resist manipulation.

THE GOAL: CATHARSIS

> Remember the goal: create the momentum of an emotional tension that builds with time until the tension is peaked. At this point a mood is created in which the tension can be released, usually through a group rush of emotional discharge—crying and then laughing. This is followed by warm feelings of relief, euphoria, and a peaceful sense of personal well-being along with a bonding with all those who underwent the same experience.

There can be no doubt that the Cursillo experience intentionally seeks to create this powerful emotional catharsis experience. The goal of the Cursillo leadership team is "to bring about *metanoia* in the candidates. The aim is a dramatic change in the candidates and the structuring of a ritual [read "set of techniques," ed.] that can inaugurate this dramatic molding of the 'new person.'"[57] The process begins with the Thursday "disorientation." It is heightened by the loss of routine and unpredictability of the schedule. This is

---

[56] Ibid., 133.
[57] Marcoux, Cursillo: Anatomy of a Movement, 49-50.

coupled with a shifting of expectations. What begins as a typical and familiar Roman Catholic retreat takes several shocking shifts that continue to disorient the participant. Admittedly, these techniques are "procedures designed to jolt the candidate" and "intended to catch the candidates off-guard."[58] Psychotherapists would describe this as stripping away defense mechanisms.

But the ultimate admission that these techniques are designed as a powerful emotional stimulus is that emotionally unstable people are prohibited from attending.

> Members consider initiation a powerful mechanism that jolts candidates into a re-evaluation of their past lives; because of this, initiation is considered too traumatic for certain individuals, causing added problems for the highly neurotic, not to mention the psychotic. In fact, there are individuals... who were institutionalized following their initiation. The stress of the cursillo weekend is realized, so that those who have problems in dealing with stress and change are prohibited.[59]

It should be noted that not all of these elements must be employed, but that if enough are omitted through poor planning, the momentum will not be created, the tension will not be peaked, and the cathartic release will fizzle out. But let me state once again that when these techniques were used with a fair degree of skill, I have never known them to fail.

And this is not to say that every aspect of every technique is manipulative or evil. Many times I have received a genuine handshake or hug from a friend, and it was offered and received with sincere gratitude. Like many, I appreciate a wide variety of music styles, from the great and majestic hymns of the faith to simple praise songs. Even emotion itself is not corrupt, nor is it to be feared. The content of our faith ought to lead us to a wide range of very genuine emotions. Contemplation of heaven ought to delight us, while thoughts of hell should shock and horrify us. The cross of Christ should fill us with grief and dismay; his resurrection should captivate us with unfailing hope.

The problem comes when these techniques are combined and the person is skillfully and perhaps unwittingly manipulated into a psycho-physiological, emotional response which is reinterpreted as a spiritual, perhaps *the* spiritual experience. The simple fact is that unscrupulous, cultic groups are doing so. Why should Christian groups be using the same techniques? As he was in the process of leaving the Moonies, former cult member and author Steven Hassan was forced to ask himself, "Does God have to use the same

---

[58] Ibid., 72.
[59] Ibid., 38-39.

tactics as Satan in order to make an ideal world?" [60] "Does the God I believe in need to use deception and mind control? Do the ends truly justify the means? I had to ask myself whether the means determine the ends."[61] The leaders of weekend religious experiences should be asking the same questions.

---

[60] Hassan, *Combatting Cult Mind Control*, 28.
[61] Ibid., 54.

4. *The Origins of the Cursillo Method*

History of the Movement

The Cursillo method was devised in the 1940s and 50s in Majorca (or Mallorca), Spain. The historical and cultural factors are integral to its perceived need and its shape and function.

The movement's unofficial historian, Ivan J. Rohloff, summarizes several historical and cultural aspects of mid-twentieth-century Spain. The Catholic Church in Spain had had a history of isolation and popular control, but at this time found itself under attack. "During the traumatic thirties [1930s] both superstition and violent anticlericalism surfaced."[62] To complicate matters further, "secular humanism and atheism were quite widespread among the intelligentsia and in academic circles."[63] What's more, Spanish men had long been absent from the church: "It was often considered childish or effeminate for men to be devout in their faith."[64] Rohloff considers the Cursillo method to be a direct reaction to these secularizing forces in an attempt to reclaim young Spanish men who had been caught up in non-Christian lifestyles.

Sociologist Ralph G. O'Sullivan would therefore place the Cursillo in the category of a social movement "centered around efforts to invalidate the sources and teachings of those beliefs which created normative disarray in order to re-form intellectual, social, moral, and ideological normalcy in a population."[65] It is a method for reviving, renewing or revitalizing a beleaguered church.

The Cursillo was originally discovered or devised as a method for training leaders for a pilgrimage to the tomb of St. James the Greater, a religious

---

[62] Ivan J. Rohloff, *The Origins and Development of Cursillo (1939-1973)* (Dallas: National Ultreya Publications of the United States National Secretariat, 1976), 19.
[63] Ibid.
[64] Ibid.
[65] Ralph G. O'Sullivan, "Cursillo in Social Movement Literature," *Free Inquiry in Sociology* 25, no. 2 (1997): 131.

Chapter 4: The Origins of the Cursillo Method 55

practice common to Spanish Catholicism. The pilgrimage was first proposed in 1932, but was frequently interrupted and postponed until 1948.

> Within this time and through the effort to organize the pilgrimage, the cursillo was formed. But the movement was an inadvertent result of the planning for the pilgrimage. So unexpected was the cursillo that the reality of its existence was not discerned by many people even when it was an ongoing phenomenon. Clearly, the cursillo originated as a process to organize, train, and enliven adolescents for a pilgrimage. It has now advanced to a method for renewing Catholic men and women throughout the world.[66]

Leaders found that the desired renewal occurred through the training courses before the pilgrimage ever took place. They began to see the usefulness of the training itself, even without the pilgrimage. "Some in the early team of men experienced a shift in attitude, realizing as they did, that the significant pilgrimage was not the one to St. James the Greater, but life itself."[67] "The Mallorcans were unaware that the cursillos in preparation for the Pilgrimage were far more important than the Pilgrimage itself."[68]

One other development was yet required in order to make the Cursillo method complete, because

> ... the courses were not without their failings. Although this method increased religious fervor and dedication, it could not sustain it. Enthusiasm and joy diminished in the months following an individual's participation in the courses. Something more was needed.[69]

The problem was that after the weekend the group was disbanded. The various participants lived apart from each other and so had no continued interaction. To make matters worse, a strict rule forbade individuals from being initiated more than once, so there was no way to sustain or renew the Cursillo experience. "Therefore, there was no basis for increasing the brotherhood and sisterhood, as well as the religious fervor fostered during the initiation."[70] In time the leadership proposed an answer.

---

[66] Marcoux, *Cursillo, Anatomy of a Movement: The Experience of Spiritual Renewal*, 8.
[67] Ibid., 9.
[68] Rohloff, *The Origins and Development of Cursillo (1939-1973)*, 59.
[69] Marcoux, *Cursillo, Anatomy of a Movement: The Experience of Spiritual Renewal*, 20.
[70] Ibid., 21.

In 1951, a solution was formulated. A follow-up program of weekly and bi-monthly meetings, called group reunions and *ultreyas*, regrouped initiates and thereby provided links of continuity.[71]

The experience could be renewed and sustained. Thus the form of the Cursillo was complete: a weekend of religious revitalization and renewal followed by regular group meetings to sustain the fervor of the original weekend.

Principal Authors and Proponents of the Movement

Rohloff describes those most responsible for the development of the Cursillo method: "One could say that Eduardo Bonnin is the principal founder of the movement; Bishop Hervas is its episcopal champion; Gabriel Segui is its historian and Juan Capo is the movement's theologian."[72] Most important of these is Bonnin, who interjected a strong psychological element into the method. Rohloff calls Bonnin "the single most influential person in the origins of the movement."[73]

Eduardo Bonnin was sought out as a potential leader and was persuaded by his friend, Jose Ferregut to make the Cursillo in 1943....His avid reading in psychology gave him a keen understanding of modern man. His creativity was to influence the Cursillo movement more than any other single person.[74]

In a private interview Segui mentioned that the Cursillo movement is really the child of Eduardo Bonnin. It is a marvelous union of psychology and theology....It was Eduardo himself, with his Jewish background (his ability to use fantasy), his intelligence, his very assiduous [*sic*] study and his knack for psychological intuition that produced Cursillo. "The Cursillo movement, this, is merely an extension of the person of Eduardo Bonnin." Segui said that if one wants to know the Cursillo movement well, it is enough to know Eduardo Bonnin well.[75]

---

[71] Ibid.
[72] Rohloff, *The Origins and Development of Cursillo (1939-1973)*, iv.
[73] Ibid., 55. A letter quoted by Rohloff is addressed to *Dr.* D. Eduardo Bonnin. According to John Hensley DeTar and Thomas M. Manion, *To Deceive...The Elect* (Reno, NV: Athanasius Press, 1966), 45, early reports described Bonnin as a psychiatrist.
[74] Ibid., 52-53.
[75] Ibid., 154, n. 107.

It is apparent that Bonnin's contemporaries considered him a capable interpreter of and apologist for the movement. His books reveal him to be a seminal thinker and persuasive communicator.[76]

The Purpose of the Movement

It is important to understand that the original movement aimed far higher than simply sponsoring weekend experiences or even creating a new movement. Indeed, according to Rohloff, "the [weekend] Cursillo exercise is the least important component of the method."[77] The ultimate goal is 1) locating the people who are the "backbone" of various "environments," 2) "converting" them into leaders during the Cursillo weekend, and 3) turning them back to evangelize their environments, all the while connecting them and supporting them through continued group reunions and ultreya meetings. These three phases are called respectively the Precursillo, the Cursillo and the Postcursillo.

> <u>The leavening of environments with the Gospel</u>, which is the purpose of the Cursillo Movement, is sought, not by means of a direct and global action on all Christians, but by choosing from among them those who have the required characteristics and give promise of being the living vertebrae that animate communities so that they can change their environments. During the Precursillo, candidates will be prepared for the three day Cursillo and Postcursillo. Such candidates should come from *an existing or potential community* and should be capable of becoming its vertebrae. They should be prepared in such a way that they will be ready to understand, live and accept the message of the three days.[78]

1. The Precursillo. Not everyone should be invited to attend a Cursillo weekend. Those sought out are "the vertebrae of their environment," those with "deep personality," who exhibit the potential for "effectiveness: The effectiveness [they] will have as... vertebrae in Christianity."[79] Of course

---

[76] See especially his *Cursillos in Christianity: The How and the Why* (Dallas: National Ultreya Publications, 1981) and *Structure of Ideas: [Vertebration]*, trans. Collice H. Portnoff and Maria J. Escudero (Dallas: National Ultreya Publications, n.d.).
[77] Rohloff, *The Origins and Development of Cursillo (1939-1973)*, 55.
[78] The National Cursillo Center, *The Fundamental Ideas of the Cursillo Movement* (Dallas: National Ultreya Publications, 1974), 98, emphasis and underlining in the original.
[79] Eduardo Bonnín, Bernardo Vadell, and Francisco Forteza, *Structure of Ideas:[Vertebration]*, 14-15. Of course this selection process raises serious questions. What place do these "backbone" people have in their local churches once they are "converted" through Cursillo? Is their primary loyalty to their Cursillo community or the church? And how can they be expected to submit to their

"standard" individuals may also go, that is "those who flow with the tide."[80] But under no circumstances are "those who have no personality at all"[81] to go, that is, those with no aptitude for affecting their environment. Apparently, the Cursillo is wasted on them.[82]

2. The Cursillo. The purpose of the Cursillo weekend is to prepare the vertebrae to evangelize their environment. "It should help those attending discover their personal calling (or vocation) in order to accomplish it in and for the community...."[83] Roman Catholic Cursillo promoter Al Blatnik offers a more candid and colorful way of saying it: "They are, facetiously, the 'whomp' on the head to get your attention." He continues:

> There is little doubt about the potentiality of the candidates to exert more of a Christian influence on their environment. The problem with most of us is that this potentiality is not exerted to its fullest. We need to become restless and fervent in our desire to effect a change in our environment. We need to center our lives around Jesus Christ and not treat Him as just another object in our existence. We need to get ourselves off center and begin to move. In a simple and uncomplicated explanation, this is what the weekend is for—to light a fire in us, to cause us to become restless, to inspire us to live the Christian ideal.[84]

3. The Postcursillo. As noted before, "Although this method increased religious fervor and dedication, it could not sustain it. Enthusiasm and joy diminished in the months following an individual's participation in the courses."[85] For this reason the Postcursillo was devised. It has two parts: the group reunion, and ultreya meeting. The group reunion is a small support group for accountability purposes. Groups meet informally and frequently and are constituted on the basis of shared interests. The ultreya ("ultreya" is a Spanish word meaning "onward") "is a gathering of all cursillistas in a given

---

church leadership who may be perceived as "non-backbone" pastors or elders if these have not "made Cursillo"?
[80] Ibid., 15.
[81] Ibid. Also listed under "Those who should not attend" are "1. Those who have psychological or emotional problems" and "2. Those whose moral life is disordered in a way which could not be remedied by a Cursillo. 102.
[82] *Lower Your Nets* by Juan Capó Bosch (Dallas: National Ultreya Publications, 1965) is a 126- page book devoted to selecting candidates, motivating them to attend the Cursillo and explaining how to overcome the resistance of those who do not want to attend.
[83] The National Cursillo Center, *The Fundamental Ideas of the Cursillo Movement*, 56.
[84] Al Blatnik, *Your Fourth Day* (Dallas: National Ultreya Publications, 1973), 27.
[85] Marcoux, *Cursillo, Anatomy of a Movement: The Experience of Spiritual Renewal*, 20.

area on a regular basis"[86] meeting ideally on a weekly basis and is a larger, more structured group meeting. After an emotional Cursillo weekend experience, the graduates are encouraged to become involved in an ultreya group but are cautioned that the ultreya will not match the emotional intensity they felt on the Cursillo, because "no experience immediately after the three days is going to duplicate the joy and emotional exultation that you felt then." In fact, after being swayed by emotion during the weekend, graduates are instructed "not to base your Christian growth on emotions alone."[87] Leaders often contact graduates, invite them to reunions, and emphasize the importance of attending ultreya meetings. They also encourage graduates to "work" at subsequent Cursillos and to sponsor friends or family.

The Format of the Cursillo Weekend.

The weekend follows an invariable pattern of three days, fifteen talks, and several "surprises." Reformed pastor and Cursillo leader Roderic Jackson describes the four states of the weekend as "preparation, proclamation, conversion and insertion."[88] Episcopalian priest and Cursillo leader Dennis C. Rydholm gives a commentary on the three days:

> Thursday evening the candidates are introduced to their new environment and new companions of the succeeding three days. All external contact with the outside world and one's normal existence is removed. The objective is to establish an insular space of contemplative and inward retreat. In some regions of the country, windows and doors have been blocked with paper or cardboard, clocks have been masked, and candidates are asked to surrender their watches. This first evening and following morning consist of quiet prayer sessions (i.e., the Stations of the Cross) and personal introductions.
>
> Friday, the first day, consists of a series of sermons or "Rollos" which set the basic pattern for the remainder of the weekend. These short half-hour "talks" build in intensity throughout the weekend and are punctuated by some form of group activity—typically poster making or the writing and enacting of skits designed to reinforce the message of the preceding talk. The content of these sermons is centered around the triadic themes of "piety," "study," and "action," the three supports on which life as a Cursillista are based.

---

[86] Blatnik, *Your Fourth Day*, 10.
[87] Ibid., 12.
[88] Roderic Douglas Jackson, "A Handbook for Leaders in the Cursillo Movement for the Reformed Church in America" (D.Min. diss., North American Baptist Seminary, 1981), 16.

At some point during the first day a candidate also learns to become the recipient of "Palanca"[89]—handwritten statements addressed personally to each candidate expressing affection and describing an act of sacrifice, usually prayer and fasting, that the author of the note is undergoing in the candidate's name. Palanca can also take the form of small gifts, typically handmade, again with the candidate "personally" in mind. Palanca is made to "appear" in the candidate's midst frequently and in great volume throughout the weekend.

The talk on "piety" and the reading of the palanca letters are described in one Leader's Manual as the "two 'shocks' of the first day when the cursillista is brought up short and made to realize that he is going to have to respond in a way that he probably never did before."

By the second day, Saturday, a sense of comraderie [sic] and community has set in—typically engendered by close physical contact in the form of holding hands or embracing during frequent singing of Cursillo songs before and after meals and in between sermons. Inhibitions have been dissipated by frequent sharing and confession, a form of communication encouraged by the presence of members of the Cursillo team—sometimes identified as such, sometimes not—who personally accompany the candidates throughout the weekend activities.

At some point during the second day candidates are served an "Agape Meal" preceded by a celebration of the eucharist. The Agape Meal can be presented to unsuspecting candidates in their usual place for taking meals, only this time with the room "magically" transformed with elaborate décor, the meal served by dozens of mysterious, loving servants who appear "out of nowhere" (the planning and engineering of these elaborate events unbeknownst to the candidates is one of the true miracles of the Cursillo weekend).

The third and final day typically begins with a Cursillo "Wake-up"—a communal converging of singing servants bearing orange juice upon sleeping candidates signaling the awakening of a new beginning and a new life for the candidate. The day proceeds with more talks, more skits and posters, more song. The event culminates in the "Clausura" or closing. Candidates, by now anxiously anticipating a climax of unknown proportion, are escorted singing to the steps of the church. As the doors are flung open, the candidates apprehend the pews filled row-upon-row with joyous cursillistas,

---

[89] "Palanca" is Spanish for "lever," perhaps a reference to its ability to pry open a resistant or unwilling candidate?

Chapter 4: The Origins of the Cursillo Method

singing or chanting, as the candidates are led in procession, numb with emotion, to the altar.

The order of events at the Clausura can vary considerably, but one procedure is to allow the candidates to testify to the congregation about the weekend experience. After a service or hymns, the church is emptied and the candidates are then led to a "Rollo Room" or prayer chamber, described to the candidates as the "power center" behind the weekend. Here it is demonstrated how other cursillistas have been conducting a 24-hour prayer vigil in the candidate's name, often with candles and incense. The candidates are presented with a tiny cross that has been held firmly in hand in the candidate's name by prayerful keepers of the weekend vigil. As each cross is presented, the weekend leader, often a clergyperson, states "Christ is counting on you,"[90] to which the candidate responds, "And I on Him."

Thus ends the weekend.[91]

---

[90] When my children heard me read the words "Christ is counting on you," they correctly responded, "No, he's not!"
[91] Daniel C. Rydholm, "Theology and Methodology in the American Episcopal Cursillo Movement" (unpublished manuscript, Berkeley, CA: Spiritual Counterfeits Project, 1987), 6-9.

5. *The Theology of the Cursillo Method*

It is evident that the Cursillo is not really about theology from the fact that the method is so readily adaptable to very divergent theological perspectives: Roman Catholicism, Lutheranism (Via de Cristo), Methodism (Walk to Emmaus), Anglicanism (Episcopal Cursillo), Presbyterianism (Presbyterian Cursillo), Pentecostalism (Tres Dias), and Dutch Reformed (Reformed Cursillo). Since I am Reformed/Presbyterian, I will critique the Cursillo from my theological tradition. Other traditions such as Roman Catholicism and Methodism might be more theologically receptive to the Cursillo method, since they are semi-Pelagian. But theologically speaking, a Presbyterian or Reformed Cursillo must certainly be considered an oxymoron.

Previous Reformed Theological Evaluations

Very little work has been published critiquing the Cursillo method from the perspective of the Reformed tradition (or from any theological tradition, for that matter). I could find only two significant sources of Reformed evaluation.

1. In 1998 Kevin R. Boyd, a minister in the Presbyterian Church (USA) wrote a Doctor of Ministry thesis for Austin Presbyterian Theological Seminary titled, "Decently De Colores: A Reformed Evaluation of the Cursillo Movement in the Presbyterian Church."[92] Boyd only evaluated the Cursillo from the perspective of Reformed ecclesiology using the "Six Great Ends of the Church":

> The great ends of the church are the proclamation of the gospel for the salvation of humankind; the shelter, nurture, and spiritual fellowship of the children of God; the maintenance of divine worship;

---

[92] Kevin R. Boyd, "Decently De Colores: A Reformed Evaluation of the Cursillo Movement in the Presbyterian Church" (D.Min. diss., Austin Presbyterian Theological Seminary, 1998).

Chapter 5: The Theology of the Cursillo Method

the preservation of the truth; the promotion of social righteousness; and the exhibition of the Kingdom of Heaven to the world.[93]

As one can see, there is nothing particularly "Reformed" about these "great ends." They could easily be affirmed by most Christian churches including the Roman Catholic tradition in which the Cursillo was developed. Even though Boyd concludes that the Cursillo method is congruent with the "great ends," his analysis sheds little light on whether the Cursillo is compatible with more distinctive aspects of Reformed theology.

2. Roderic Jackson, a pastor in the Reformed Church in America, authored the 43-page "Handbook for Leaders in the Cursillo Movement for the Reformed Church in America"[94] a guide presumably still used as a blueprint for Reformed Cursillos in Northwest Iowa. In Chapter III Jackson raises the question of theology:

> Can this instrument of renewal which comes out of a Roman Catholic background be used with integrity and without fear of compromise by the RCA? Are there theological differences at the very foundation which make such usage unwise or even dangerous?[95]

Jackson answers his own questions: he sees no incompatibilities between the Cursillo method and the Reformed tradition.

> The writer believes, after eleven years of working in the Cursillo movement, studying the literature it has produced, and studying the scriptures and theological documents of the Reformed Church, that there is nothing basically incompatible between the RCA and the Cursillo method.[96]

How is it possible that a renewal method birthed in the stridently Roman Catholic milieu of mid-twentieth century Spain can be considered compatible with Reformed theology? Jackson makes it clear that his version of "Reformed" theology has made many concessions to Roman theology by avoiding Reformed (even *Protestant*) distinctives. For example:

---

[93] Office of the General Assembly of the PC(USA), *The Constitution of the Presbyterian Church (U.S.A.), Part II, Book of Order* (Louisville, KY: Office of the General Assembly of the PC(USA), 1999), G-1.0200.
[94] Jackson, "A Handbook for Leaders in the Cursillo Movement for the Reformed Church in America."
[95] Ibid., 9.
[96] Ibid.

> The old arguments about whether grace is imputed or infused are avoided. Grace is not spoken of quantitatively as a 'thing' or substance or even a 'state' which was the older Roman Catholic terminology; rather, it is a dynamic relationship between persons. The language of commerce or the courtroom are [*sic*.] not used of grace in the Cursillos.[97]

It is remarkable that Jackson could so lightly dismiss the imputation (crediting, reckoning) of Christ's righteousness which was considered essential to the Gospel by the magisterial reformers. And without "the language of commerce or the courtroom" (redemption and forensic justification), it is hard to see how the Gospel can be proclaimed at all.

To what extent has Jackson modified the Cursillo in order to make it fit the Reformed Church in America? He asserts that his version is virtually identical to the Roman Catholic variety:

> ...(E)very attempt has been made to present a picture of authentic Cursillos in Christianity, the movement as the founders envisioned and developed it. Though written for a non-Roman Catholic readership, specifically the Reformed Church in America, it does not present a hybrid event or program which we simply call "Cursillo." Though some terminology has been changed and some specifically Roman Catholic ideas omitted, the basic structure and details are intact.[98]

Judging from his prior statements about "infused" grace and not using "the language of commerce or the courtroom," it is obvious that very little has been changed not only from the Roman Catholic theology which is taught during Cursillos, but also from the underlying theological assumptions that would make the Cursillos required or even desirable. In fact, the only explicit theological difference between the original, Roman Catholic version and Jackson's *Handbook* for the Reformed Church in America is a denial of "the Roman Catholic doctrine of baptismal regeneration."[99]

Jackson and other Protestants might be surprised to learn that one of the main promoters of the first Cursillos considered any Protestant version to

---

[97] Ibid., 10.
[98] Ibid., 1.
[99] Ibid., 13. Elements of distinctive Roman Catholic doctrine apparently persist in the Reformed Cursillo in Northwest Iowa. For example, in an email to the author dated December 2, 2005, a pastor who has for many years shared in leadership in the Reformed Cursillo in Northwest Iowa said he recently taught the Cursillo rollo on the "seven main sacraments." Of course most Protestants recognize only two sacraments.

Chapter 5: The Theology of the Cursillo Method

be illegitimate. In his defense of the Catholic Cursillo, Bishop Juan Hervas offers two criteria for assessing the genuineness of a spiritual renewal movement:

> 1) *orthodoxy in the doctrine* guaranteed by the infallible Magisterium of the Church—a close and universal rule of faith and
> 2) *obedience to the lawful shepherds,* who through divine right, are the Pope and the Bishops in communion with him.[100]

Martin Luther is explicitly mentioned (and presumably John Calvin would be as well) as one of the "pseudo-reformers"[101] or "so-called reformers"[102] along with Marcion and Montano (Montanus) who are all (Luther included) deemed "false prophets and teachers of evil, who, though presenting themselves in sheep's clothing, are ravenous wolves."[103] To this early co-founder of the movement, a *Protestant* Cursillo would be an impossibility, or at the very least, a false reform movement.

Jackson does, however, inadvertently reveal a crucial theological assumption, one in which he shows his affirmation of Roman Catholic theology as opposed to the Reformed theology he professes. Jackson lists five "implications" for the church as it seeks to address an "essentially non-Christian" world "as we believe it is in this last quarter of the 20th century" (Jackson writes in 1981). The second of these implications is telling: "The church must awaken a hunger for God, rather than presume there is a hunger which doesn't exist." [104]

Classical Reformed theology declares the unregenerate not simply to be asleep and in need of awakening, but altogether dead in their sins (Ephesians 2:1-3); not merely disinterested in God, but actively hostile to God and incapable of submitting to him (Romans 8:7); and not merely ambivalent toward God, but definitely not seeking after God (Romans 3:11). Reformed theology has never presumed that people are hungry for God nor believed that the church can awaken such a hunger for God. To do so is humanly impossible, absolutely under the purview of God alone. Such a statement reveals Jackson's non-Reformed, semi-Pelagian convictions which he shares with Roman Catholic theology.

---

[100] Juan Hervás, *Leaders' Manual for Cursillos in Christianity*, 3rd ed. (Madrid: Ultreya Press for Euramerica, S.A., 1967), 65, emphasis original.
[101] Ibid., 63.
[102] Ibid., 64.
[103] Ibid., 65.
[104] Jackson, "A Handbook for Leaders in the Cursillo Movement for the Reformed Church in America," 6.

How does Jackson suggest the church accomplish what the Bible declares to be impossible (awakening a hunger for God in the unregenerate)? The Cursillo method.

> Everything that is humanly possible, from the best insights of psychology, pedagogy and group dynamics to the clearest understanding of Scripture is put together in an orderly sequence to achieve the aims of the Cursillo.[105]

This is truly to the heart of the matter. The unacknowledged theological assumption on the part of Jackson, one that makes the Cursillo method not only possible or permissible but even necessary, is that which is essentially Roman Catholic, but which is emphatically denied by every branch of Reformed theology: semi-Pelagianism.

The Semi-Pelagian Foundation for the Cursillo Method

The founders of the Cursillo method make clear their semi-Pelagian orientation. The format for the Cursillo is a psychologically intense weekend admittedly intended first to cause a "complete disorientation"[106] in the candidate and then to re-form that person into a new way of thinking and living. According to the founder of the Cursillo, Eduardo Bonnin, "the technique is merely 'preparing the way of the Lord,' making the trenches ready to receive the Grace which will flow into man as a result of prayer and to ease his journey toward Grace."[107] Of course (according to Bonnin) this is not accomplished by coercion, but rather the Cursillo technique "awakens and animates desire."[108] It does not make a response necessary, but merely points the way to the right decision, "without ever losing sight of the fact that his decision, the acceptance of Grace, is always a free act of man, and that even God respects this freedom."[109]

Bonnin also describes the purpose of the technique in terms of creating the "right atmosphere and surroundings."

> Here technique is the organization of circumstances, which does not mean that the cursillistas (those undergoing the initiation weekend) are exposed to a series of tricks or psychological reactions, but to make them live in truth and by the truth in surroundings that are

---

[105] Ibid., 10.
[106] Hervas, *Leaders' Manual for Cursillos in Christianity*, 94.
[107] Eduardo Bonnin, *The How and the Why* (Dallas: National Ultreya Publications, 1981), 34.
[108] Ibid.
[109] Ibid.

Chapter 5: The Theology of the Cursillo Method

most conducive to deep penetration of the soul by this truth.[110]

Why is a technique which completely controls the environment of the initiates and which employs what critics perceive as "a series of tricks or psychological reactions" necessary? Bonnin explains: "Everyone knows that words penetrate effectively only when the doors of our souls are open to them and these doors are opened only under favorable circumstances."[111] And how are these "favorable circumstances" created? Sometimes providentially, but also sometimes with the aid of human engineering. "It would be well to remember that there are both unforeseen circumstances and planned circumstances."[112]

And these "planned circumstances" are described as "managing a group" through the use of "merited respect." "To have authority does not mean to give orders, but, rather, to know how to serve."[113] And what is "serving"?

> In this case the technique consists in using authority to steer all moments of collective activity toward a concrete and precise goal. We must delineate the features of the collective reality which begins to take shape; it is our place to lead the way, building fences around dangerous spots in the path so that others may take warning and avoid these places....[114]

Who is able to provide such "steering," "delineating," and "leading"?

> These things can be accomplished only by someone who has learned to understand people, to know their reactions and preferences; someone who knows how to adapt this authority or prestige to the situations in which men will yield freely, but which they will not tolerate if force is applied.[115]

Hopefully even this limited exposure to the stated rationale for and defense of the Cursillo technique prompts the reader to ask many questions.[116]

---

[110] Ibid., 36.
[111] Ibid.
[112] Ibid.
[113] Ibid.
[114] Ibid.
[115] Ibid.
[116] Some questions that would be appropriate include the following: If the decision to accept Grace is a free act of man (a freedom which even God respects) why must a technique be employed beyond merely explaining the options available? That is, why must the additional pressure of "steering," "delineating," and "leading" by those especially skilled in "understanding people," knowing their "reactions and preferences" and how to "adapt their authority or prestige"

The Reformed perspective of the human will as fallen throws into question the legitimacy, and so the propriety and even efficacy, of the Cursillo technique. Several questions are worth consideration:

    1. Is it the required and necessary work of ministers or Christian leaders to "make the trenches of the heart or will ready to receive Grace"? Is it even possible for Christian ministers to "ease (the sinner's) journey toward Grace"?

    2. Similarly, are certain surroundings more "conducive to deep penetration of the soul by (the) truth" than others? Is it to be the work of Christian ministers and leaders to discover, prepare, and provide these more conducive surroundings? Is it the work of Christian ministers to "open the doors of souls" by creating the favorable circumstances?

    3. If the answers to the former two questions are in the negative, what might be the result of Christian ministers and leaders attempting to "make trenches ready" to receive grace and "open the doors of souls" for "deep penetration of the soul by this truth"?

It is my contention that the Cursillo technique by design attempts to do what the unwavering and unanimous voice of all classical Reformed theology, from Calvin through the later standards of Reformed and Presbyterian Churches, insists cannot be done. As such it contradicts professed beliefs, diminishes God's power in salvation (thus dishonoring God), and inevitably produces unhealthy or counterfeit fruit.

The Rejection of Semi-Pelagianism by Reformed Theology

1. Martin Luther on Human Inability.

It could be said that the Protestant Reformation really turned on the question of the extent of the human will in its fallen condition. In the fifth century, the Roman Catholic Church resolutely condemned Pelagius and his views on the freedom and ability of the will to achieve salvation unaided by grace. But the church never fully adopted the counterview of Pelagius' arch-critic, Augustine; namely that the fallen will is completely unable to cooperate

---

be added if the will is truly free? How much additional pressure is permitted before it becomes psychological manipulation? What would distinguish the Cursillo technique from what would elsewhere and in other contexts be recognized as "a series of tricks or psychological reactions"?

Chapter 5: The Theology of the Cursillo Method

with or even to desire the grace required for salvation. So the church remained in an ambiguous position, somewhere between Pelagius and Augustine: semi-Pelagian (or perhaps semi-Augustinian). This was the situation at the time of the Reformation when an Augustinian monk named Martin Luther answered a treatise on the freedom of the will by the renowned Roman Catholic and humanist scholar Erasmus. Erasmus's book was titled *Diatribe seu collatio de libero arbitrio* or *Diatribe Concerning Free Will*. Fittingly, Luther called his response, *De servo arbitrio*, or *The Bondage of the Will*, and he considered it "his most important book, because it spoke to issues that he regarded as being the *cor ecclesiae*, the very heart of the church."[117]

Luther compliments Erasmus on seeing the central importance of the issue of "free-will."

> You alone have attacked the real thing, that is, the essential issue. You have not worried me with those extraneous issues about the Papacy, purgatory, indulgences and such like—trifles, rather than issues—in respect of which almost all to date have sought my blood...you, and you alone, have seen the hinge on which all turns, and aimed for the vital spot. For that I heartily thank you; for it is gratifying to me to deal with this issue....[118]

The importance of this issue for Luther and for the larger Reformation cannot be underestimated.

> 'Free-will' was no academic question to Luther; the whole gospel of the grace of God, he held, was bound up with it, and stood or fell according to the way one decided it. In *The Bondage of the Will*, therefore, Luther believes himself to be fighting for the truth of God, the only hope of man; and his earnestness and energy in prosecuting the argument bear witness to the strength of his conviction that the faith once delivered to the saints, and in consequence the salvation of precious souls, is here at stake.[119]

Luther and Erasmus were clashing over the Scholastic tradition which was decidedly semi-Pelagian. In this view the will is admittedly weakened by sin, but not utterly so. And therefore the will is capable of some small, meritorious action, without divine assistance, which would of itself merit further

---

[117] R.C. Sproul, *Willing to Believe: The Controversy over Free Will* trans., J. I. Packer and O. R. Johnston (Grand Rapids, Mich.: Baker Books, 1997), 87.
[118] Martin Luther, *The Bondage of the Will. A New Translation of De Servo Arbitrio (1525), Martin Luther's Reply to Erasmus of Rotterdam* (Westwood, NJ: Fleming H. Revell, 1957), 42.
[119] Ibid.

and needed grace from God leading to salvation. In this small work a person would make him or herself worthy and prepared for this gift of inward grace. "Grace (i.e. supernatural spiritual energy) having thus been given, its recipient could use it to do works of a quality of goodness previously out of his reach, works which God was necessarily bound, as a matter of justice, to reward with further supplies of grace and, ultimately, with heavenly glory."[120]

To this Luther responded, that according to this view, "man performs some action independently of God which does in fact elicit a reward from God. On this basis salvation comes to man through God's response to what man has done. Man earns his passage; man, in the last analysis saves himself. And this is in principle Pelagianism."[121]

At that time not just Luther but the entire Protestant Church (Lutheran and Reformed, both Zwinglian and Calvinist) embraced the Augustinian view of the enslavement to sin of the fallen human will and the absolute inability of that will to prepare itself for or even to desire the grace of salvation.[122] This meant that salvation was entirely a work of God, not by forcing sinners to repent against their wills, but by enlightening the minds of the elect to believe the Gospel and making their hearts willing to repent and turn to Christ in saving faith.

And the ordinary and appointed means or instruments God used to effect this transformation were understood to be preaching the gospel and prayer. External preaching, in itself useless and lifeless, was aided by the inward work of the Spirit, enlightening the darkened mind and renewing the corrupt will, making the person willing and able to respond to the gospel with saving faith.

The Cursillo technique denies these two central truths by resorting to means other than preaching and prayer to "make trenches ready" to receive grace and "open the doors of souls" for "deep penetration of the soul by this truth." The Cursillo method 1) denies the inability of the fallen will to prepare itself or to be prepared by human effort or persuasive technique, and it 2) denies the sufficiency of preaching as the appointed means God uses to awaken a dead and wholly unwilling will through the sovereign power of his Spirit. This is what makes the Cursillo technique so offensive to the grace of God and dangerous to the souls of the lost, as it aspires artificially to force open the soul by manipulative technique that often precipitates a spurious "conversion": it attempts to accomplish by human technique what God alone can do by his Spirit.

---

[120] Ibid., 49.
[121] Ibid.
[122] Sproul, *Willing to Believe: the Controversy Over Free Will*, 22.

2. John Calvin on Human Inability.

As Luther responded to Erasmus on the bondage of the will, so in turn John Calvin answered Albert Pighius on the same subject. When Calvin's second edition of the *Institutes of the Christian Religion* appeared in 1539, his treatment of the human will alarmed Roman Catholic leaders, who considered it "more dangerous than other 'Lutheran' writings."[123] These leaders in turn showed Calvin's work to the Dutch Roman Catholic theologian Albert Pighius. In 1542, Pighius published *Ten Books* (chapters) *on Human Free Choice and Divine Grace*, a critique of Calvin by name. Calvin quickly responded to the first six chapters, those dealing with the human will, in *Defense of the Sound and Orthodox Doctrine of the Bondage and Liberation of Human Choice against the Misrepresentations of Albert Pighius of Kampen* (1543) This work has recently (1996) been translated into English for the first time as *The Bondage and Liberation of the Will*.

a. The Condition of the Will before the Fall: The Freedom of the Will.

In his response to Pighius one of Calvin's most important distinctions to which he returns repeatedly is between the will as originally created and the will after Adam's fall into sin. "...(I)t is one thing to ask what abilities man received at the beginning and another [to ask] what remains now that he has been derived of his abilities and reduced to utter poverty. The very different condition in which he now is ought not in the least to be confused with that earlier state."[124] And again,

> However, lest I should seem thereby to be evading the issue, I reply that both Luther and all of us define nature in two ways: first as it was established by God, which we declare to have been pure and perfect, and second as, corrupted through man's fall, it lost its perfection. We assign blame for this corruption to man; we do not ascribe it to God.[125]

In fact, much of Pighius's complaint against Calvin's view of the bondage of the will in sin is easily resolved as a confusion of the condition of the will before and after the fall.

Before the fall, Adam was created with a mind, "by which to

---

[123] John Calvin, *The Bondage and Liberation of the Will: A Defense of the Orthodox Doctrine of Human Choice against Pighius*, Texts and Studies in Reformation and Post-Reformation Thought, vol. 2, Edited by A. N. S. Lane, trans. Graham I. Davies, (Grand Rapids, MI: Baker Books, 1996), xiv.
[124] Ibid., 156.
[125] Ibid., 40.

distinguish good from evil, right from wrong; and, with the light of reason as guide, to distinguish what should be followed from what should be avoided."[126] To this God added the will, "under whose control is choice."[127] In Adam's original state, the mind was sufficiently enlightened to direct his life in a godly direction, and his will likewise desired holiness and happiness: "men mounted up even to God and eternal bliss."[128] The power of choice faithfully directed all the appetites of life, and the result was to "make the will completely amenable to the guidance of the reason."[129]

So Adam could have persevered in goodness and attained eternal life if he so willed. But his will was not unchangeable, but "capable of being bent to one side or the other."[130] Likewise, he was not given the power to persevere in goodness and could fall into sin. Calvin insists that Adam's choice was a free choice and that his mind and will were "rightly composed to obedience, until in destroying himself he corrupted his own blessings."[131]

According to Calvin, this solves a great puzzle of the philosophers. They reasoned (correctly) that for a man to be a rational creature he must possess the power of "free choice of good and evil," and that "the distinction between virtues and vices would be obliterated if man did not order his life by his own planning."[132] What they did not perceive was the distinction between man as created and man as fallen; that in this great change man is "said to have ruined himself totally."[133] So in looking for free will in fallen man, the philosophers were "seeking in a ruin for a building and in scattered fragments for a well-knit structure."[134] In this stark image, all that remains of the fallen human will is a "ruin" and "scattered fragments."

b. The Condition of the Will after the Fall: The Bondage of the Will.

By a "voluntary rebellion" our first ancestor "brought upon himself his

---

[126] John Calvin, *Institutes of the Christian Religion,* The Library of Christian Classics, vol. 20-21, Edited by John Thomas McNeill, trans. Ford Lewis Battles (Philadelphia: Westminster Press, 1960), 195.
[127] Ibid.
[128] Ibid.
[129] Ibid.
[130] Ibid.
[131] Ibid., 196.
[132] Ibid.
[133] Calvin, *The Bondage and Liberation of the Will: A Defense of the Orthodox Doctrine of Human Choice against Pighius,* 172.
[134] Calvin, *Institutes of the Christian Religion,* 196.

wretched condition of bondage, since he had been created free."[135] But it was not only upon himself alone, but rather "he consigned his race to ruin by his rebellion when he perverted that whole order of nature in heaven and on earth."[136] This was the original sin, but also the origin of sin in all of Adam's posterity, "the inherited corruption, which the church fathers termed 'original sin,' meaning by the word 'sin' the depravation of a nature previously good and pure."[137] Calvin defines "original sin" as "a hereditary depravity or corruption of our nature, diffused into all parts of the soul, which first makes us liable to God's wrath, then also brings forth in us those works which Scripture calls 'works of the flesh' [Gal. 5:19]."[138]

The consequences of this original sin upon Adam's race are dire. First, we are condemned and convicted before God "to whom nothing is acceptable but righteousness, innocence, and purity."[139] Not that we are liable for another's sin, but we are "entangled" with Adam's sin to the degree that a "contagion imparted by him resides in us, which justly deserves punishment."[140] Even in the case of infants who have done no good or evil, "they carry their condemnation along with them from the mother's womb" so that they are "guilty not of another's fault but of their own."[141]

> For, even though the fruits of their iniquity have not yet come forth, they have the seed enclosed within them. Indeed, their whole nature is a seed of sin; hence it can only be hateful and abhorrent to God. From this it follows that it is rightly considered sin in God's sight, for without sin there would be no accusation.[142]

But second, "this perversity never ceases in us, but continually bears new fruits."[143] The fallen nature is not merely deprived, but wantonly depraved: "For our nature is not only destitute and empty of good, but so fertile and fruitful in every evil that it cannot be idle."[144]

As a further result of the fall, both the mind and the will are corrupted, but not extinguished altogether. Because the mind is an essential part of human nature (a natural gift), "it could not be completely wiped out; but it was partly

---

[135] Calvin, *The Bondage and Liberation of the Will: A Defense of the Orthodox Doctrine of Human Choice against Pighius*, 172.
[136] Calvin, *Institutes of the Christian Religion*, 246.
[137] Ibid.
[138] Ibid, 251.
[139] Ibid.
[140] Ibid.
[141] Ibid.
[142] Ibid.
[143] Ibid.
[144] Ibid., 252.

weakened and partly corrupted, so that its misshapen ruins appear."[145] Though "some sparks still gleam," these merely "show him to be a rational being, differing from brute beasts, because he is endowed with understanding. Yet, secondly, they show his light choked with dense ignorance, so that it cannot come forth effectively."[146] And similarly the will, as an essential part of human nature, "did not perish, but was so bound to wicked desires that it cannot strive after the right."[147] In summary: "we say that man's mind is smitten with blindness, so that of itself it can in no way reach the knowledge of the truth; we say that his will is corrupted by wickedness, so that he can neither love God nor obey his righteousness."[148] This is indeed a hopeless condition, one of utter human inability, which leads Calvin to conclude with Augustine's words: "whatever good you have is from him; whatever evil, from yourself." And also, "Nothing is ours but sin."[149]

This brings us to the subject proper of the will in bondage to sin. And in a key passage[150] Calvin defines his terms and distinguishes his view from the semi-Pelagian Pighius. The four critical descriptions are of the will as (1) free, (2) coerced, (3) self-determined and (4) bound.

(1) For the will to be "free" it must "have in its power to choose good or evil"[151] This is the view of Pighius (and the view of Eduardo Bonnin, the founder of Cursillo). While Calvin would apply this understanding to humanity in his created, unspoiled state, he would deny that this view of the will is possible for people in their fallen state.

(2) A "coerced will" Calvin considers to be a logical impossibility since the ideas are contradictory. But for completeness and contrast Calvin defines a coerced will as one that "does not incline this way or that of its own accord or by an internal movement of decision, but is forcibly driven by an external impulse."[152] We might say that a coerced will, controlled from the outside like a puppet, is "forced to will," which lacks any intelligible meaning.

(3) A "self-determined" will is one that is not coerced by any external forces or impulses, but one which "of itself directs itself in the direction in which it is led."[153]

(4) And a "bound will" is "one which because of its corruptness is held

---

[145] Ibid., 270.
[146] Ibid.
[147] Ibid., 271.
[148] Calvin, *The Bondage and Liberation of the Will: A Defense of the Orthodox Doctrine of Human Choice against Pighius*, 128.
[149] Calvin, *Institutes of the Christian Religion*, 289.
[150] Calvin, *The Bondage and Liberation of the Will: A Defense of the Orthodox Doctrine of Human Choice against Pighius*, 69.
[151] Ibid.
[152] Ibid.
[153] Ibid.

Chapter 5: The Theology of the Cursillo Method 75

captive under the authority of evil desires, so that it can choose nothing but evil, even if it does so of its own accord and gladly, without being driven by any external impulse."[154] R. C. Sproul summarizes this view of the will as a "voluntary slave."[155]

The reason these definitions are important is that Calvin uses these terms to define his own position on the fallen will and to distinguish his view from that of Pighius. Pighius claims that human nature was not corrupted in the fall, and so the will is free, that is, able to choose good or evil. This, by the way, is a fully Pelagian position, and Pigihus was later condemned even by the Roman Catholic Church for it.[156] Calvin of course denies that the will is free.

But if the will is not free, what is it? It cannot be "coerced" because "this contradicts the nature of will and cannot coexist with it."[157] So, according to Calvin, the will is "self-determined," but is also "bound," enslaved by its own sinful corruption. Therefore the will sins "of necessity": "it is driven to evil and cannot seek anything but evil."[158] Yet this is vastly different from coercion for the simple fact that the bound will also sins "willingly."

> For we do not say that man is dragged unwillingly into sinning, but that because his will is corrupt he is held captive under the yoke of sin and therefore of necessity wills in an evil way. For where there is bondage, there is necessity. But it makes a great difference whether the bondage is voluntary or coerced. We locate the necessity to sin precisely in corruption of the will, from which it follows that it is self-determined.[159]

The main objection to the idea that we sin of necessity is the notion that "being voluntary is inconsistent with being necessary,"[160] that is, that if an action is necessary, it would cease to be voluntary. So that would mean that "there is no sin or virtue where there is necessity."[161] In other words, if a person can do no other than to sin, he is not responsible for that sin, and should not be blamed. And likewise, if a person could do no other than the good, he would not be responsible for the good, and should not be praised. Calvin dismisses this point easily by use of a comparison. Who could deny that God is good of necessity? Yet who would suggest that God's goodness is not

---

[154] Ibid.
[155] Sproul, *Willing to Believe: the Controversy Over Free Will*, 105.
[156] Calvin, *The Bondage and Liberation of the Will: A Defense of the Orthodox Doctrine of Human Choice against Pighius*, xvii.
[157] Ibid., 69.
[158] Ibid.
[159] Ibid., 68-69.
[160] Ibid., 147.
[161] Ibid., 146-147.

voluntary? Therefore, "necessity" and "voluntary" are not inconsistent. "We reply that God is good of necessity, but he obtains no less praise for his goodness because of the fact that he can only be good."[162] Therefore, Calvin concludes, humans sin of necessity and voluntarily, and so are entirely culpable for their sins. And because we sin of necessity, and this by nature, we can do no other as long as our nature remains corrupt.

> We say that (man) is evil because he comes from an evil descent, like a bad branch from a bad, corrupt root. Therefore, as long as he continues in his own nature, he cannot will and act except in an evil way. Indeed, we deny that it is in his power to abandon his wickedness and turn to the good.[163]

This is summarized in four points, to which Calvin refers repeatedly[164] (not, perhaps "the five points of Calvinism" but "the four points of Calvin.")

(1). Because of sin, the whole of human nature has been corrupted: "Of course, since man has sinned not with some part of himself but with his whole being, why should it be surprising if he be said to have ruined himself totally?"[165] For this corruption, man himself, and not God, is entirely responsible.

> For we do not locate the origin of our wickedness in creation or in the work of God, but in the fault of our first ancestor. For by a voluntary rebellion he brought upon himself his wretched condition of bondage, since he had been created free.[166]

The result of this whole corruption is a complete inability to turn to God: "As for our saying that the whole person is corrupted in such a way that he cannot with any part of himself come near to God by himself, we affirm nothing other than that to which God himself bears witness (in Scripture)."[167]

(2). From this it follows that the sinner can make no preparation to receive God's grace.

> But who cannot see that what I then add is the [logical] consequence of this? Namely that it is not in man's power to prepare himself to receive the grace of God, but his whole conversion is the gift of

---

[162] Ibid., 147. Calvin makes the same point about the devil and evil.
[163] Ibid., 149.
[164] See, for example, Ibid., 114, 128-131, 172-178.
[165] Ibid., 172.
[166] Ibid.
[167] Ibid., 172-173.

God.[168]

As evidence of this, Calvin turns to a favorite biblical image, the unregenerate "heart of stone" in Ezekiel 11:19 and 36:26.

> For when the Lord promises that he will give us a heart of flesh in place of our heart of stone, what room is left for preparation? How shall he who is made willing instead of unwilling, ready to obey instead of rebellious and obstinate, claim for himself the praise for his preparation?[169]

God must prepare us himself.

> So it is God's work to go before us, to convert us to himself. No wonder, for although it is a much lesser thing to think than to will, Paul does not even leave us the capacity to think anything good (referring to 1 Cor. 2:14).[170]

If the unregenerate could somehow prepare themselves to receive grace, then they might receive at least some of the credit for their salvation, but this is by no means true:

> For he cries that it is his work that we who were blind are enlightened, that we are brought over from darkness into his light, that we were renewed in mind, and finally we are roused from death to life. What kind of preparation will one who is dead use to call forth the grace of God?[171]

For support, Calvin calls upon pertinent declarations of the Council of Orange (529).

> If anyone argues that God waits for our desire that we should be cleansed from sin, and does not acknowledge that it is by the work of the Holy Spirit in us that we are even caused to want cleansing, he resists the Holy Spirit as he speaks through Solomon: The will is prepared by the Lord.[172]

---

[168] Ibid., 173.
[169] Ibid., 173-174.
[170] Ibid., 174.
[171] Ibid.
[172] Ibid., 81.

> If anyone says that mercy is bestowed on us because apart from the grace of God we will, toil, desire, try, ask, seek, or knock, and does not acknowledge that it is from God through the Spirit that we are enabled to believe, will, ask, and do all these things as we should, he resists the apostle when he says: What do you have that you have not received?[173]

> If anyone says that both the beginning and the increase of faith and the very desire to believe come not as a gift of grace (i.e. through the working of the Holy Spirit reforming our will from unbelief to belief, from irreligion to religion), but are innate in us by nature, he is opposed to the apostle when he says: He who began a good work in you will complete it at the day of the Lord Jesus.[174]

Calvin approvingly quotes Augustine, who explains why we pray for those who are "hostile to the Christian cause":

> We pray for them. What then do we ask but that instead of being unwilling they should be made willing, instead of rebelling be made acquiescent, instead of attackers be made loving? But by whom, except by him of whom it is written: 'By the Lord the will is prepared'?[175]

Augustine agrees that conversion is God's work, not our own:

> We pray for the wicked, that their evil will may be changed to a good one. And by the secret grace of God many are drawn to Christ. Those who reject this are in conflict not with me but with Christ who cries: no one can come to me unless my Father draws him.[176]

And Calvin concludes, "Do you see that people can only will evil until by a wonderful transformation their will is changed from evil to good?"[177]

(3). A third point is that grace is efficacious, that is, God's grace always accomplishes salvation when God intends it so. The reason for this is that God's grace effects a true conversion. First, to be clear, Calvin states what he does not mean:

---

[173] Ibid., 82.
[174] Ibid.
[175] Ibid., 110.
[176] Ibid.
[177] Ibid., 110-111.

Chapter 5: The Theology of the Cursillo Method 79

> I say, then, that grace is not offered to us in such a way that afterwards we have the option either to submit or to resist, I say that it is not given merely to aid our weakness by its support as though anything depended on us apart from it.[178]

Rather, "it is entirely the work of grace and a benefit conferred by it that our heart is changed from a stony one to a heart of flesh, that our will is made new, and that we, created anew in heart and mind, at length will what we ought to will."[179] God does not merely offer us the option of transformation if we choose, but actually transforms us so that we do choose. Calvin quotes Augustine in support of this: "Indeed in our receiving good and holding perseveringly to it by means of this grace, there is in us not just the ability to do what we will to do, but also the will to do what we are able to do."[180] In salvation God gives us both the ability to believe and the willingness to do so. It is entirely the work of grace.

(4). And fourthly, Calvin maintains that the perseverance of the converted unto life's end is also a gift of God. "Moreover, what we say about one action should be extended to cover our whole of life. For it would not be enough if God guided man's heart once, and did not always maintain it in a similar way and strengthen it to persevere."[181] Calvin wants to be clear that this does not mean that a person once awakened will now cooperate with grace on his own power, nor that subsequent grace is a reward merited by the awakened will. "For I do not allow that human beings have any ability but that which has been given to them. And [I say] that God unceasingly so accomplishes his work in them that whatever he bestows on them right to the end is freely given."[182] Quoting himself from the *Institutes* he concludes "And [I say], lest man fail, he is strengthened in such a way by the power of God that the course of pure, undeserved grace continues right up to the end of his life."[183]

Calvin summarizes these points:

> But all that we say amounts to this. First, that what a person is or has or is capable of is entirely empty and useless for the spiritual righteousness which God requires, unless one is directed to the good by the grace of God. Secondly, that the human will is of itself evil and therefore needs transformation and renewal so that it may begin to be good, but that grace itself is not merely a tool which can help

---

[178] Ibid., 174.
[179] Ibid.
[180] Ibid., 187.
[181] Ibid., 175.
[182] Ibid.
[183] Ibid., 178.

someone if he is pleased to stretch out his hand to [take] it. That is, [God] does not merely offer it, leaving [to man] the choice between receiving it and rejecting it, but he steers the mind to choose what is right, he moves the will also effectively to obedience, he arouses and advances the endeavor until the actual completion of the work is attained. Then again, that [grace] is not sufficient if it is just once conferred upon someone, unless it accompanies him without interruption.[184]

3. John Calvin on the Means of Grace.

If salvation is all of grace, if it is of God's "steering the mind" and "moving the will," not making a person simply able to choose, but also willing to choose, what part is there for human agency in effecting this great change? Certainly not to make the unwilling "more willing"[185] so that the unconverted reach out in their own strength or are convinced to choose grace. The "unwilling" are not at all willing, and cannot be made "more willing" by human works. As Calvin insists: "...people can only will evil until by a wonderful transformation their will is changed from evil to good." The unregenerate are inconvincible because they have no ability whatsoever even to want to be convinced.

Yet God has ordained some outward means which the Holy Spirit uses to effect this inward transformation, namely preaching the gospel and prayer. Calvin flatly asserts that "faith is not obtained through human efforts at persuasion, but is the special work of the Holy Spirit."[186] To this Pighius objects; then why bother to preach? "He (Pighius) says that we labour in vain in urging and exhorting people to believe, if it is really the case that they do not conceive [faith] themselves of their own power, but God inspires it by his grace."[187] To this, Calvin answers that the farmer does not labor in vain by sowing seed, even though he knows full well that without God's blessing his seed will not bear fruit. In truth, "all labour is in vain without the blessing of God," even "worth nothing."[188] In fact, since "man does not live by bread alone but by the power of [God's] word," "bread does not have any power of itself, but only the blessing of God is sufficient to nourish us."[189] God only uses bread as a means by which he sustains us. "But where [God's power] is

---

[184] Ibid., 114.
[185] Or, in the words of Bonnin, "'preparing the way of the Lord', making the trenches ready to receive the Grace" or to awaken and animate desire (*The How and the Why*, 34).
[186] Ibid., 31.
[187] Ibid., 32.
[188] Ibid.
[189] Ibid.

Chapter 5: The Theology of the Cursillo Method   81

present, it supports and sustains us no less effectively without bread than with bread."[190] God ordinarily chooses to use means to accomplish his work, but the means are of no importance.

Calvin comes to the point with an obvious reference to 1 Corinthians 3:7:

> Now it remains to apply those comparisons to the present case. Paul, when he speaks about the task of the apostles, compares them to gardeners who plant or water. And immediately he adds that they are nothing, God alone, who gives the increase is everything.[191]
>
> Now let [Pighius] bare his teeth at Paul. Let him mockingly ask what he achieves by writing and speaking so, why he undergoes so many trials, exposes himself to so many troubles and cares, makes no end of traveling around, if all these are nothing. To all these questions Paul replies that he has a ministry of the Spirit by which he is to write the preaching of the gospel on human hearts, not by his own activity and effort or (as they say) by his own exertions, but by the Spirit of the living God. Now you hear where the effectiveness of his ministry comes from, namely from the secret action of the Holy Spirit, not by human labour or desire. You hear also that the instrument which the hand of God uses to complete his work is thereby of no importance. So then let the holy apostle adapt this defense of his to us too in our common cause. Pighius asks, What is the point of our labour in writing and public speaking if man, before he believes, is held captive in Satan's bonds so that he cannot by himself receive and embrace sound teaching but when he is enlightened by the Spirit of God he effectually and necessarily receives it? Let Paul reply here: it is because God appointed the gospel to be the means to display the power of his Spirit. What more do you want? It is God alone who acts; but because he willed that the power of his Spirit should in some way be enclosed in the preaching of the gospel, our work which serves his providence is not empty or useless.[192]

So preaching is nothing, and only the power of the Spirit matters. And yet God has "willed that the power of his Spirit should in some way be enclosed in the preaching of the gospel." For this reason the gospel is preached. In fact, preaching alone is to build the church.

---

[190] Ibid., 32-33.
[191] Ibid., 33.
[192] Ibid.

We must hold to what we have quoted from Paul (2 Cor. 4:6)–that the church is built solely by outward preaching, and that the saints are held together by one bond only: that with common accord, through learning and advancement, they keep the church order established by God.[193]

Calvin is unequivocal: preaching is God's chosen and approved means of converting the lost.

...(A)lthough he is able to accomplish the secret work of his Holy Spirit without any means or assistance, he has nevertheless ordained outward preaching to use it as it were as a means. But to make such a means effective and fruitful he inscribes in our hearts with his own finger those very words which he speaks in our ears by the mouth of a human being. So he makes his work spiritual and living, when it would otherwise be of the letter and dead.[194]

We should always be clear "how big a difference there is between the outward preaching of a human being, which strikes only the ears, and that secret, more inward instruction of the Holy Spirit by which the mind is enlightened and the heart touched."[195] This means that "teaching is fruitful only when both the light of understanding and the disposition to obey are given by God"[196] and these are only given to the elect. "(T)he ungodly are also taught, but in a different way, with the result of course that they hear only a man, not that they learn from God."[197]

So two things must happen simultaneously for preaching to be effective.

God works in the elect on two levels, externally through the word, and internally through the Spirit. By enlightening our minds by his Spirit and forming our hearts to love and cultivate righteousness, he makes a new creation; and by the word he arouses us to seek, search for, and pursue renewal.[198]

In human preaching, God speaks through the preacher to those who are being

---

[193] Calvin, *Institutes of the Christian Religion*, 1019.
[194] Calvin, *The Bondage and Liberation of the Will: A Defense of the Orthodox Doctrine of Human Choice against Pighius*, 215.
[195] Ibid., 233.
[196] Ibid.
[197] Ibid.
[198] Ibid., 163-164.

saved:

> That is of course that God by his Spirit engraves on human hearts what he speaks through his mouth to their ears, not before or after but at the same time. So in preaching the seed is being sown, but that it puts out roots, germinates, and bears fruit is brought about by the Spirit of God inwardly.[199]

And since we have no way of knowing who are or are not elect, we preach the gospel to all:

> But as far as we are concerned, we cannot distinguish those who are predestined from those who are not, and so we ought to want everyone to be saved. We ought therefore to administer a harsh rebuke to all as a medicine, lest they perish or lest they cause others to perish. But it is God's work to make it beneficial to those whom he has foreknown and predestined.[200]

> God speaks through the preacher's voice:

> Those who think the authority of the Word is dragged down by the baseness of the men called to teach it disclose their own ungratefulness. For, among the many excellent gifts with which God has adorned the human race, it is a singular privilege that he deigns to consecrate to himself the mouths and tongues of men in order that his voice may resound in them. Let us accordingly not in turn dislike to embrace obediently the doctrine of salvation put forth by his command and by his own mouth. For, although God's power is not bound to outward means, he has nonetheless bound us to this ordinary manner of teaching....No one—not even a fanatical beast—ever existed who would tell us to close our ears to God. But in every age the prophets and godly teachers have had a difficult struggle with the ungodly, who in their stubbornness can never submit to the yoke of being taught by human word and ministry. This is like blotting out the face of God which shines upon us in teaching.[201]

The Apostles understood that Christ was speaking through them, and took great comfort from it:

---

[199] Ibid., 164-165
[200] Ibid., 160.
[201] Calvin, *Institutes of the Christian Religion*, 1018.

It was important for the apostles to have constant and perfect assurance in their preaching, which they were not only to carry out in infinite labors, cares, troubles, and dangers, but at last to seal with their own blood. In order that they might know, I say, that this assurance was not in vain or empty, but full of power and strength, it was important for them to be convinced that in such anxiety, difficulty and danger they were doing God's work; also, for them to recognize that God stood beside them while the whole world opposed and attacked them; for them, not having Christ, the Author of their doctrine before their eyes on earth, to know that he, in heaven, confirms the truth of the doctrine which he had delivered to them. On the other hand, it was necessary to give the unmistakable witness to their hearers that the doctrine of the gospel was not the word of the apostles but of God himself; not a voice born on earth but one descended from heaven. For these things—forgiveness of sins, the promise of eternal life, the good news of salvation—cannot be in man's power. Therefore, Christ has testified that in the preaching of the gospel the apostles have no part save that of ministry; that it was he himself who would speak and promise all things through their lips as his instruments.[202]

But why "preaching"? Why does God use this means alone to proclaim the Gospel and convert the sinner? One intriguing answer Calvin gives is that since paradise was lost through our ears, by listening to temptation, it is fittingly regained in the same way, by hearing the Gospel. "Hence Bernard rightly teaches that the door of salvation is opened to us when we receive the gospel today with our ears, even as death was then admitted by those same windows when they were opened to Satan (cf. Jer. 9:21)."[203]

But more importantly, this divine arrangement ensures that God alone receives the glory in salvation. Referring again to 1 Corinthians 3:7, Calvin notes: "Paul declares that all those who plant or water are nothing. How so, except that the ministers of Christ achieve nothing more by their teaching and preaching than they would if they were striking the air with their breath?"[204] Why does Calvin consider preaching so utterly ineffective apart from God's power? "...(B)ecause they are speaking to stones until, by his miraculous and secret operation, God introduces into people's minds and breathes into their hearts what, by their own efforts, could not reach beyond their ears...."[205] And

---

[202] Ibid., 1213.
[203] Ibid., 246.
[204] Calvin, *The Bondage and Liberation of the Will: A Defense of the Orthodox Doctrine of Human Choice against Pighius*, 163.
[205] Ibid.

this inevitably leads to God's glory alone:

> This is not because in doing everything by the power of his Spirit [God] excludes the ministry of his servants, but so as to secure the entire praise for the action for himself, just as the effectiveness derives from him alone, and whatever labour people do without him is empty and barren.[206]

The inventor of the Cursillo technique, Eduardo Bonnin, argues that his technique is "not only an essential element in the efficacy of the Cursillos but also of its specific, distinguishing qualities."[207] And lest the reader confuse this technique with other, more ordinary methods (such as preaching and prayer), Bonnin contends that his methods "are distinctly different from the other apostolic realizations or methods with which they have been compared."[208] In other words, Bonnin insists that his Cursillo technique is quite new and novel, something far beyond the time-honored, God-ordained, biblical means of grace in preaching and prayer, or anything else that has heretofore been tried, for that matter. And this previously undiscovered technique is "essential" to the Cursillo. Remarkably, something unknown in Scripture is now "essential" to effective ministry!

This perspective of Calvin has been preserved and even amplified in all of the Reformed Creeds and Catechisms, documents which Reformed and Presbyterian ministers and elders profess to believe to be reliable expositions of what the Scriptures teach. (A summary of the pertinent portions of these documents appears in Appendix A.) To be clear: the doctrinal standards of virtually all Reformed churches demonstrate that the Cursillo method is not only unnecessary and irrelevant to truly biblical ministry, but also attempts to do what we profess cannot be done. The Cursillo Method is certainly incompatible with Reformed theology on this ground alone. Perhaps the chart below can best display the distinction.

---

[206] Ibid.
[207] Bonnin, *The How and the Why*, 33.
[208] Ibid.

The Formula for Effective Ministry According to Theological Tradition

Roman Catholic **(Cursillo) Theology** (Semi-Pelagian)	Traditional Means of Grace (Word, Sacraments & Prayer) +	God's Grace +	"the best insights of psychology, pedagogy and group dynamics ... put together in an orderly sequence"[209] =	Effective Ministry
Classic Reformed Theology (Augustinian)	Traditional Means of Grace (Word, Sacraments & Prayer) +	God's Grace +	(nothing else) =	Effective Ministry

The Cursillo method irreconcilably contradicts distinctive and central doctrines of the Reformed faith. One could easily understand a Roman Catholic (semi-Pelagian) Cursillo, or an Arminian Cursillo, a Wesleyan-Arminian Cursillo, or a Freewill Baptist Cursillo. But a Reformed/Presbyterian Cursillo is a virtual oxymoron—a contradiction of terms and an attempted union of irreconcilables. One must choose: Reformed or Cursillo, but one may not claim both.

---

[209] Jackson, "A Handbook for Leaders in the Cursillo Movement for the Reformed Church in America," 10.

6. *The Techniques of the Cursillo Method*

The effects of the Cursillo method are undeniable. There is too much anecdotal evidence to dispute them.[210] The founder of the Cursillo method, Eduardo Bonnin, could boast: "Eleven years after the first Cursillo, its efficacy has been verified a hundred times over."[211] Bonnin is certain that this is a genuine work of God and claims "the authoritative voice of the Bishop of Cuidad Real, Juan Hervas," has described it as a "'divine work, inspired by God, moved by the Holy Spirit, governed by the hierarchy.'"[212] Indeed, Bishop Hervas claims more as he quotes approvingly an unnamed psychologist who has studied the Cursillo method.

> The Cursillo possesses a technique which we have studied from a psychological viewpoint, with the researcher's eagerness to explain by natural means whatever is humanly explicable...a detailed explanation and a minute analysis would be a task for a book, and no small one....As a summary, and placing the effectiveness of grace in the first place, we think that the technique of the Cursillos in Christianity is based on psychological elements so effective and so skillfully wielded, that even from a purely psychological and material point of view, a good part of their undeniable individual and collective success can be explained.[213]

In other words, the Cursillo method employs such powerful psychological elements so skillfully that God is practically unnecessary.

In the same context, Hervas chides the church for failing to adopt these kinds of techniques.

---

[210] The *genuine and lasting* efficacy of the Cursillo method is not conceded, however, and awaits further analysis.
[211] Bonnin, *The How and the Why*, 1.
[212] Ibid.
[213] Juan Hervás, *Cursillos in Christianity, Instrument of Christian Renewal*, 2nd. ed. (Madrid: Ultreya Publications for Euramerica, 1967), 293.

> Having carelessly ignored or overlooked the natural means and resources which psychology, pedagogy and didactics place at the disposal of man, can we not find an explanation—always making allowance for supernatural factors—for the lack of continuity and perseverance in the work realized, of the little or no efficacy of the apostolate carried on by many pastors of souls and educators? We are convinced that it is so.[214]

The church's efforts fail, opines Hervas, not so much for lack of God's grace, but for neglect of or refusal to adopt and employ new discoveries in the fields of psychology, social dynamics and educational technique.

American Catholic Cursillo leader, Al Blatnik explains to newly made Cursillistas:

> It may have seemed to you something that was just thrown together and just happened to "jell" because a group of good fellows were [*sic*] there and because the Holy Spirit made his presence felt. There were [*sic*] a group of good fellows there, and the Holy Spirit certainly made His presence felt. But something thrown together, it was not!
>
> The weekend is the result of long years of work, experience and prayer. The psychology involved, the schedule, order of talks and events, and the content are carefully planned. Nothing is left to chance.[215]

In fact, Blatnik is willing to admit that it is the method itself and not the content of the messages which makes the difference. "The presentation of Christianity in the talks by the priests and the laymen contained nothing that you did not already know about your faith. It is the unique manner in which it is presented that is so effective."[216] As we have seen, this was affirmed by Jackson in his *Handbook for Leaders in the Cursillo Movement for the Reformed Church in America*. "Everything that is humanly possible, from the best insights of psychology, pedagogy and group dynamics to the clearest understanding of Scripture is put together in an orderly sequence to achieve the aims of the Cursillo."[217]

And so it is important for us to consider what these almost miraculous psychological elements are that can produce such results, almost apart from the power of God.

We have already seen one important point. Cursillo is not really about

---

[214] Ibid., 292.
[215] Blatnik, *Your Fourth Day*, 25.
[216] Ibid., 26.
[217] Jackson, "A Handbook for Leaders in the Cursillo Movement for the Reformed Church in America," 10.

Chapter 6: The Techniques of the Cursillo Method

theology. It is a *method*. By all reports, the method produces a powerful, sometimes overwhelming, usually pleasant, emotional experience in most participants. Presbyterian Cursillo advocate and pastor Kevin Boyd laments the problem some call "weekend-itis," "a condition in which Cursillo weekends become the center of a person's religious life." He explains: "The emotional appeal can be so powerful that the part of the program which is supposed to prepare the participants for something greater (i.e., a life of leadership within the church) becomes the ultimate goal."[218] He also notes the familiar problem of cliquishness, in which participants only socialize with each other and exclude non-initiates. This, too, Boyd explains, is an unintended result of the emotional weekend experience. "To be fair, this is probably not intentional. Those who have participated share the bond of a powerful experience with Christ and are naturally drawn to one another."[219]

Jackson states that one of the messages during the weekend titled "Total Security" explains how the pleasurable experience of the weekend can be maintained: "The rector of the weekend gives this rollo which tells the candidates how they can preserve the experience of the Cursillo for the rest of their lives."[220] Blatnik clarifies that this experience can be renewed in the post-Cursillo gatherings: "The spirit of the weekend is perhaps only captured again in vital ultreyas, and then for only short periods of time due to the length of these weekly gatherings."[221] Hughes highlights the need for emotional balance, or the weekend can become overly emotional.

> When a participant leaves a weekend that was an excessively emotional one, then he/she may be inclined to feel a victim of his/her emotions. Yet, if the structure of the weekend is properly balanced so that the emotional element is not overdone, it can be seen that the weekend reveals a spirit of Christian love, genuine friendship, and the presentation of the simple truths of the gospel do involve love.[222]

What can account for this powerful, usually pleasant emotional experience that bonds participants together? What are the acclaimed psychological elements and techniques? Juan Hervas notes that the full study of these methods is yet to be completed.

---

[218] Boyd, "Decently De Colores: A Reformed Evaluation of the Cursillo Movement in the Presbyterian Church," 123.
[219] Ibid., 128.
[220] Jackson, "A Handbook for Leaders in the Cursillo Movement for the Reformed Church in America," 24.
[221] Blatnik, *Your Fourth Day*, 25.
[222] Gerry Hughes, ed. *Our Fourth Day for the New Cursillista* (Dallas: National Ultreya Publications, 1985), 2.

> What are these resources, these natural means which are employed in the Cursillos? The profound and complete study of them should not be our task, but rather that of specialists in pedagogy and psychology. We trust that some day a profound and thorough analysis will be made which will reveal these values to priests and lay leaders so that they may use them with maximum exactness and efficacy.[223]

Since Bishop Hervas has invited evaluation, we should turn to the limited studies that have been done, several of which are not at all positive.

A. William Sargant: *Tension Relief and Group Bonding Through a Physiological Abreaction or Catharsis.*

William Sargant was a British psychiatrist who published a book titled *Battle for the Mind, A Physiology of Conversion and Brainwashing*. He noted the various ways that excessive anxiety could create hysteria and especially states of increased suggestibility through the inhibition of critical faculties. In Sargant's view these reactions were physiological and not so much psychological in nature.

One such reaction is called an abreaction or catharsis in which repressed, unpleasant feelings are suddenly released bringing understandable relief. Such abreactions could be stimulated through hypnosis, alcohol or other drugs, or through vigorous and rhythmic dancing. Sargant's main concern in his book was to expose how unscrupulous leaders could manipulate such techniques to create desired responses on the unsuspecting.

> Abreaction is a time-worn physiological trick which has been used, for better or worse, by generations of preachers and demagogues to soften up their listeners' minds and help them take on desired patterns of belief and behaviour. Whether the appeal has more often been to noble and heroic deeds, or to cruelty and folly, is a matter for the historian rather than the physiologist to decide.[224]

Sargant did not write specifically concerning the Cursillo method, but his thesis relates to every method which employs these techniques, including the Cursillo. It is interesting that even though he calls Sargant's views "extreme," the usually cautious David F. Wells gives credence to his theories.

---

[223] Hervas, *Cursillos in Christianity: Instrument of Christian Renewal*, 293-294.
[224] William Sargant, *Battle for the Mind: A Physiology of Conversion and Brain-Washing* (New York: Doubleday, 1957; repr., Cambridge, MA: Malor Books, 1997), 59.

Chapter 6: The Techniques of the Cursillo Method

Most noteworthy in Sargant's contributions were his attempts to link psychological studies of brainwashing with religious conversion. He believed that suggestion and brainwashing operate in large evangelistic meetings, and he attempted to identify some of the effective ingredients. Evangelists were given considerable prestige, build-up, and wide publicity beforehand. They spoke with great conviction and fervor in a meeting preceded by the repetitive singing of emotional hymns and choruses and a background of bright lights, massed choirs, and stirring music with a strong rhythmic beat. It was in these circumstances, said Sargant, that physical and psychological stresses are skillfully applied, so that they produce dramatic changes in feeling, behavior, and ultimately, beliefs. Sargant argued that brainwashing phenomena are especially evident in the meetings of snake-handling sects in the southern states of America. When emotional exhaustion had paved the way to heightened suggestibility, beliefs were implanted and commitment was called for. *There may well be some truth in some of the speculations that Sargant gave about possible psychological processes underlying the behavior going on in these meetings*, but it certainly does not tell us anything about the truth of the beliefs that were arrived at.[225]

Revival scholar, Iain H. Murray, likewise urges that Sargant's cautions be heard. In relation to crusade evangelism (the "invitation system"), Murray writes:

It has not, however, escaped the notice of some who are also interested in psychology, but who do not claim to be evangelicals, that the very fact that the invitation system harmonizes with certain features in our psychological make-up leaves it open to serious objections. These critics argue that the way conversions are produced under this system by a pressure on the will is little different from the way in which 'conversions' which make no claim to be Christian at all often take place. The 'conditioning' of a large crowd of people in a controlled environment, with methods of persuasive suggestion leading to a demand for a public response—an emotional release—is psychologically certain, they say, to produce results regardless of whether the crowd meets in the name of religion, entertainment or politics. Modern psychiatrists like William Sargant have analyzed some of the physiological processes which make this the case....

---

[225] David F. Wells, *Turning to God: Biblical Conversion in the Modern World* (Grand Rapids, MI: Baker Book House, 1989), 70-71, emphasis added.

When during the religious crusade the call to respond is issued, with these powerful techniques employed, "the wonder is that so few obey."[226]

Sargant's observations, as well as Wells's and Murray's endorsements should give pause to all who promote such techniques.[227]

B. DeTar and Manion: *Pyschological Manipulation Using Covert Pressures Induced Through Techniques of Psychodrama and Sociometry.*

In 1965 John H. DeTar, a medical doctor with some knowledge of psychology and sociology, along with Thomas M. Manion, conducted an early examination[228] and concluded that the Cursillo method is a deceitful application of the group dynamics of sociometry and the emotional techniques of psychodrama applied in a manipulative way that enforces compliance and restricts dissent:

> During the Cursillo, the closing ceremonies (the Clausura) and after the Cursillo (Post-Cursillo) intense pressures are applied to the individual to prevent the development of deviationist tendencies. In a real sense, Cursillo becomes a way of life lasting far longer than the seventy two hour period to which the novice cursillista thinks he is committed. At the time of invitation there is considerable misrepresentation about the time which the novice will be expected to give after the Cursillo. Nor is he told of the intense group pressures used to keep him under Cursillo guidance after attending. The prospective novice is reassured that he will have no subsequent obligations or responsibilities—true from a contractual standpoint,

---

[226] Iain Hamish Murray, *The Invitation System*, (Edinburgh: The Banner of Truth Trust, 1973), 13-14. For D. Martyn Lloyd-Jones's partial-endorsement of Sargant's thesis, see Appendix B.
[227] Sargant is not the only one to note the physiological or psychological factors at work in some sudden "conversions." See also Marybeth F. Ayella, *Insane Therapy: Portrait of a Psychotherapy Cult* (Philadelphia, PA: Temple University Press, 1998); Steven Hassan, *Combatting Cult Mind Control*, (Rochester, VT: Park Street Press, 1988); Michael D. Langone, ed., *Recovery from Cults: Help for Victims of Psychological and Spiritual Abuse* (New York: W.W. Norton & Company, 1993); Robert Jay Lifton, *Thought Reform and the Psychology of Totalism* (Chapel Hill, NC: The University of North Carolina Press, 1989); Margaret Thaler Singer with Janja Lalich, *Cults in OurMidst*, 1st ed. (San Francisco: Jossey-Bass Publishers, 1995) and Margaret Thaler Singer and Janja Lalich, *"Crazy" Therapies: What Are They? Do They Work?* (San Francisco: Jossey-Bass Publishers, 1996). For a detailed discussions of both the pros and cons of the brainwashing model, see Benjamin D. Zablocki and Thomas Robbins, eds., *Misunderstanding Cults: Searching for Objectivity in a Controversial Field* (Toronto: University of Toronto Press Inc., 2001). For a comparison of the Cursillo method and its effects with other non-Christian or non-religious methods which employ the similar techniques and achieve similar results, see chapter 8 of this book.
[228] DeTar and Manion, *To Deceive...The Elect*.

Chapter 6: The Techniques of the Cursillo Method 93

> but untrue from a standpoint of persuasion. As the Cursillo progresses, he is led to believe that he will fail to be true to Christ if he does not continue the work of the Cursillo, and to most people failing Christ is tantamount to mortal sin....It should be noted that the entire three days is carefully planned and conducted, much like a large concert orchestra, the instruments being mortals who are gently manipulated by the trained members of each section.[229]

In the view of DeTar and Manion, the candidate "is gradually molded from a resistant skeptic through the successive stages of non-resistance, insecurity, security and finally to a condition of total commitment to Cursillo."[230]

If their statement seems extreme, DeTar and Manion may be excused. Hervas himself admits to arguably manipulative practices. The first day's activities are to commence with little emotional pressure. Why? To overcome natural resistance: "One must really take into consideration the fact that one of the main points of resistance on the part of the cursillista will usually stem from his shying away from their 'desire to convert him.'"[231] After a night of introspective silence, the next morning the desired mood of the candidates is to be

> ...marked by a complete disorientation of the cursillistas, caused by their lack of knowledge of what the Cursillo is to be and by the diverse and contrary impressions that they have already gained. The distribution by *'Decurias'* [table groupings of only candidates who are strangers to each other, ed.] will probably have added to the disorientation; the termination of the period of silence and the first contacts with instructors and companions, generally strangers to them, will contribute also to the disorientation in the new environment that is beginning to be created.[232]

The first speaker on the first morning is instructed to

> proceed furtively like one who intends to place a bomb inside a castle. He enters it like a peaceful visitor who goes about examining each of the rooms until he reaches the interior of the fortress where he furtively places the explosive which in this case is the question that,

---

[229] Ibid., 65.
[230] Ibid., 68.
[231] Hervas, *Leaders' Manual for Cursillos in Christianity*, 93. Here is one of the first of numerous indications in the *Leaders' Manual* that the main purpose of the Cursillo method is to overcome the resistance or the "defense mechanisms" of the candidate.
[232] Ibid., 94.

put at the end of the *'rollo'*, [short talk or sermon, ed.] produces the effect of a real surprise and causes many false ideals to collapse.[233]

After the "bomb" is exploded, "the instructor leaves immediately in order to avoid unnecessary or premature discussions and questions,"[234] thus effectively preventing critical evaluation.

The purpose of these techniques of disorienting and dropping "bombs" that have been "furtively" placed is obviously and even explicitly in order to overcome defenses. By the last half of the first day, Hervas notes that in the ideal situation, "The temper of the cursillista has been changing perceptively. He has abandoned his defensive position, placing himself each time on more accessible ground."[235] It should be noted that all of these attempts at overcoming resistance are to be done "furtively."

Remarkably, Eduardo Bonnin maintains that the Cursillo method is valid because it is "an instrument of something greater" (i.e. its greater goal of spiritual renewal). Without that worthy goal, the method would be "tantamount…to a psychological trick." And without that greater goal we can be sure that God would not use this method, and so "it would be unfruitful in everything supernatural."[236] But since God obviously does use it, he argues, it must be legitimate.

C. Marcene Marcoux: *"Breaking" the Candidate with Psychological Jolts and Shocks.*

Marcene Marcoux conducted a sociological study of the Cursillo method, and her findings were eventually recorded in the book, *Cursillo: Anatomy of a Movement*.[237] In Chapter 3, she describes the Cursillo weekend experience giving special attention to the intended emotional effect on the participant.

> The weekend begins on Thursday night. The candidates arrive, usually in a heightened emotional state. "Enthused or hesitant, optimistic or somewhat dejected—in whatever mood, the candidates arrive Thursday to begin their initiation, where they will remain until Sunday evening. What will fill the space and time in this period is the

---

[233] Ibid. Though Hervas wrote in a day when terrorist bombings were not commonplace, the reference sounds chilling in our post-911 climate.
[234] Ibid. One Methodist Cursillo or "Walk to Emmaus" leader told me the motto for the weekend is "Don't evaluate, just participate."
[235] Ibid., 113.
[236] Bonnin, *The How and the Why*, 32-33.
[237] Marcoux, *Cursillo, Anatomy of a Movement: The Experience of Spiritual Renewal*.

question they all face. What they experience is the answer."[238]

What they find on the Thursday night is a dark mood:

> The tone is somber, and the atmosphere meditative as individuals examine their past lives. The themes of this night are helplessness, loneliness, and salvation through self-denial and self-surrender which are pointedly expressed in the three meditations preached that evening.[239]

This design is calculated to "disorient" the candidate:

> Clearly, Thursday is structured to effect a disorientation of the candidates, that is, to plunge them into a shocking state of self-awakening. The individuals must handle this shock in isolation since they are prohibited from speaking with other candidates and must maintain silence. They are segregated from others and left without any supportive group to share their frustrations and anxieties. Candidates listen to words that may upset them and are designed to do exactly this. The images and examples are purposefully selected to instil [sic] aloneness and helplessness.[240]

The effect can be dramatic:

> It is not surprising that certain individuals experience a break with their past that very night. All though most individuals experience a shock Friday or Saturday, there are some drastically affected by the events of the first night.[241]

But the mood is suddenly transformed in the morning.

> The following morning, the somber and individually centered format is punctured by a tone of happiness and an atmosphere of shared fellowship. Each person now surprisingly gathers that social interaction, discussions, and a joyful spirit are vital. Unprepared for this transition, many are startled and confused....[242]

---

[238] Ibid., 66.
[239] Ibid.
[240] Ibid., 69.
[241] Ibid.
[242] Ibid., 70.

The sudden shifting of moods is not the only unsettling element awaiting the candidate.

> Predictably, relinquishing the Thursday night atmosphere creates a feeling of unpredictability that is reinforced throughout the initiation by similar procedures designed to jolt the candidates. The style and content of the rollos, which encapsulate in fifteen presentations the cursillo doctrine, are also intended to catch the candidates off-guard. Rollos are given in a room where candidates sit around tables bearing the names of particular saints. Each table, called a *decuria*, consists of ten individuals who remain grouped for every rollo. Although there are ten persons per decuria, only eight are initiates, for the other two are team members, and their identities are revealed only at the moment they present their rollos.[243]

These rollos or talks are not merely lectures but contain many statements of intimate, emotional and perhaps even shameful self-revelation, for "without doubt, the cursillo understands the power of disclosure, of revealing one's feelings in the process of communication."[244] Such openness often produces discomfort for the candidates: "Especially in a society where religion is considered private and spiritual feelings remain undisclosed, the rollos break this norm, and the shock of personal revelation overwhelms many candidates."[245]

Another "surprise" awaits the candidates in the form of "palanca." Palanca are "symbolic offerings to candidates implying some sacrifice by the giver and handed to the candidate as a public statement of caring."[246] These may be from people known to the candidates or from complete strangers. The purpose of such gifts is to remind the candidate "that someone outside the sphere of initiation is thinking about them and will continue to keep them in mind until Sunday evening."[247]

> The palanca catch the initiates by surprise with an overflow of Christian love and concern. Some, overwhelmed with the palanca, begin to cry as individuals at their table comfort them and share in the intensity of the experience. Others take the impact less emotionally, but even among these, many are dramatically affected by the

---

[243] Ibid., 72-73.
[244] Ibid., 77.
[245] Ibid.
[246] Ibid., 80.
[247] Ibid., 81.

sacrifices.[248]

The palanca serve another purpose, however, and that is decreasing resistance to conversion: "the palanca affects many so deeply that they begin lowering their defenses as they experience the care of others and Christian love."[249] But the palanca also adds a pressure to convert as "'…the cursillista is brought up short and made to realize that he is going to have to respond in a way that he probably never did before.'"[250]

These "shocks" or "jolts" are essential to the Cursillo method according to Marcoux.

> The team aims at shocking the candidates to alter their everyday consciousness. That which is taken for granted, now is confronted. General notions of Christian love are placed in a new perspective. Individuals are jolted, caught off guard, but more important, they experience a shock to their everyday sense of the world.[251]

In the process, the candidate is hopefully "broken":

> For the cursillista, the shock or "breaking" as it is called within the movement, is the necessary rupture with a traditional perspective on the self, the church, and society, preparing the initiate for a transition into a different religious model of social reality—a realm with contrasting religious emphases and distinctive social consequences. The cursillo initiation is consciously structured to produce a break with the things that are taken for granted, and each aspect of the initiation: the Thursday retreat, the rollos, and these palanca, are designed to achieve this dramatic outcome.[252]

This induced "breaking" can usually be timed to the very day.

A few candidates are aware of personal changes Friday evening; some begin to feel different Sunday or even weeks later. But it is assumed and carefully planned that Saturday will prove to be, for most of the candidates, the day of conversion; it generally is.[253]

---

[248] Ibid., 85.
[249] Ibid., 90.
[250] Ibid., 85. Marcoux attributes this quotation to S. Martin and R. Clark. "An Overview of the Cursillo Talks," mimeographed, 2.
[251] Ibid., 86.
[252] Ibid. Al Blatnik more candidly and colorfully calls this process "the 'whomp' on the head to get your attention." *Your Fourth Day*, 28.
[253] Ibid., 90-91.

She describes the breaking:

> The inner doors open; unexpected breezes blow through, and the person experiences the breakthrough. Some never knew of these inner dimensions; several failed to open the door; and others searched for years looking for the key that would unlock the door. For some, the cursillo triggers the quest and the discovery.[254]

But now the all-consuming question becomes how to maintain this powerful, mountaintop experience. After the breakthrough on Saturday, Sunday then becomes the day "to proclaim the cursillo's strength by illustrating to the initiates that it can maintain the Saturday experience as a permanent way of life."[255] During the lectures Sunday "(i)nitiates discover the importance of contact with Christ and with the brothers and recognize that the weekly meetings can sustain some of the fervor of the initiation."[256] The last lecture, called "The Fourth Day" is "framed as an intimate testimony."[257] "The speaker is enthusiastic and definitive, intending to demonstrate that Christian joyfulness can be, and is, sustained after initiation."[258]

And yet it is not over. The last act of initiation, the closing ceremony or the "clausura, as with the retreat phase, the palanca, and the presentation of rollos, continues the element of shock." That is because the "initiates, now accustomed to the cursillo style, do not expect any new surprises on this weekend."[259] But what they get instead is truly overwhelming:

> As the doors open, hundreds of people rush through to welcome the initiates into the cursillo membership. Spouses, friends, family members, neighbors, parishioners, acquaintances, and those strangers who have written palanca meet face-to-face. It is a moment of friendship, harmony, intense emotional responses and Christian love as people embrace intoning the by now familiar phrase: de colores. Initiates are held, hugged, and welcomed; here new members and older ones assemble, come into contact and partake in the circle of this spiritual community.[260]

Having experienced one such clausura as a candidate, I noticed an additional

---

[254] Ibid., 92.
[255] Ibid., 93.
[256] Ibid., 95.
[257] Ibid.
[258] Ibid., 96.
[259] Ibid.
[260] Ibid., 96-97.

result. Those who attend as past participants also seem to re-live the glow and re-capture some of the experience for themselves.

D. Ralph G. O'Sullivan: *A Predictable Pattern, Psychological Surprises, Group Dynamics, and Positive Reinforcement.*

Ralph G. O'Sullivan is a sociologist who has taught at Illinois State University and Bradley University and who attended a Roman Catholic Cursillo weekend in Peoria, Illinois, in 1982. From 1988-1999 he wrote journal articles analyzing the methodology and impact of the Cursillo method. In his analysis, several factors contribute to the Cursillo effect.

One element is the structure of the weekend itself which follows a recognized pattern of personality development encompassing three stages: 1) the preparatory, 2) the interactional, and 3) the participatory, roughly corresponding to the three days of Cursillo. The first day, Friday,

> is both a preparatory day and a destructive day, because the talks, or *rollos* of the day are intended to create a sense of unrest in the religious seeker or cursillo candidate/initiate. It is also a time period wherein the seeker is introduced to cursillo language structure, the history and philosophy of cursillo, and alternative sets of beliefs with which the religious seeker may align oneself to replace the beliefs of a secular lifestyle.[261]

The second day is likened to the interactional stage because on this day the "candidate is provided with information concerning the development of new learning skills by which to become an informed Christian activist."[262] It is noted that the theme of the second day is "Study." The third day, which is entitled "Action" is similar to the participatory stage. The "candidates are now asked to return to their respective communities to work for themselves, their families, their home churches and denominations, and cursillo itself." Accordingly "outreach skills and, cautions, are instilled into candidates during the day."[263]

A second element are the "surprises" which occur during the weekend.

> There are also several gatherings during the course of a cursillo weekend of which candidates should not be aware during their sponsor's presocialization. Such secretive occurrences may be, and

---

[261] Ralph G. O'Sullivan, "Structure, Function, and Cognitive Development in Cursillo: An Interactionist Analysis," *Sociological Spectrum* 8, no. 3 (1988), 262.
[262] Ibid., 263.
[263] Ibid.

sometimes are, the "significant emotional events" (Massey 1976) in the lives of cursillo initiates which serve as sufficient stimuli to bring about the religious conversion or religious revitalization.[264]

And a third element stems from the intensity of the group dynamics.

> (M)any religious conversions or revitalizations are not the direct product of cursillo's structure, but rather result from informal networks of human relationships that develop when large numbers of people are sequestered from the larger society, and when they have only themselves with whom to interact during three uninterrupted days of religious instruction.[265]

O'Sullivan describes a fourth element in the success of the Cursillo method as "positive reinforcement" or "stroking," i.e. the rewards for proper behavior. Similar to the Alcoholics Anonymous's "drunk-a-log," an important element in the weekend is the "sin-a-log" or "witnessing," in which one's sinful life is publicly recounted and then repudiated. Psychologists call this "renunciation." Such renunciation "has two types of reward structures built into it….the actions relieve psychological pressures and guilt from the seeker so that personal well-being becomes possible….(and) the seeker now has an external source of pressure affecting conformity to the new lifestyle and the new referent group."[266] The speaker then enjoys the approval (positive reinforcement) of the group, but has also become accountable to the group for continued fidelity to his promises.

This also works to solidify the speaker's place within the group. In the words of "Hirschi's (1985) fourfold components of internal and external mechanisms for social control" O'Sullivan writes:

> The religious seeker has developed a cathetic *attachment* to the new group. The seeker becomes *committed* to the group members because they may have replaced old friends. The seeker becomes *involved* in working for self and the group. The religious seeker begins to internalize the *belief* structure of the new group.[267]

A fifth element in the success of the Cursillo method O'Sullivan describes as "upward mobility." Candidates must learn a new vocabulary of

---

[264] Ibid., 269.
[265] Ibid.
[266] Ralph G. O'Sullivan, "Climbing Jacob's Ladder: Symbolic Renunciation, Reference-Group Identification, and Status Mobility in Cursillo," *Sociological Spectrum* 9, no. 3 (1989): 333-4.
[267] Ibid., 334, emphasis original.

unique terms, "buzz words," used in Cursillo for integration into the group. But the most important language, according to O'Sullivan, is to be able "to tell the right kind of witnessing stories as a form of *palanca* to the right kinds of audiences, so that referent others will label the religious seeker or new cursillista as a peer." This is how a person "achieves upward mobility within a cursillo center,"[268] another powerful incentive of positive reinforcement or reward. O'Sullivan describes within the Cursillo community a "bureaucratic structure" in which there "is a hierarchy of authority and social influence, and there are specific methods by which ranked social status changes in cursillo communities occur."[269] Those possessing the highest statuses are marked during the weekend with "colorful clothing, such as vests" and/or unique identification badges, for example. "While such paraphernalia are not specifically intended to denote status differences among cursillistas, they connote such variations"[270] thus effectively identifying those who have achieved greater positions of prestige within the movement.

E. Sigmund Dragostin: *"Conversion" Through Social Psychological Mechanisms.*

Sigmund Dragostin (or "Dragastin"), O.F.M., has extensive experience as spiritual director at Franciscan centers. After completing his doctoral work in sociology at the University of Chicago he joined the faculty. His evaluation of the Cursillo method came through personal involvement: Dragostin made Cursillo in 1962.

> As a priest-sociologist with some acquaintance with current social psychology, I am disturbed by what seem to me to be undue pressures exerted on those making the exercises. A study of Bishop Hervas's *Leaders' Manual,* an extensive description of the *cursillo* running to some 300 pages, has done little to change this reaction.
> Read from the viewpoint of pastoral theology, Bishop Hervas's manual does take some pains to achieve balance and points the way to obviate the more apparent pitfalls, e.g., lack of perseverance, cliquishness, and misdirected fervor. One should not blame on the *cursillo* the various mistakes that have been made in its name. On the other hand, I did not get the impression that the Bishop—whether by design or by accident—gives a fair description of the social psychological techniques involved. To be sure, there are enough

---

[268] Ibid., 336.
[269] Ibid.
[270] Ibid., 339.

general references to methods of good pedagogy and the lessons of modern psychology. But the actual description of the techniques of influence are mostly smothered in a smoke screen of pious vocabulary.[271]

After describing the Cursillo weekend, Dragostin notes: "From the foregoing brief description, the perceptive reader can see that the *Cursillo* is in large measure an exercise in 'group dynamics.'"[272] He then details "some of the social psychological mechanisms being employed."[273] Dragostin lists seven.

The first is isolation, which serves two purposes: "men are removed from any social support they might receive from friends and relatives, persons who might confirm their resistance to a more fervent Christianity," and so that they "will feel less constrained in expressing religious sentiments."[274]

The second is affirmation, as "lay leadership, masculine atmosphere, mixed social groupings, contrived conviviality, and great personal acceptance all seem functional in reducing ego-defensiveness toward 'conversion' on the part of candidates."[275]

The third factor could be called peer pressure. "New attitudes and beliefs will develop out of the ordinary process of social interaction provided that the majority opinion is large, that the opinion is made public, that the group is especially friendly and close-knit, and that the object of opinion is ambiguous." Dragostin notes that these "well known facts of small-group dynamics are very much utilized in the Cursillo."[276] That would also mean that the expression of contrary or discordant viewpoints would be detrimental to the process, which would explain the discouragement of questions and open discussion and placing a "plant" at each table to keep the conversation on track.

The fourth factor is the religious atmosphere or setting of the weekend. The candidate "becomes acutely aware of his religious identity by the fact that he has placed himself in a religious setting." The candidates, therefore, "put their best religious foot forward," acting in a manner suitable to the surroundings and the expectations of the group.[277]

The fifth element leading to "conversion" is the structure and design of

---

[271] Sigmund Dragostin, "The Cursillo as a Social Movement," in *Catholics/U.S.A.; Perspectives on Social Change,* ed. William Thomas Liu and Nathaniel J. Pallone, 479-489 (New York: John Wiley & Sons, Inc., 1970), 481. It would seem that Hervas has written "furtively" even to those who would lead Cursillo events.
[272] Sigmund Dragostin, "All That Glistens Isn't: A Look at the Cursillo Exercise," *Una sancta* 23 (1966): 48.
[273] Ibid.
[274] Ibid. 49.
[275] Ibid.
[276] Ibid.
[277] Ibid.

Chapter 6: The Techniques of the Cursillo Method

the weekend itself. Dragostin notes that the group "goes through phases roughly equivalent to the empirically tested ones of collecting information, evaluating information, and pressing for a decision." The emotional state of the group is carefully guided to match each step in the process, "the decision point being the critical bottleneck." "(C)andidates are introduced to *palanca* (reports of sacrifices or prayers made by others on their behalf, ed.) just as they reach the decision point." This is usually quite moving: "The idea that others are suffering on their behalf is instrumental in getting trainees to choose a more fervent Christian commitment."[278]

The sixth factor, according to Dragostin, is the discomfort of cognitive dissonance and the tendency toward cognitive consistency. Those who are "converted" by these dynamic techniques may seek to persuade others in order to defend their decision and/or to keep on persuading themselves.

> Sudden changes in attitudes and beliefs may leave one in a state of cognitive dissonance because former attitudes and beliefs retain some of their attractiveness. Persons who change after a personal struggle and who harbor some unconscious reservations will be more enthusiastic about their new beliefs and more zealous in spreading them. This may account, in part, for the extraordinary zeal shown by some candidates.[279]

The seventh and final element listed by Dragostin (though he by no means intends to be exhaustive) is pragmatic. This weekend has been costly to the candidate, therefore it must be valuable. "(A) person values his group membership in proportion to the difficulty of his initiation into the group."[280] I made Cursillo in a prison setting as the only non-prisoner candidate among inmates. At the conclusion, one candidate in my table group said with tears how proud he was of himself because this was the first prison "program" he had ever completed. It had become valuable to him because of the hard work he had put into it.

After examining these seven social psychological mechanisms, Dragostin carefully offers this disclaimer, "I have no intention of limiting the power of divine grace to empirical models;" nevertheless, he concludes, "It does, however, seem clear to me that much of the *Cursillo's* dramatic effect can be accounted for through natural causes."[281] Elsewhere, Dragostin declares:

> I would welcome an atmosphere that provides a free and open

---

[278] Ibid., 49-50.
[279] Ibid., 50.
[280] Ibid.
[281] Ibid.

opportunity for an individual to broaden his religious experience. But the extraordinary dramatic effect of the *cursillo* as well as its excesses seem directly related to the element of social manipulation.[282]

SUMMARY

Experts in their fields, Sargant, Murray, DeTar and Manion, Marcoux, O'Sullivan and Dragostin have all noted the physiological, psychological, and sociological dynamics at work in Cursillo. How much of the Cursillo effect is dependent on these psychological elements and how much on divine grace would be difficult to determine. What one could do as a test is to create a Cursillo experience where the content of the message (Christian teaching) is replaced with some other content, say, the teachings of Islam, Buddhism or a non-Christian philosophy. Of course, such an experiment would be problematic and should not be attempted by Christians.

But what if such "experiments" were already being conducted? What if non-Christian, even non-religious groups could be found using the same psychological and sociological dynamics as the Cursillo method and achieving similar results, all without any Christian teaching? Would this not demonstrate that most, if not all, of the Cursillo effect is due to the natural method and not to "divine grace"? And, in point of fact, just such "experiments" have been and are being conducted by non-Christian and even non-religious groups and are achieving the same results (see chapter 8 for examples).

The physiological, psychological and sociological elements employed should cause us to question the use of the Cursillo method. From a Reformed perspective as described in chapter 5, these techniques would be completely unnecessary. But much worse, they would tend to produce spurious conversions: those who have had intense emotional experiences which are interpreted for them as religious conversions or revitalizations, but are purely the result of the physiological, psychological and sociological techniques employed, and not true conversions at all.[283] It should be observed that this

---

[282] Dragostin, "The Cursillo as a Social Movement," 488.
[283] Over a century ago, Charles H. Spurgeon laments these spurious conversions produced by revivalism: "We have had plenty of revivals of the human sort, and their results have been sadly disappointing. Under excitement nominal converts have been multiplied: but where are they after a little testing? I am sadly compelled to own that, so far as I can observe, there has been much sown, and very little reaped that was worth reaping, from much of that which has been called revival. Our hopes were flattering as a dream: but the apparent result has vanished like a vision of the night." And "If, for a moment, our improvements [of revivalistic techniques] seem to produce a larger result than the old gospel, it will be the growth of mushrooms, it may even be of toadstools; but it is not growth of trees of the Lord." Quoted in Iain Hamish Murray, *Revival and Revivalism: The Making and Marring of American Evangelicalism 1750-1858*, 409. In this worthy book Murray distinguishes between revival as a sovereign and unexpected work of God and revivalism,

serious problem would not be due to a misapplication of the Cursillo method, nor in spite of the Cursillo method, but precisely as a result of the Cursillo method as it was originally devised.

In 1957 American journalist and social critic Vance Packard published a landmark book demonstrating how unscrupulous advertisers sought to influence consumers through deceptive manipulation. He described "large-scale efforts…to channel our unthinking habits, our purchasing decisions, and our thought processes by the use of insights gleaned from psychiatry and the social sciences."[284] Many of these efforts took place "beneath our level of awareness" hence they were "hidden." If these efforts were not underhanded, they were at least under the radar. He called this method the "depth approach." Packard hoped that by revealing the techniques of the "hidden persuaders" he could neutralize their effects, as he explains in his concluding chapter:

> We still have a strong defense available against such persuaders: we can choose not to be persuaded. In virtually all situations we still have the choice, and we cannot be too seriously manipulated if we know what is going on. It is my hope that this book may contribute to this general awareness. As Clyde Miller pointed out in *The Process of Persuasion*, when we learn to recognize the devices of the persuaders, we build up a "recognition reflex." Such a recognition reflex, he said, "can protect us against the petty trickery of small-time persuaders operating in the common-place affairs of everyday life, *but also against the mistaken or false persuasion of powerful leaders*…."[285]

It is my hope that his book will help to create a similar "recognition reflex" and offer similar protection.

---

a planned, human work using natural means of persuasion. The Cursillo method would clearly be an example of the latter.
[284] Vance Packard, *The Hidden Persuaders* (Brooklyn, NY: Ig Publishing, 2007), 31.
[285] Ibid., 239, emphasis added.

7. *The Effects of the Cursillo Method*

If one were to judge only by the anecdotal evidence supplied by Cursillo promoters, one would conclude that the method produces unfailingly positive results. People are spiritually awakened, feel great emotional relief and renewed fervor for religion, experience love and bonding with fellow participants, and readily plunge into Christian service, becoming the best workers for Christ the church has ever known. Official Cursillo literature[286] is overflowing with such boasts.

But there are other voices which are not so enthusiastic. In fact, the complaints about the Cursillo method start to sound familiar. Rather than focusing on the positive claims concerning the effects of the movement, which are available in abundance from the aforementioned official Cursillo literature, it would be helpful to examine what is often buried in obscure journal articles and other works which evaluate the movement from a more neutral or critical viewpoint.

A. Bishop Juan Hervas: *Questions and Problems.*

One Cursillo leader who is somewhat forthright about the problems associated with the Cursillo method is one of the original leaders and promoters from Majorca, Spain, Juan Hervas. He wrote an entire book explaining the various problems and how they might be remedied.[287] The book appears to have two aims. One is to guard the Cursillo method against abuses that may cause problems. The other is to defend the Cursillo method against its critics.

With respect to guarding the method, Hervas suggests avoiding being

---

[286] See, for example, Hervas, *Cursillos in Christianity: Instrument of Christian Renewal* and *Leaders' Manual for Cursillos in Christianity*, Bonnin, *The How and the Why*, Blatnik, *Your Fourth Day*, Hughes, *Our Fourth Day*, Rohloff, The *Origins and Development of the Cursillo (1939-1973)*, etc. Some of these may mention problems but will, like Jackson, quickly dismiss them as the result of misuse of the method. None of them consider that the method itself may actually precipitate the problems.

[287] Juan Hervás, *Questions and Problems Concerning Cursillos in Christianity* (Tucson, AZ: Ultreya Publication for Euramerica S.A. - Madrid Spain, 1963).

Chapter 7: The Effects of the Cursillo Method

overly zealous in the desire to make many more cursillistas, avoiding elitism (Cursillism), avoiding making the Cursillo about strong personalities (personalism), and avoiding spiritual pride.

Hervas also defends against charges of emotionalism (sentimentalism), psychological manipulation (suggestion), and brain-washing. His apology against this last charge is remarkable. Though he is not quite sure what brain-washing means, he is quite sure that the Cursillo does not practice it: "I do not know exactly in what a brain-washing consists....To say that Cursillos in Christianity are a brain-washing is to speak absolute nonsense."[288] Hervas implies in the same context that the Cursillo method is to be considered immune from criticism because it is so good and effective: "to call it brain-washing in passing judgment on the method of the Cursillos in Christianity is, besides being false, offensive to so useful and effective an instrument in the work of the Church in extending the kingdom of Christ."[289]

This "beyond criticism" mindset is made clear in Hervas's catch-all response to any problems arising in the Cursillo method: "Whenever something rare or shocking is observed in the Cursillos in Christianity—whether in the pre-Cursillo, in the Cursillos proper or in the post-Cursillo—we can be confident that some falsification has been introduced."[290] In other words, the method itself is perfect and infallible. Any difficulties must stem from some innovation in the method or error in its application.

And critics of the Cursillo method are dismissed with *ad hominem* attacks. Critics are grouped into three categories: 1) the prejudiced, 2) the alienated, and 3) the resentful. The prejudiced are further subdivided as a) enemies of the church, b) those reacting to a false understanding of the Cursillo method or to excesses by incompetent cursillistas, and c) those who are resistant to change.[291] The alienated are the "rare cases" of those who fail to continue in the Cursillo (Hervas claims a success rate of almost 100% of those who persevere after the weekend).[292]

The resentful (drop outs who turn against the movement) are harder to explain, according to Hervas. Though he does allow that some of the fault may be on the part of uncaring cursillistas, he never considers that the criticism of the "resentful" could be valid. Rather, they are probably cases of "willful obstinacy and conscious rebellion"[293] and to be made the special objects of prayer, "hoping from the omnipotent power of Grace what human effort

---

[288] Ibid., 309-310.
[289] Ibid., 310.
[290] Ibid., 319.
[291] Ibid., 325-328.
[292] Ibid., 328.
[293] Ibid., 332.

cannot achieve."²⁹⁴

B. Roderic Jackson: *Misuse and Misunderstanding May Create Problems.*

Jackson is so altogether positive about the Cursillo method that he seems oblivious to any problems that may be caused by the Cursillo. On the last page of his *Handbook*, however, he does suggest that problems may arise from its misapplication. "If used properly, it may serve well the Reformed Church and any church which embraces it. If misused, it will only bring misunderstanding and suspicion on the name "Cursillo" and on the church itself."²⁹⁵ Jackson apparently never considers that the Cursillo method itself could ever "cause" any problems, only its "misuse."

Jackson also hints that some may have expected too much out of the Cursillo sessions, and so have misrepresented them:

> Let us, therefore, make it very clear what Cursillos are <u>not</u> intended to accomplish. They do not give [a] full course of catechetical instruction. They do not give specific answers to individual problems and ought not to be used as a substitute for psychological counseling. They are not a social action group, a charismatic prayer group or any special elitist organization. They ought never to be used as a substitute for one's own church or an underground church. To see the Cursillo movement as any of these things is to misunderstand its essence and purpose.²⁹⁶

Once again, it should be noted that a supporter of Cursillo believes that any difficulties from the method stem from its misuse or misunderstanding. The method itself, if used properly, can only be "a tremendous asset to any pastor who is concerned about renewal."²⁹⁷

C. Marcene Marcoux: *Potential Disaffection with the Local Church.*

Sociologist Marcene Marcoux spent several years studying a Massachusetts Roman Catholic Cursillo community which had initiated over

---

²⁹⁴ Ibid.
²⁹⁵ Jackson, "A Handbook for Leaders in the Cursillo Movement for the Reformed Church in America." 42.
²⁹⁶ Ibid.
²⁹⁷ Ibid.

Chapter 7: The Effects of the Cursillo Method

3,500 people from 1964 to 1980. Even though she reports that some Cursillo participants have been "institutionalized following their initiation,"[298] she is generally supportive of the Cursillo method and could even be considered an advocate for it (she points out that now "persons assessed as mentally unstable"[299] are not permitted to attend). She does recognize that there are those who object to its methodology (for instance, she mentions DeTar and Manion,[300] whom she disparages as "rigid" and "negative"). However, Marcoux does note one potential problem: that of disaffection with the local church. "The cursillo potentially does affect the parish by weakening its bonds; parishioners may become more intertwined with the cursillo community as they join ultreyas and find enthusiasm, friendships, and spiritual guidance within the cursillo."[301] She explains why this may become the case:

> Many begin to become more critical of their parish and become more demanding of what they require of a good parish. Being exposed to significant rituals, they expect more from the Mass and from the other sacraments. Affected by learning and studying in the cursillo, they insist on more than pat sermons and repetitive stories from their parish priests. Thus they frequently encounter dissatisfactions with the way of life in the parish, although they previously may have held few complaints.[302]

Quoting one Cursillo participant with regard to attendance at his local church, she demonstrates this affective detachment: "But now we are like a bunch of gypsies on Sundays. We go where there is a young curate. He is freer, has ways of expressing himself and is not afraid. Or if he is, he doesn't show it."[303] (This disaffection from the local church will be expanded later in the Boyd critique below.)

D. Ralph G. O'Sullivan: *Perceptions of Manipulation.*

Sociologist Ralph G. O'Sullivan notes that not all is well with Cursillo. Contrary to popular belief, he writes, not all respond positively to the Cursillo method.

The preceeding [*sic*] discussions may have led the reader to believe

---

[298] Marcoux, *Cursillo, Anatomy of a Movement: The Experience of Spiritual Renewal*, 39.
[299] Ibid., 38.
[300] Ibid., 150-151.
[301] Ibid., 146.
[302] Ibid., 147.
[303] Ibid., 148.

that all people who attend cursillo are positively affected by it, or that they decide to dedicate themselves to cursillo and its religion. Such is not the case, however.

Some people leave cursillo, either during the weekend or in its aftermath, perhaps because they feel it is too restrictive, being like a total institution in nature. The days begin at predesignated times and end late at night. The hours between are strictly scheduled in accordance with the needs of the day. Many complaints have been registered by candidates which, in summary, contain the following kinds of comments: "We were brainwashed;" "They tried to make Roman Catholics of us" (or members of any host denomination); "It's run by a tight clique (a 'power elite') of cursillistas;" "By the time the long weekend was over we were apt to believe in anything because we became so tired," and so on.[304]

(This theme of manipulation will be expanded in Boyd's critique below.)

E. Kevin R. Boyd: *Areas Which Need Fresh Thought and Improvement.*

Presbyterian pastor and Cursillo participant Kevin Boyd, though generally favorable toward Cursillo, does suggest some modifications for improvement. He lists nine potential problem areas and offers practical solutions. It would be helpful briefly to summarize the problems he sees and the solutions he proposes and to make appropriate comment on each.

1. "Weekend-itis" or living for the weekend experience. "The emotional appeal can be so powerful that the part of the program which is supposed to prepare the participants for something much greater (i.e., a life of leadership within the Church) becomes the ultimate goal."[305] Boyd's solution to this dilemma is to get the Cursillo graduates more involved in the after-the-weekend Cursillo activities such as the group reunions and the ultreyas. Of course this would only serve to get them more and more involved in other aspects of the Cursillo movement.

2. Exclusivism or restricting friendships and relationships only to Cursillo people. "It is therefore regrettable that in some instances Cursillo-related communities have developed exclusive tendencies."[306] Boyd protests that this exclusivism is not the intended aim of the Cursillo. What's interesting

---

[304] O'Sullivan, "Structure, Function, and Cognitive Development in Cursillo: An Interactionist Analysis," 271.
[305] Boyd, "Decently De Colores: A Reformed Evaluation of the Cursillo Movement in the Presbyterian Church," 123.
[306] Ibid., 128.

Chapter 7: The Effects of the Cursillo Method 111

is that almost every critic and (even several proponents) admit to this exclusivistic tendency. Cursillo almost universally causes exclusivism. Here is an example of the method working contrary to its expressed aim. Boyd's solution to this problem is to open the after-the-weekend activities to those who are not a part of Cursillo and to "counsel with those who have become more active in Cursillo than in the regular worship and service life of their congregation."[307] What is quite revealing is who Boyd thinks should provide such counsel. He says that "the Cursillo leadership" should be the ones to offer this counsel. Here is a practical admission that, for many Cursillo graduates, "the Cursillo leadership" becomes their spiritual authorities, their *de facto* pastors. And it should be noted that while the solution to the first problem is "greater involvement in the Cursillo movement," the second problem is actually caused by the same thing that is the solution to the first, "greater involvement in the Cursillo movement."

    3. A third problem Boyd addresses is the difficulty many Cursillo graduates find in going back to dull, congregational worship services. "It is somewhat disturbing for me, as a pastor, to hear comments to the effect that while the participants' congregations use old outdated hymns, the music in Cursillo is fresh, joyful, singable and meaningful.... Sunday mornings are tolerated, but monthly Ultreyas are exciting."[308] Boyd's solution is to work within the church's already existing structure to reform the church's worship, understanding that the church's worship may never match the zeal of Cursillo worship. "While it is neither possible nor desirable to make congregational worship have the same zeal as worship at Cursillo events, participants need to learn that worship will be exciting during times of great emotional and spiritual zeal. This is not the everyday experience of the Fourth Day."[309]

    While such caution is wise, I doubt very much if it will pacify the excited Cursillo graduate. And notice the assumption that the Church is in need of reforming its worship to make its worship more like Cursillo worship.

    4. A fourth problem is the re-entry of the Cursillo graduates into a church which might not appreciate their experience. "One often repeated theme in the survey and focus groups was that participants returned to the Church excited and ready to participate in a much fuller way, only to be ignored or misunderstood by the pastor."[310] Cursillo graduates are told that they are now leaders (after one weekend of training) and have great responsibility. "Cursillo identifies potential leaders and trains them to be 'backbones' of the Church for the purpose of evangelizing our environments."[311] Boyd's solution

---

[307] Ibid., 130.
[308] Ibid., 132-133.
[309] Ibid., 135.
[310] Ibid.
[311] Ibid., 136.

is to better educate pastors and churches so they will be more ready to accommodate these new "backbones," and to find ways to redirect the passion of the overly zealous graduate. Once again, however, notice that the church must change to accommodate Cursillo.

5. A fifth problem is that secrecy creates suspicion. The weekends have for too long been shrouded in secrecy. "The issue of secrecy is one of the most difficult problems Cursillo faces....Yet, through the years it has been well demonstrated that secrecy does not serve Cursillo well. It causes major misunderstandings for those who have not been."[312] Boyd's solution is to do away with secrecy entirely. Publish the schedule ahead of time and "encourage participants to share freely their experiences." With this suggestion, Boyd shows an amazing lack of understanding about the psychological factors that make Cursillo "work" (i.e., Marcoux's "jolts and shocks"). This suggestion would successfully eviscerate the Cursillo effect.

6. A sixth problem area is that of the expectation of specific emotional responses.

> A particular concern of the clergy was that there seemed to be times when a certain emotion was expected out of all participants. Kleenex was everywhere. Hugs were forced when the group had not developed to that point. Even specific reactions to certain songs were seen as milestones of how well the weekend was going. This is unfortunate and unfair.[313]

Boyd recognizes the problem but offers no concrete solution beyond a simple caution to note that "everyone is unique and so don't expect everyone to respond the same way." Once again, this betrays a profound misunderstanding of the Cursillo effect. Every action on the Cursillo weekend is calculated with a view toward its expected emotional reaction.[314]

7. Cursillo graduates often have trouble translating the weekend experience into practical service outside the Cursillo community. "The founders of Cursillo...sought to make a difference in this world by training leaders who would, through the Church, impact the world by evangelizing their environments."[315] But Boyd's research found something far different.

---

[312] Ibid., 139.
[313] Ibid., 143.
[314] See, for example, Blatnik's comment "Nothing is left to chance" (*Your Fourth Day*, 25), or Hervas's fixation on the emotional response of the candidates during the various phases of the weekend in his *Leaders' Manual for Cursillos in Christianity*: 94—"complete disorientation;" 113—"abandoned his defenses;" 137—"there is very little resistance left to overcome;" and 166—"burning with fervor and enthusiasm."
[315] Boyd, "Decently De Colores a Reformed Evaluation of the Cursillo Movement in the Presbyterian Church," 144.

"Contrary to the program design, the survey indicates that among the issues with which Cursillo was deemed to have been helpful, those which touch on social righteousness were among the least indicated."[316] Boyd's solution is to call for more education for Cursillo graduates in their new social responsibilities and opportunities for service. Yet, what if the weekend is so emotionally powerful that it rather awakens a desire for more emotionally powerful experiences? This surely is a prime example of "emotionalism," emotion for emotion's sake.

    8. An eighth problem area comes in the perceived manipulation caused by a rigid schedule.

> When asked if there were any elements of the program which were manipulative (in a negative sense), the majority said no. However, as was pointed out, a significant minority (31% of clergy and 26% of lay persons) said yes. Nearly all of the responses in this category dealt with the weekend schedule. It was seen as inflexible, too exhaustive and secret. Many mentioned the need for some free time to process what had occurred.[317]

Boyd's solution is to relax the schedule, and especially incorporate more free time. As stated before, such a suggestion reveals a lack of understanding on Boyd's part and will fundamentally change the psychological intensity of the weekend, greatly inhibiting the Cursillo effect.

    9. Boyd's last concern is that there is on the part of the participants a general lack of clarity on what it is that transforms lives: human means or the work of the Holy Spirit? They participate in a well orchestrated weekend that uses powerful, psychological techniques; yet they are told that the effects are all produced by the Holy Spirit. Boyd quotes a personal conversation with a Presbyterian Cursillo leader who opines: "Perhaps we've made the weekends so slick that they're too seductive. The early Cursillos were held in very sparse settings and the impact was just as strong. We need to help people understand just Who has changed their lives."[318] Boyd agrees adding, "If all of the benefits happen purely through human agency, we might as well not offer Cursillo in the name of the church."[319]

    But here Boyd finds himself on the horns of a dilemma encountered by all who employ revivalistic techniques. How much can be attributed to natural means, and how much to God's working? If the psychological manipulations to which Boyd objects are all removed, the Cursillo would be destroyed, and

---

[316] Ibid., 145.
[317] Ibid., 148.
[318] Ibid., 151.
[319] Ibid., 152.

presumably, its effects negated. Boyd apparently wishes to avoid "throwing the baby out with the bath water," but he seems to have trouble distinguishing between the two.

But what if there is no baby in the bath water? In other words, what if these problems are not merely ancillary but systemic? Boyd makes several suggestions for changes that will alleviate perceived problems, but which will fundamentally change the essential nature and outcome of the weekend experience. In essence he wants a Cursillo that is not a Cursillo, which would indicate that the problems are caused by that which is essential to the Cursillo method (i.e., that the problems are indeed not ancillary but systemic).

F. Dennis C. Rydholm: *Psychological "Razzle-Dazzle" Akin to Brainwashing, Requiring Modification*

A similar conclusion was reached by Episcopal priest Dennis C. Rydholm. In an unpublished paper,[320] he addresses the question of whether or not the Cursillo weekend could be considered "Brainwashing." He references Robert J. Lifton's book *Thought Reform and the Psychology of Totalism: A Study of Brainwashing in China*.[321] Lifton describes a "totalist environment" consisting of eight factors which lends itself to brainwashing. Due to the brevity of his paper, Rydholm discusses only four of the eight factors.

1. The first factor is called "milieu control," "whereby the totalist environment exerts a somewhat rigid control over one's communication with the outside world as well as one's communication with oneself, the ability for any prolonged internal reflection."[322] Rydholm notes that the Cursillo method makes a concentrated effort to exploit this factor in both respects. The cloistered environment of the Cursillo weekend, the seating at table groups with complete strangers, and in some cases, covering the windows and removing clocks and wristwatches effectively cuts the participant off from the outside world. And the relentless schedule and a lack of free time, even the "constant conspicuous presence of team members" prevents "prolonged internal reflection."

2. The second factor in a totalist environment is called "Mystical Manipulation,"

> referring to the sense of a "mystical aura" surrounding a given institution, a "higher purpose" or imperative in which the

---

[320] Daniel C. Rydholm, "Theology and Methodology in the American Episcopal Cursillo Movement."
[321] Robet Jay Lifton, *Thought Reform and the Psychology of Totalism* (Chapel Hill, NC: The University of North Carolina Press, 1989).
[322] Rydholm, "Theology and Methodology in the American Episcopal Cursillo Movement," 12.

Chapter 7: The Effects of the Cursillo Method

practitioners are the sole agents and the vanguard of some "imminent law of social development." One is asked to accept this higher purpose on a basis of ultimate trust (or faith), "like a child in the arms of its mother," as Lifton quotes one of his sources.[323]

The effect on those unprepared for it is to further inhibit the ability to question the leaders or act independently. The Cursillo method likewise fosters this sense of "mystical manipulation." Participants are told that they have been selected for this weekend, that they are to become the "backbone" of their environment with a special mission to carry out the directives and experiences attained on the weekend. Rydholm considers this sense of mystical manipulation unavoidable since it is contained, by definition, in the mission of the Cursillo.

3. A third factor is called the "Cult of Confession," "whereby the pressure created by the totalist environment prompts repeated emotional sharing and confession turned into 'command performances, the element of histrionic public display (taking) precedence over genuine inner experience.'"[324] During the Cursillo weekend there are many opportunities for "emotional sharing and confession": participation at table groups, presentation of posters and skits, emotional singing, and the sharing during the clausura. Participation is "optional," but strongly encouraged, and almost all participate. Rydholm describes this as an "inexorable unmasking process" which "creates an initial conflict over which 'self' to preserve and which to surrender to the group. As the conflict increases, boundaries between the private-self and the group-self become blurred and resistance to total self-surrender is worn away."[325]

4. A fourth factor in the totalist environment (the last one Rydholm discusses) is that of "Sacred Science," "whereby an institution's methods are tied to exaggerated claims of airtight logic and absolute scientific precision."[326] This implies that opposition or even criticism is not only disrespectful and immoral but also "unscientific." The result of this, according to Lifton, is "continuous pressure toward personal closure and self-surrender, stifling genuine self-expression and creative development." We have seen how the Cursillo method is described as being "based on psychological elements so effective and so skillfully wielded,"[327] how much emphasis is placed on the great preparation that goes into the weekend, how the "most modern pedagogic, religious, sociological and psychological methods are brought into harmonious

---

[323] Ibid., 12-13.
[324] Ibid., 13.
[325] Ibid.
[326] Ibid.
[327] Hervas, *Cursillos in Christianity: Instrument of Christian Renewal*, 293.

fusion with the traditional doctrine of the church"[328] and how "nothing was left to chance."[329] Rydholm concludes: "The Sacred Science idea is an inherent part of the Cursillo weekend and as such renders even this formal critique of the process a profound violation of Cursillo norms."[330]

The point is that, according to Lifton, the more these totalist factors are present, "the greater the ability to change people and institute thought reform or 'brainwashing.'"[331] To remove these totalist factors and lessen the chance of thought reform occuring, Rydholm offers three reforms of the Cursillo weekend. As with Boyd, however, the reforms he offers would fundamentally alter the essential character of the Cursillo method and suppress the Cursillo effect. Rydholm also wants a Cursillo that is not a Cursillo, indicating that the flaws of the Cursillo method are systemic in nature.

G. Ralph Barker: *Disenchanted with the Group Dynamics and Mind Control.*

In a 1980 article titled, "Is the Cursillo Movement Winding Down?" university professor Ralph Barker is quoted describing first his involvement with the Cursillo, and his later disenchantment. Barker and his wife made their Cursillo in 1964 and were faithfully involved in the after meetings and in promoting the Cursillo for five years. Then they withdrew:

> "None of the people I made it with are still in it," he says. "Some have left the Catholic Church altogether. In our city, which has half a million people, there are some remnants of older groups but not many."

At first Barker welcomed the Cursillo as the most important thing in his life. He was an evangelist, a persistent recruiter.

> "I think we started with a good idea, with a lot of brotherhood. Then we became elitist, in-bred, feeling sorry for the poor souls—including priests and the bishops—who weren't with it. We moved from *a* message to *the* message. We felt duty-bound to make all the other Catholics understand."

When a priest whom he admired rejected his Cursillo overtures, Barker began to have his doubts. Not much later, he was out.

> Salinas [a priest and veteran of the movement, head of a Cursillo center in Phoenix, ed.] explains much of the "falling away" as the

---

[328] Quoted in DeTar, *To Deceive...The Elect*, 84.
[329] Blatnik, *Your Fourth Day*, 25.
[330] Rydholm, "Theology and Methodology in the American Episcopal Cursillo Movement," 14.
[331] Ibid., 14-15.

Chapter 7: The Effects of the Cursillo Method

result of expectations being unfulfilled, of change not occurring fast enough.

"They thought they were going to solve all the problems of the world but found they couldn't," he says. "Then they gave up."

Barker doesn't agree.

"I think our enthusiasm just ran ahead of our brains," he feels. "We began to do all sorts of things in the name of the Cursillo. The end really justified the means."

Now he experiences some discomfort when he recalls the selling job he did, equating it with some of the secular marketing tools.

"If you can be swayed by group dynamics, you'll be taken in," he says, with a trace of bitterness. "There's a lot of power in a group. It isn't until later, when you're alone, that you begin to see the flaws in some of your reasoning."

Among the things that bothered Barker was the meeting of the team leaders each night of the Cursillo during which time they discussed individual cursillistas and how they were reacting to the sessions and how they could get them to react the way they wanted.

"I'm not sure now that this was a good idea," he says. "We justified it because it was a good cause but it was still mind control. A lot of people became unglued."

He also found fault with the "rather stern" manual which was followed religiously, despite arguments for change by some members. And he began to despise the person he had become.

"We fed on ourselves. The movement became important and we felt important because we were in the movement."

Another aspect he now questions is the openness that developed as a result of community, the trust that encouraged you to share everything, to expose yourself to the ultreya group.

"Sharing turns me off now," he states. "I think it's phony."[332]

With his opening line, Barker suggests that his story could be echoed by many, and that some have even left the Catholic Church as a result of their Cursillo involvement.[333]

---

[332] Ralph T. Reilly, "Is the Cursillo Movement Winding Down?" *U.S. Catholic* (January, 1980), 27-28.

[333] Virginia McDowell writes approvingly of the Cursillo method in describing case studies of nine people who have experienced "growth" through the Cursillo method, even though several of the people she describes are no longer a part of the Catholic Church. McDowell herself was a veteran of ten years of Cursillo involvement and is likewise no longer a part of Christianity, "a tradition that was no longer meaningful or believable for me" (xv). She notes that from her research she found two long-term effects on Cursillo participants: "the institutional church had largely ceased to be meaningful to these Cursillistas," and "attitudes toward sexuality were

H. Sigmund Dragostin: *An Affront to Human Dignity, Autonomy and Freedom.*

Perhaps the most serious, eloquent, and stinging indictment of the effects of the Cursillo method is found at the pen of sociologist Sigmund Dragostin. He sees the Cursillo as an indefensible and inexcusable "affront to human dignity, autonomy and freedom." I quote him at length.

> The fact that the cursillo inspires great enthusiasm as well as violent reaction seems to me to be related to several underlying issues.
>
> First there is the question of the relative weight given to the free and transcendental character of the human person. There has been an historical development in man's consciousness of his own dignity. While the Church has come to see that political force is an improper instrument for bringing about religious consent, there are those within the Church who give very little attention to the moral and psychological means used to insure religious conformity. Between hyp[n]otism at the one end of the scale and true education at the other there is available a whole bag of social psychological techniques that can be used to change people. Used by one person on another without his knowledge and consent, most of them are an affront to human dignity, autonomy, and freedom.
>
> Second, there is the degree to which one realizes that social-psychological mechanisms can be as imperious as physical force. If a college fraternity on a prestigious campus were to use the *cursillo* structure to initiate Roman Catholic students into agnosticism, we would certainly consider it a violation of fair play. No organization considering itself an educational institution would resort to such tactics.
>
> Finally, there is the extent to which one emphasizes that the effects of the *cursillo* are the result of divine grace or the natural outcome of well-known social psychological techniques. This is not a question that lends itself to empirical evidence. If you insist that the effects of the *cursillo* are entirely the effect of Divine grace, then to whom do you attribute the non-random instances of fanaticism and the rare instances of complete personality disorganization? I would also like to know why God's grace habitually stops short with whole classes of people for whom the *cursillo* is not "a fitting means." The

---

reported to have shifted toward liberalism," including a greater approval of premarital cohabitation (24). See Virginia H. McDowell, *Re-Creating: The Experience of Life-Change and Religion* (Boston: Beacon Press, 1978).

Chapter 7: The Effects of the Cursillo Method 119

maximalists will answer that only the good effects are to be attributed to the Holy Spirit. When things go wrong, the human element is to blame. As I said, the question does not lend itself to empirical evidence.

As I read Scripture, it says that the truth shall make you free. The *cursillo* implies that if you give up just a little of your freedom, it will make you true. They used to call that, "The end justifies the means."[334]

SUMMARY

We have surveyed the conclusions of eight persons of some expertise who have evaluated the effects of the Cursillo. All see potential or actual problems. Some, like Boyd and Rydholm would suggest radical modifications in the Cursillo method, effectively producing "a Cursillo that is not a Cursillo." Others, like Barker and Dragostin would suggest an even more radical solution: discontinuing the program altogether.

---

[334] Dragostin, "The Cursillo as a Social Movement," 489.

8. *Other Forms of Cathartic Experiences*

The Cursillo could be described as a cathartic event carefully orchestrated during an emotionally stressful weekend by using well-known, psychologically disorienting and distressing techniques. Since some Cursillo participants have been "institutionalized following their initiation,"[335] and since "persons assessed as mentally unstable"[336] are regularly weeded out of consideration, it would be helpful to understand the long-term effects of initiating such a catharsis experience. Unfortunately this particular phenomenon (the Cursillo-generated catharsis) has never been studied before, so this information is not available. However, similar studies of the effectiveness of catharsis as a tool of psychotherapy in other contexts are available, and so I will turn to these.

Three psychological phenomena most closely resemble the techniques used on the Cursillo weekend and achieve the same effect of a (usually) pleasurable catharsis and its resulting sense of euphoria, personal well-being and closeness to others: encounter groups, Arthur Janov's Primal Therapy and Large Group Awareness Training weekends (LGATs) such as those sponsored by est, Lifespring and Mind Dynamics. Each of these will be considered with respect to their use of catharsis and the consequent effects.

Catharsis

What is catharsis? It consists in the relief of tension. Psychologists and authors Michael P. Nichols and Melvin Zax see both a cognitive and somatic aspect to catharsis: "catharsis has two related but separate components: one is relatively intellectual—the recall of forgotten material; the second is physical—

---

[335] Marcoux, *Cursillo, Anatomy of a Movement: the Experience of Spiritual Renewal*, 39.
[336] Ibid., 38. See also Juan Hervas' caution in his *Leaders' Manual*, 201, "Be extremely careful not to admit those who because of psychological or psychopathic conditions might harm [be harmed by?] the intense spiritual and emotional activity that is developing in the Cursillos."

Chapter 8: Other Forms of Cathartic Experiences

the discharge of emotion in tears, laughter, or angry yelling."[337] At times, they suggest, tension relief may occur cognitively without the accompanying physical manifestations, while other times the emotion may be expressed without any awareness of the precipitating cause. But ordinarily catharsis is the combination of the cognitive and the somatic. Interestingly persons may erroneously perceive a cathartic reaction as precipitated by the wrong cause. "People sometimes focus their thoughts on a remote calamitous event and cry about it as a way of justifying tears which in fact may have been provoked by some other event, or by the accumulation of numerous small frustrations."[338]

Recognition of the catharsis experience is truly ancient.

> Etymologically, *catharsis* derives from the Greek *katharsis*. The essential meaning of *katharsis* was "to clean or purify," but it had shades of other meanings as well. In a medical context, the word meant purgation, or the elimination of offensive humors. In a religious context, it referred to rebirth or initiation; and in a moral and spiritual context, it meant relief of the soul and spirit by purification. Thus, its semantic origins suggest that catharsis has always included two ideas: purgation or purification; and rebirth or initiation into a new state.[339]

Aristotle wrote of the positive effect of music and drama because of their cathartic function. In Greek tragedy, for example, "Emotions are aroused and then purged because the audience is able to identify with the tragic hero to the extent that his pain has relevance and meaning to them."[340] Early psychologists such as Freud "used catharsis to describe the process of a sudden recall of a previously forgotten memory, together with the expression of feeling associated with it, when this event was accompanied by a release of repressed psychic energy and followed by a feeling of relief."[341]

There are numerous techniques which may be employed in precipitating a cathartic event, but most are aimed at defeating or circumventing "defense mechanisms" which prevent emotional expression. The Cursillo is a masterful combination of such techniques which regularly produce disorientation, emotional distress, emotional release, followed by a pleasant feeling of relief and euphoria. Some of the techniques of the Cursillo initially provoke or heighten the normal, day-to-day tensions of life, thus creating a

---

[337] Michael P. Nichols and Melvin Zax, *Catharsis in Psychotherapy* (New York: Gardiner Press, 1977), 8.
[338] Ibid.
[339] Ibid., 2.
[340] Ibid.
[341] Ibid, 2-3.

more dramatic cathartic impact later on. Again, since there has been no analysis of the effect of catharsis in the Cursillo, we must consider studies of similar experiences which depend on catharsis as a tool of therapy or change agent.

Catharsis in Encounter Groups

The similarities between encounter groups and the Cursillo are uncanny. Both utilize similar techniques and both achieve similar results (and both suffer from similar problems, too). So in evaluating the lasting effect of the Cursillo-catharsis, one may gain some insight from more clinical evaluations of the encounter group.

Encounter groups must be understood as a diverse movement rather than a monolithic and singular approach to psychotherapy. In the 1960s and 1970s such groups became quite popular and were employed by therapists and non-therapists alike from various psychological approaches. Terminology associated with this movement include: Basic Human Relations Groups, T-groups, Psychodrama, Esalen Eclectic, sensitivity training, Synanon, Gestalt therapy, and Rogerian Marathon Trainings. But encounter groups share certain commonalities:

> Despite their varied form and function, encounter groups do share common features. They attempt to provide an intensive, high contact, group experience; they are generally small enough (six to twenty members) to permit considerable face-to-face interaction; they focus on the here-and-now (the behavior of members as it unfolds in the group); they encourage openness, honesty, interpersonal confrontation, self-disclosure, and strong emotional expression. The participant is usually not labeled a "patient" and the experience is not ordinarily labeled "therapy," though the groups strive to increase self and social awareness and to change behavior. The specific goals of the groups may vary from reducing juvenile delinquency to reducing weight. Occasionally they seek only to entertain, to "turn-on," to give experience in joy, but generally the overall goals involve some type of personal change—change of behavior, of attitudes, of values, of life-style.[342]

Nichols and Zax agree that encounter groups place a premium "on openness, honesty, interpersonal confrontation, and self-disclosure." Then they

---

[342] Morton A. Lieberman, Irvin D. Yalom, and Matthew B. Miles, *Encounter Groups: First Facts* (New York: Basic Books, 1973), 4. It should be noted that almost every feature of this description of encounter groups could be said of the Cursillo as well.

Chapter 8: Other Forms of Cathartic Experiences

observe: "These interpersonal procedures *almost guarantee strong emotional expression*. In fact, the central theme of encounter groups may be expressivity, which includes self-disclosure and interpersonal confrontation, as well as emotional expression, ventilation, and discharge."[343]

They note the techniques of defeating defense mechanisms:

> Like cathartic psychotherapy, hypnotherapy, drug-induced abreactions, and emotive religious rituals, encounter groups function to liberate emotionality by disrupting everyday defenses to emotional responding. In encounter groups this disruption of everyday, socially-reinforced patterns of interaction is achieved through concentration on the immediate group process and emphasis on personal relations and personal remarks. The resultant subjective experience is infused with intense emotional experiencing.[344]

The following observations about encounter groups could equally apply to the Cursillo:

> Most of the conditions and procedures of encounter groups are designed to strip away defenses. The shock of the initial encounter with a group of strangers, the minimization of outside roles and status, the ambiguity and lack of structure, and the separation from usual surroundings all act to breach defenses. A powerful set is also created in members, most of whom have previously heard or read that encounter groups generate a highly expressive atmosphere. In addition to the set and setting, various techniques enhance the expectancy that something impactful is going to happen. *Under such conditions, affective arousal is bound to occur.* Attempts to reconstitute defenses or to escape from the emotional atmosphere of the group by discussing outside problems are sharply curtailed. Furthermore, affectively charged interactions cannot be sidestepped or ignored, since the norms of the encounter groups pressure the participants to say the unspeakable and to feel the emotions that in ordinary life are suppressed. Feedback is used to highlight transactions, to intensify emotions, and to bring to completion interactional gestalts.[345]

What is the purpose of such groups? Encounter groups ostensibly seek to enhance skills of interpersonal relations by connecting emotional expression with personal insight. "At its best the encounter group methodology integrates

---

[343] Nichols and Zax, *Catharsis in Psychotherapy*, 81, emphasis added.
[344] Ibid.
[345] Ibid, 81-82, emphasis added.

emotional expression with intellectual understanding of the value of that expression."[346] And yet the goal is to be able to recapitulate this learning in regular life. "Ideally this produces not only an impactful experience, but also insight that can be transferred to life outside the group."[347]

But the supposed education that is to occur in these encounter groups often becomes sidetracked by the powerful pleasurable-ness of the experience itself: "Although there is as yet little evidence that such learning does take place, some encounter group participants argue that groups provide a moving experience which is desirable for itself and has no need to be justified by evidence of lasting change."[348] So Nichols and Zax observe that "By fostering strong emotional expression they create a unique experience which is relief from emptiness and boredom. *For many, the group experience may be an end in itself, independent of its effectiveness in solving personal problems or changing behaviors.*"[349] Nichols and Zax are quick to note the difficulty with such a perspective:

> The trouble is that such groups are generally advertised as vehicles for change. It is this claim, explicit or implicit, that legitimizes, no, necessitates careful evaluation of the effects of encounter group experiences. The theorist must explain how intense interactions with other people, direct feedback, and emotional expression have an effect on participants and modify their behavior. The researcher must document both that such changes occur and that other, unwanted, effects do not.[350]

The parallels with Cursillo should not be underestimated. Cursillo is advertised as a great tool of revival and spiritual growth, or, in the words of the Reformed Church in America pastor cited earlier, Cursillo is the "king of revival and miracles and movement of the Holy Spirit." In fact, like encounter groups, it is a pleasurable (for most people), highly-charged, emotional, weekend retreat, which likewise often becomes "an end in itself, independent of its effectiveness in solving personal problems or changing behaviors." This sobering observation by Nichols and Zax should be noted:

> The vacuum left by lack of objective evaluation has been filled by subjective opinion, generated more often by visceral reaction than by thoughtful consideration. Some extol the human potential movement as the definitive cure for modern man's alienation; others see in it a

---

[346] Ibid., 82.
[347] Ibid.
[348] Ibid. (Is this a practical admission that such groups produce no lasting change?)
[349] Ibid., emphasis added.
[350] Ibid., 82-83.

Chapter 8: Other Forms of Cathartic Experiences 125

dangerous forum and license for quackery that leads to irresponsible and primitive expression of impulse. Carl Rogers, for instance, has described encounter groups as "an avenue to fulfillment" and a life remedy. *Bruce Maliver, on the other hand, points to suicides and psychoses precipitated by such experiences, and describes the group culture as fostering profound emotional fascism.*[351]

But do encounter groups produce lasting positive change as they claim? A massive study of the effects of encounter groups was undertaken by Lieberman, Yalom, and Miles. Without denying the often pleasurable effects of encounter groups, the study is not flattering concerning the ability of such groups to provide lasting change. In one measurement, the efficacy of encounter groups was compared to that of other forms of psychotherapy in general. Citing nine studies of the effectiveness of psychotherapy published between 1952 and 1969, they conclude:

> The percentage of improvement (in psychotherapy) … ranges from a low of 33 percent to a high of 87 percent, yielding a mean of 67 percent and a median of 71 percent. In the encounter groups, the success rate ranged from zero per group to 80 percent with a mean of 33 percent and a median of 33 percent.[352]

The difficulties inherent in such a comparison are acknowledged. "Nevertheless, taken this way, these rates of effectiveness suggest that across all the encounter groups studied, the ability to effect change is modest when compared to that of psychotherapy."[353]

Of more concern, though, is the negative effect of encounter groups. Citing the same studies of the effectiveness of psychotherapy mentioned above, the various psychotherapy approaches "report a figure of approximately 10 percent overall negative impact for the studies they have reviewed."[354] In assessing encounter groups, on the other hand, they found that "the rates of 8 percent Casualties and 11 percent Negative Changers, or an overall rate of 19 percent (omitting Dropouts), is close to double that of the overall rate of negative impact reported in psychotherapy literature."[355] This led Lieberman, et. al., to conclude:

> It appears, thus, that, overall, encounter groups are less successful in

---

[351] Ibid, 83, emphasis added.
[352] Lieberman, et al., *Encounter Groups: First Facts*, 444.
[353] Ibid.
[354] Lieberman, et. al., *Encounter Groups: First Facts*, 445.
[355] Ibid.

positively changing individuals when compared to psychotherapy and are more likely to induce deteriorative effects than psychotherapy.[356]

If encounter groups were largely ineffective in achieving purported goals, why were they so well-liked? Nichols and Zax postulate: "The great difficulty people in our culture have in experiencing and expressing intense emotions helps explain why they are so popular."[357] Lieberman, et. al., offer suggestions of their own. One is that the experiences themselves are so pleasurable that the participants confuse "liking" with "learning."

> The findings presented in Chapter 12 clearly suggest that the expressions of strong positive or negative feeling, a great amount of self-disclosure in and of itself, and the experience of intense emotional events are not mechanisms that uniquely maximize member learning. They are, however, vivid, intense experiences in participants' minds, and thus the leaders whose techniques are oriented toward producing them come to believe that they are "right on." Perhaps both members and leaders have contributed to the construction of an elaborate mythology which specifies that where there is stimulation (or expressivity, or self-disclosure) there also will be learning; a mythology for which there is evidence, not of learning, but of involvement, of liking what is happening. [358]

The authors then suggest that this might be reason enough to justify the encounter groups.

> Perhaps we have demanded evidence that is inappropriate to the major meaning of encounter groups as enterprises *not for people-changing, but for people-providing*. Perhaps the import of encounter groups lies not in how many people leave them with new ways of thinking about and responding to themselves and the world they live in and new strategies for coping with life. Perhaps there is a much simpler need that encounter groups are engineered to provide efficiently and effectively—that of momentary relief from alienation, which some have called the most prevalent illness of our times.[359]

Once again we observe the problem that the encounter group is billed as one thing, a vehicle of personal change, when it amounts to something else,

---

[356] Ibid.
[357] Nichols and Zax, *Catharsis in Psychotherapy*, 81.
[358] Lieberman, et. al., *Encounter Groups: First Facts*, 452.
[359] Ibid, emphasis in the original.

Chapter 8: Other Forms of Cathartic Experiences

"momentary relief from alienation." One might suggest the same to be true of the Cursillo. It is presented as "the living of Christianity, the grandeur of the life in grace sincerely and fervently lived"[360] and the "king of revival and miracles and movement of the Holy Spirit," when what it amounts to is a pleasurable, intense weekend experience, perhaps no more than "momentary relief from alienation."

Lieberman, et. al., also suggest that encounter groups also provide "commitmentless communion":

> "Sensitivity training is thus an excellent *synthetic community experience* for a population that has lost the meaning of community but not its sentimental appeal." (Back, 1972) Those aspects of leader strategy that are characteristic of encounter groups are superbly engineered to provide intense, *meaningful, transitory relationships to others*. They satisfy a deep hunger for the individual who experiences a sense of normlessness, a chronic boredom, or any other symptoms usually associated with the term alienation. This quality of encounter groups should not be associated with irresponsibility for, at their best, encounter groups provide intense, personal experiences with others in a responsible manner. *People are bound together and do feel responsible for one another....*
>
> What is unique to the situation is that *the responsibility and feelings for others are severely limited in space and time*. Encounter groups are *happenings that are salient and significant and meaningful for most of the participants at the time they take place and perhaps understood by all as being sufficient as such*. Unlike the case with many other institutions to which people have looked for communion—most notably the family and the church—*no pledge to the future is exacted as the price of belonging, no permanent commitment to particular individuals or particular ideas is required to experience the joys of membership*. Blessed as "the tie that binds" may be, it is a satisfaction won at a higher price in more enduring social systems than encounter groups.
>
> The techniques encounter leaders use to create excitement, to create closeness, to create openness become more understandable viewed in this perspective. The psychological meaning to participants of the well-known "trust-walk," the exercise which perhaps most epitomizes the encounter movement, may be clearer when viewed as functioning not to change people but to provide them with *a replica of an experience felt to be too rare or too costly to acquire from the interactions of*

---

[360] Juan Hervas, *Cursillos in Christianity Instrument of Christian Renewal*, 60.

everyday life.[361]

I would suggest that the Cursillo likewise offers the same transitory experience of community that usually falls far short of the real thing. Lieberman, et. al., appear quite enthusiastic about "commitmentless communion" and a "synthetic community experience" and about "a replica of an experience felt to be too rare or too costly to acquire from the interactions of everyday life." Scripture offers communion *through* commitment as well as *authentic* community experience. Scripture urges Christians to pay the cost to acquire *true* community and not merely a *replica*.

Catharsis in Primal Therapy

Yet another way to achieve catharsis was developed by Arthur Janov, who called his method Primal Therapy. Primal Therapy is another form of emotive therapy using a method other than a group experience to produce a cathartic effect. Janov claims to have discovered Primal Therapy inadvertently in a counseling session with a patient named Danny.

> During a lull in our group therapy session, he [Danny] told us the story about a man named Ortiz who was currently doing an act on the London stage in which he paraded around in diapers drinking bottles of milk. Throughout his number, Ortiz is shouting "Mommy! Daddy! Mommy! Daddy!" at the top of his lungs. At the end of his act he vomits. Plastic bags are passed out, and the audience is requested to follow suit.
>
> Danny's fascination with the act impelled me to try something elementary, but which previously had escaped my notice. I asked him to call out, "Mommy! Daddy!" Danny refused, saying that he couldn't see the sense in such a childish act, and frankly, neither could I. But I persisted, and finally, he gave in. As he began, he became noticeably upset. Suddenly he was writhing on the floor in agony. His breathing was rapid, spasmodic; "Mommy! Daddy!" came out of his mouth almost involuntarily in loud screeches. He appeared to be in a coma or hypnotic state. The writhing gave way to small convulsions, and finally, he released a piecing, deathlike scream that rattled the walls of my office. The entire episode lasted only a few minutes, and neither Danny nor I had any idea what had happened. All he could say afterward was: "I made it! I don't know what, but I

---

[361] Lieberman, et. al., *Encounter Groups: First Facts*, 452-453, emphasis added.

Chapter 8: Other Forms of Cathartic Experiences

can *feel*."[362]

Janov was later to conclude that neurotic people are suffering from Primal Pain, from painful experiences which stem from the earliest moments of life.

> I have come to regard that scream as the product of central and universal pains which reside in all neurotics. I call them Primal Pains because they are all original, early hurts upon which all later neurosis is built. It is my contention that these pains exist in every neurotic each minute of his later life, irrespective of the form of his neurosis. These pains often are not consciously felt because they are diffused throughout the entire nervous system where they affect body organs, muscles, the blood and lymph system and, finally, the distorted way we behave.[363]

This may sound far removed from the Cursillo experience, and as far as the theory of Primal Therapy, it is. What is of salient interest is the technique Janov uses to expose this Primal Pain and to elicit the cathartic, Primal Scream experience. It begins with disorientation and removal of all customary supports and comforts.

> Twenty-four hours before we begin, the patient is isolated in a hotel room and asked not to leave that room until his therapy hour the following day. He may not read, watch television, or make phone calls during this twenty-four hour period. He is permitted to write. If we have reason to believe this is a well-defended patient, we ask that he stay up all night. This technique may be used occasionally during the first two weeks of individual therapy.
>
> The isolation and sleeplessness are important techniques which often bring patients close to a Primal. The aim of the isolation is to deprive the patient of all his usual outlets for tension, while the sleeplessness tends to weaken his remaining defenses; he has fewer resources to fight off his feelings. The aim is not to allow the patient to become distracted from himself....[364]

The effect can be quite disturbing:

---

[362] Arthur Janov, *The Primal Scream: Primal Therapy: The Cure for Neurosis* (New York: Dell Publishing Co., 1970, Laurel Edition, 1972), 11-12.
[363] Ibid, 13.
[364] Ibid, 80.

> Aloneness often can make the neurotic desperate. For many patients that night in the hotel room is the first time in years that they have sat still, been completely alone, and thought about themselves. There is no place to go and nothing to do. There is no place to act out the unreality. One of the important functions of keeping the patient awake during the night is to prevent him from acting out his unreality in his dreams. Lack of sleep helps crumble defenses, partly because plain fatigue renders the person less able to carry on his act, but mainly because he cannot act out symbolically via his dreams, and thus is unable to relieve tension. By stopping this symbolic act awake and asleep, we bring the person closer to his feelings. In addition to this point, a number of research studies have found that isolation itself lowers one's threshold for pain.[365]

Similarly, the first night of the Cursillo is one of darkness, isolation, and enforced silence. Windows are blocked out with opaque coverings and wristwatches are collected in order to disorient the subject with respect to time. No schedule is announced; events unfold without notice; several disorienting or shocking "surprises" occur throughout the weekend. The effect is one of surrender to and dependency on the Cursillo leaders who completely control the environment for the duration. Those who undergo the Cursillo regularly report a lack of sleep. One Teens Encounter Christ (TEC) graduate testifies to being "on fire" for God after a sleepless weekend. "From the kidnapping from our cars and the run through the church to the *lack of sleep* and no showers—I am on fire for the Lord!...I haven't been this on fire—ever."[366] Janov claims that by using the same or similar techniques, he is able to weaken defenses and make neurotics "desperate."

The authors of the Cursillo admit a similar interest in overcoming defenses through disorienting candidates. Bishop Juan Hervas, chief promoter of the Roman Catholic Cursillo in its infancy, writes of the intended effect of the Cursillo technique during the first phase of the weekend.

> The environment of the Cursillo, at this initial moment, is marked by a complete disorientation of the cursillistas, caused by their lack of knowledge of what the Cursillo is to be and by the diverse and contrary impressions that they have probably already gained.
>
> The distribution by "Decurias" (being grouped together at tables with complete strangers) will probably have added to the disorientation; the termination of the period of silence and the first

---

[365] Ibid.
[366] From an undated Northwest Iowa TEC (Teens Encounter Christ) newsletter, distributed late 2001 or early 2002. Available at www.nwiowatec.org. Emphasis added.

Chapter 8: Other Forms of Cathartic Experiences

contacts with instructors and companions, generally strangers to them, will contribute also to the disorientation in the new environment that is beginning to be created.[367]

Later in the weekend, the stated desire is to create a more submissive attitude in the candidate. "The temper of the cursillista is changing perceptively. He has abandoned his defensive position, placing himself each time on more accessible ground."[368]

During the third and last phase of the Cursillo weekend, complete submission of the candidate should have been achieved:

> At the time of this meditation (a talk given by a leader), it most frequently and normally happens that all the cursillistas (candidates) have a complete feeling of inner surrender and are filled with enthusiasm before the greatness of the ideals they have been catching a glimmer of.[369]

But what if some have not had the cathartic experience yet? The now-isolated candidate is often in distress because he has failed to attain the ostensibly religious experience enjoyed by the others.

> It very frequently happens that some cursillistas go to the priest and also seek for more time with the lay leaders themselves, driven by their concern at not "feeling" anything, a concern that sometimes turns into torture in contrast to the overflowing joy of the others. They would willingly share in the common joy and they blame themselves inwardly for their possible or imaginary shortcomings and could easily be dragged down into despair. Could the others be exaggerating? Could these be better than they? Why these differences? Could they be to blame in the sight of God for the lack of feeling they are experiencing?[370]

How is one to counsel participants who have failed to achieve the religious/cathartic experience? According to Bishop Hervas, Cursillo leaders should blame such participants for their lack of commitment and urge upon them a more humble confession for their sins.

---

[367] Juan Hervas, *Leaders' Manual for Cursillos in Christianity*, 94.
[368] Ibid, 113.
[369] Ibid, 144.
[370] Ibid.

> It is not enough to tell them to do certain things and then fervor will automatically come. Perhaps the deep-seated reason is that although they have been living in Grace for many years, their lack of commitment has caused them to bury the talents they have received from God; they were close to the Lord, but they lacked the idealism, self-surrender and spirit of charity that are the normal conditions for the cultivation of Grace and spiritual progress. Their reaction, therefore, – they will have to be told – cannot be the same as that of their companions in the Cursillo who stand fascinated before a Christ Whom they did not know or had lost and Whom they have just found again. Also their personal attitude is necessarily different: with humility and compunction, they must ask pardon for the years in which, without being cut-off branches, they have given only scanty fruits; during the time that they possessed the vital fluid of Grace, they lacked the irrigation water of generosity and sacrifice to make it exuberant and fertile. This humble attitude will, without doubt, attract them to Graces of the Lord and will bring them to the joy of total surrender.[371]

To my mind, this is one of the most insidious and harmful effects of the Cursillo. The real point of the Cursillo is to achieve a pleasurable catharsis. Those who for various reasons (superior resistance to the tricks and techniques, previous familiarity with or burnout from similar weekends, the use of prescription, psycho-active medications, for example) are unable to achieve the catharsis are told that they are spiritually inferior or lacking in commitment to Christ. The catharsis becomes equated with the reality of one's commitment to or experience with Christ. Those who do not "get it" must not be as committed to Christ as those who do "get it."

In the same way, every aspect of Primal Therapy is calculated to heighten tension and cause psychological distress, with a view toward achieving an intense catharsis.

> The patient arrives suffering. He is neither smoking nor taking tranquilizers, and he is tired and apprehensive. He is not sure what to expect. He may be kept waiting five to ten minutes beyond his appointed time in order to allow more tension to build. The sound-proof office is semi darkened; the phone is off the hook. The patient lies on the couch. He is instructed to lie spread-eagle because I want the body in as defenseless a physical position as possible. The importance of position and carriage was brought home to me by

---

[371] Ibid, 145.

Chapter 8: Other Forms of Cathartic Experiences

> observing new jailbirds who often spend their first days in jail with their legs crossed, arms folded across the abdomen and body hunched over their knees, as if to protect themselves against their aloneness, despair and hurt.[372]

Notice how carefully the patient is prepared for a cathartic experience. Tension, apprehension and vulnerability are at their premium, while coping defenses and familiar supports are stripped away. During the first session, Janov encourages the patient to talk about his problems:

> The point is that the patient is unhappy and suffering. If he is very tense and afraid, I will ask him to let that feeling overtake him. If he gets panicked, I encourage him to call one of his parents for help. On occasion that will produce a painful feeling within the first fifteen minutes of his first session. I will ask him to discuss his early life. He will say that he cannot remember very much. I push for whatever can be remembered.[373]

One of the goals of this exercise is to discover the patient's defense strategy: "As he speaks, I am gathering information. The patient is revealing his defense system...."[374] And then Janov works to defeat that defense system through making him relive a painful childhood memory:

> The patient is encouraged to sink into an early situation that seems to have evoked a good deal of feeling in him. "I was sitting there, letting him beat up my brother and—Gee, I feel tense...I don't know what it is...." He is again encouraged to sink into the feeling. He may not discover what the feeling is, or he may say, "I think I began to feel that this thing could happen to me if I spoke back like my brother did....Ooh, I've got a knot in my stomach. Was I afraid?" The patient begins to twitch a bit. He moves his legs and hands. His eyelids flutter, and his brow is furrowed. He sighs or grinds his teeth. I urge him to: "Feel that! Stay with it!" Sometimes he will say, "It's gone. The feeling has passed." This sparring process may go on for hours or days, but here I will telescope the situation and assume that the feeling stays so we can go on to the next stage.
>
> "I feel tight all over. Yeah, I think I was really afraid of the old man" may be the patient's next statement. At this point, when I see that he is into the feeling and is holding on tight, I will ask him to

---

[372] Janov, *The Primal Scream*, 81.
[373] Ibid.
[374] Ibid.

breathe deeply and hard from the belly. I will say, "Open your mouth as wide as possible and keep it that way! Now pull, pull that feeling from your belly!" The patient will begin to breathe deeply, writhing and then shaking. When the breathing seems to be happening automatically, I will urge, "Tell Daddy you're afraid!" "I'm not going to tell that son of a bitch anything!" he may answer. I urge him on. "Say it! Say It!" Usually, during the first hour, as simple as that task seems, the patient will not be able to say it. If he does scream it out, it will usually bring a stream of tears and stomach-wrenching gasps. He may immediately begin talking afterward about the kind of person his father was. Chances are good that he will also have several insights as he speaks.

This initial reaction is called the pre-Primal. The pre-Primals may go on for several days or even a week or so. It is essentially a chipping-away process, the aim of which is to open up the patient and get him ready to have him surrender his defense system. No one simply comes in and allows that to happen. The body gives up neurosis in begrudging stages.[375]

This kind of intense encounter may go for weeks with daily interviews, uncovering more painful memories, defeating more defensive behavior, and preparing for the ultimate effect, the Primal, in which the patient experiences the original pain of deprivation or abandonment that has caused his life of neurosis. Once this pain is expressed, through the original Primal Scream that was blocked, the neurosis is gone and Janov considers the patient cured. Janov is so convinced of this that he subtitles his book, *The Primal Scream*, with "Primal Therapy: The Cure for Neurosis."

What Janov's approach demonstrates is that facing or reliving painful memories can provoke an intense, cathartic event. But is it effective? Janov claims it is:

Primal Therapy purports to *cure* mental illness (psychophysical illness, to be exact). Moreover, it claims to be the *only* cure. By implication, this renders all other psychologic theories obsolete and invalid. It means that there can be only one valid approach to treating neuroses and psychoses.[376]

---

[375] Ibid., 81-82.
[376] Singer and Lalich, *"Crazy" Therapies: What are they? Do they work?* (San Francisco: Jossey-Bass Publishers, 1996), 121-122.

Chapter 8: Other Forms of Cathartic Experiences 135

He affirms that his results can be replicated by any competent primal therapist. But then he cautions: "It must be emphasized that this *therapy is dangerous in untrained hands.*"[377]

These high claims aside, the evidence does not warrant such a boast. Nichols and Zax note the rigor of the therapy as the "therapist constantly batters the patient's defenses" and then observe:

> Some patients may be ready for this onslaught—capable of experiencing and integrating their emerging feelings, and of growing through the process. Others, however, may be debilitated. There are no studies of Janov's procedures, so we cannot know if any or many of his patients become suicidally depressed. However, data that show a relatively high number of psychological casualties resulting from encounter groups suggest that primal therapy may very well also produce some walking wounded.[378]

The evidence regarding the helpfulness of primal therapy is uneven.

> Much of the positive evidence for the effectiveness of primal therapy is testimonial; on the other side of the ledger, some of Janov's patients report his approach as an intolerable emotional brainwashing.[379]

Nichols and Zax conclude:

> In sum, Janov seems to have developed an efficient procedure for helping people to achieve access to and to express feelings. They are helped to couple feelings with memories and perceptions in a manner that generates a great deal of ventilation. Whether this emotive discharge is a sufficient antidote for unhappiness by itself is yet unclear.[380]

Yet the ventilation of anger advocated by Janov's method can have the effect of increasing anger.

Leonard Berkowitz of the University of Wisconsin points out that acting out hostile feelings in the ways advocated by such therapists actually increases hostility: "The therapist or group members approve

---

[377] Ibid., 122, (emphasis added).
[378] Nichols and Zax, *Catharsis in Psychotherapy*, 139.
[379] Ibid., 141.
[380] Ibid., 144.

the patient's display of aggression. As a number of researchers have shown, *these rewards heighten the likelihood of subsequent violence.*"[381]

Reporting on a 1975 study of patients who had received primal therapy, Prochaska concludes:

> Holden (1975) does not report the percentage of patients who were cured by primal therapy. From his inadequate data, however, *it is clear that even after two years of primal therapy, there are patients who are not free from neurotic symptoms, which is contrary to the original claims of 100 percent effectiveness.* From a survey of 83 men and women between the ages of 25 and 50 who had completed at least three months of primal therapy, Holden cites individual case reports of changes in weight, height, sleeping, eating, and other signs. He summarizes his data by claiming that a majority of the primal patients showed the following patterns of changes: straightening of posture; clearing of sinuses and nose; fuller, deeper respiration; normalization of appetite and food intake; marked decrease in sex urge with increased enjoyment of sex; marked decrease in muscle tension; and insight into the relationship between symptoms of illness and primal pain. *A closer examination of the patients' reports, however, does indicate that some patients have increased fear of sex, increased muscle tension, more sleeping problems, and an increase in a variety of other symptoms following months of primal therapy.*[382]

While primal therapy may lead to a greater relaxation of tensions, its claims of being "the cure for neurosis" are demonstrably false.

Catharsis in Large Group Awareness Trainings (LGATs)

Another type of cathartic experience is not billed as religious in nature, though it is often used as a recruitment front for cult organizations.[383] Large Group Awareness Trainings (LGATs) follow a format and use techniques remarkably similar to the Cursillo initiation weekend. When I first began to read about LGATs, I found these similarities astounding. To my knowledge, of all of the other cathartic experience methods, the one employed by the LGAT is the one that most closely resembles the Cursillo in technique, format, and effect. And the LGATs method could rightly be understood as a combination of both the encounter group dynamics and the more radical elements of

---

[381] Singer and Lalich, *"Crazy" Therapies: What are they? Do they work?* 128 (emphasis added).
[382] James O. Prochaska, *Systems of Psychotherapy: A Transtheoretical Analysis*, 289, emphasis added.
[383] Singer with Lalich, *Cults in Our Midst*, 183.

Chapter 8: Other Forms of Cathartic Experiences

emotive therapy as in Janov's primal therapy.

LGATs grew out of the encounter group movement of the 1960s. But LGATs take group therapy to another level. LGATs are psychotherapy in the hands of enterprising entrepreneurs, and have become a multi-million dollar business. Most LGATs have their intellectual roots in a course called "Mind Dynamics," taught in California in the late 60s and early 70s. The two largest are est (Erhard Seminar Training), founded by Werner Erhard, also called Forum or Landmark, and Lifespring founded by John Handley. Others include Insight Seminars, Actualizations, PSI World, Silva Mind Control, and Transformational Technologies, to name a few. Often these courses seek to inculcate New Age ideology,[384] and Christians should be forewarned.

Usually for exorbitant amounts of money, people are promised they can develop their leadership or interpersonal skills, or "get in touch with themselves," or "achieve personal power," if they will only attend a "weekend training seminar." The seminar will teach "secrets" of leadership, persuasion, influence, or self-awareness. Often mid-level corporate employees are sent as part of their "leadership training," with the expectation of a promotion on the other end. While there are many legitimate leadership workshops and seminars, LGATs have little to do with acquiring leadership or other skills.

Berkley Psychology professor Dr. Margaret T. Singer writes,

> Because of the popularity of training programs and seminars, countless employees are sent to courses thinking that they are going to learn management techniques or specific job-related skills. Instead, they find themselves in high-confrontation, psychologically intense programs that are supposedly going to transform them, not just train them, but literally make them over into a new breed.[385]

The LGAT usually involves an extended weekend, four or five days in duration, which employs features similar to Janov's Primal Therapy. According to one LGAT attendee, the experience follows a three-step pattern:

1) Psychological breakdown/opening up the subconscious mind.
2) Catharsis or the releasing of repressed emotions usually caused by interpretations of childhood events.
3) A rebirthing or psychological buildup with processes designed to make participants feel good about themselves, the trainer and the course.[386]

---

[384] For a more complete discussion, see Douglas R. Groothuis, *Unmasking the New Age* (Downer's Grove, IL: InterVarsity Press, 1986).
[385] Singer with Lalich, *Cults in Our Midst,* 190.
[386] From an anonymous description of an LGAT weekend.

The First Day of the LGAT

The first day (often a Thursday night) is devoted to establishing the authority of the leader, called a facilitator or trainer. This is accomplished through a rigorous control of all aspects of the schedule, seating arrangement, restroom and other breaks and through berating and belittling any dissenters. One aspect of the seating arrangement is that participants may not sit near anyone they already know, effectively neutralizing any potential support system. The participant is alone and isolated in a room of strangers.

On the first evening each participant is required to sign or otherwise commit to a "contract" which includes the promise to participate in the entire weekend, to be on time, to obey the trainer, and especially not to reveal the processes, techniques, or surprises of the weekend.

> The program trainers and leaders typically get agreement from participants that they will not tell anyone about the processes that occur. To do so "will spoil it for your friends, family, co-workers when they take the course. Tell them what you got out of it," trainers advise. This means be vague about the actual content and provide glowing endorsements telling others that the training turned your life around, but do not tell them how emotional, dramatic, confrontational, and unnerving the sessions can be for some people. Because of this promise, consumers who buy and attend these seminars do so without information about how psychologically, socially, and sometimes physically stressing the event can be.[387]

After the lengthy, even tiresome explanation of the contract and ground rules (establishing the authority of the trainer), a brief break is often allowed, followed by a lecture on the pop psychology and/or New Age philosophy upon which the particular LGAT is based, usually having to do with "expanding your potential" or "overcoming limits internalized in childhood."

Later, the participants are directed through "awareness exercises" which often involve such discomfiting practices as gazing into the eyes of a stranger and disclosing personal information. A large part of the weekend includes "guided imagery": closing the eyes and following the trainer's description of an inward journey of self-discovery, a technique common to hypnosis, producing a heightened suggestibility.

Remarkably, most participants perform all of the exercises and submit completely to the trainer. But there are reasons for this. For one thing, many of the participants are really returnees who have already experienced the

---

http://www.caic.org.au/psyther/lgat/lgat1.htm
[387]Singer with Lalich, *Cults in our Midst*, 193.

Chapter 8: Other Forms of Cathartic Experiences

weekend and know the routine. Dr. Singer writes:

> New customers are unaware that most LGATs allow or even encourage those who have taken the training before to reattend. These people serve as a claque or modeling section. They clap, speak the same jargon as the leader, make endorsing statements, and are models for the new customers to pattern themselves after. Because the returners talk the talk and walk the walk, they get good responses from the trainer when they make comments. New customers begin to pattern their language and demeanor after the behavior of these others who, they notice, receive praise for using certain language or revealing personal material.[388]

But the more obvious incentive to conform is the verbal mashing objectors receive from the trainer. And some participants genuinely accept the trainer's promises of enlightenment or new awareness or personal power if they will only submit to the trainer's correctives and instruction. Those who attempt to walk out are met at the door by specially trained handlers, staff who try to coax them back into the session.

By this time (well after midnight) the participants are worn out. Even after they are dismissed, many are so disturbed that they sleep poorly that night. If they must work the next day, they arrive for their second day, usually Friday night, in an already compromised condition.

The Second Day of the LGAT

The second day (or night) aims at instilling whatever new philosophy the LGAT is espousing. Guilt becomes a powerful tool of manipulation. Participants are told that they are really responsible for all of the pain and tragedies of their lives. Dr. Singer describes the process:

> The well-known LGATs claim that you have caused everything that ever happened to you, from choosing your parents to breaking your leg, from getting yourself jilted to having been molested by your stepfather as a child. Trainers use the terms accountable and responsible, but not with their ordinary meaning. Trainers mean that you will, if you "get it," start to make your choices patterned after the way the organization advocates. They create guilt and fear in you that you have caused all the bad things that have happened in your life. "Your life is not working!" the trainer or leader yells, while he implies his is. If you just "get it," you'll be able to "make your life work."

---

[388] Ibid., 193-4.

What they teach about how to get your life to work is that there is a magical thinking that allows you to create whatever you want. You are told that you can create parking spaces, money to buy the next courses, and so on. Since creativity is in, you create just by thinking.[389]

This breaking down process is usually painful. After being directed to play an un-winnable competition game, an LGAT participant writes:

> By this time it was after 1 AM and we were told to file back into the main ballroom in silence. The trainer had a look that would kill. When we got to our seats we were ordered to close our eyes and the trainer yelled at us for 30 minutes straight. We were told that what we did in the game amounted to war and the way we played that game was the way we lived our lives. That lecture was filled with just about every negative behavior imaginable. You would have thought we were the leaders of Russia and America who just fired off an all-out nuclear exchange at each other and were now being called to account for it in hell.
>
> After a night of sleep deprivation and now another late night plus all the psychological opening exercises, this screaming lecture sends thunderbolts through your subconscious. I felt like with every sentence that a powerful jolt of electricity was sent through my nervous system.[390]

This participant then says that the group was dismissed about 2:00 a.m. with the instruction to "spend an hour reflecting on what we just did and to be back at 10 a.m."

The Third Day of the LGAT

The third day involves more guided imagery, dredging up unpleasant personal memories or failures and disappointments of early childhood. These exercises often involve one's mother or father, broken promises, sad events, lost dreams. The purpose is to open one up emotionally and psychologically. The demeanor of the trainer is also transformed from the domineering master to the seductive, loving mommy or daddy. The third day also involves "sharing." Some are sufficiently opened up to desire to share their darkest secrets. An LGAT participant describes the first person to share, a woman who was sexually molested by her father.

---

[389] Ibid., 194.
[390] http://www.caic.org.au/psyther/lgat/lgat1.htm

Chapter 8: Other Forms of Cathartic Experiences

The woman confesses the entire story of being raped by her father and is crying like a little child. The trainer nods and acts like they have heard it all before. Several people in the room (myself included) are crying in sympathy. The emotion is way too intense. Tension is extremely high in the room.

The trainer walks up on stage next to the woman and screams in her face "TELL YOUR FATHER HOW YOU FEEL ABOUT THIS! TELL HIM!. The woman screams out "I HATE YOU! WHY ARE YOU DOING THIS TO ME?"

The trainer yells "WHAT ARE YOU FEELING? WHERE IS THAT ENERGY IN YOUR BODY?" The woman points to her solar plexus. The trainer demands "HAVE THAT ENERGY MAKE A SOUND AND LET IT OUT." The woman lets out a long scream into the mike and then bursts into tears. One of the assistants helps her back to her seat.[391]

The "sharing" continues:

Person after person gets processed in this fashion by the trainer. They all end up screaming and crying into the microphone. Amplified by a PA system it has a powerful effect on the rest of us. This type of "sharing," more accurately described as "catharsis" is what the previous two days of aggressive awareness exercises produces in the participants. These exercises, along with the sleep deprivation, have opened people up psychologically and have produced a strong altered state of consciousness such that the childhood traumas that have been long buried in the subconscious are now surfacing.[392]

The transformation of the trainer into the kindly helper has another goal. Remember, these LGATs are a multi-million dollar industry. By the end, this must become a pleasant experience to encourage participants to return for "advanced training," and to invite their friends to take the basic weekend seminar. So after the deep and painful catharsis, the mood turns light. The guided imagery exercises turn positive. Dancing is often encouraged in the newly felt euphoria. An LGAT participant describes the "love bombing" process:

This process involves a long snaking circular line. Where we are given the opportunity to silently interact with every person in the room

---

[391] Ibid.
[392] Ibid.

including the staff. We are instructed to vote with our fingers: one finger means no contact, Two means to look the other person in the eyes, three fingers for a handshake, and four to give a full body hug. None of this lean over and keep your pelvis away type of hug stuff. This is full contact head to toe. Most everyone votes to hug. It is a very moving experience.[393]

Dismissal is early by comparison, 10:00 p.m. But then the goal has been reached: the catharsis and euphoria.

The Fourth Day of the LGAT

The final day is the celebration and solidification day. The mood is light. Further "sharing" from the microphone is encouraged. Participants are guided in setting goals for the future. There is more hugging and dancing. And during the afternoon there is a sales pitch for the advanced courses. "It was presented like the good feelings we had would not stick and we would fall back into our old ways of doing things unless we signed up for advanced (courses)."[394]

The weekend is concluded with a "graduation" ceremony. It may include symbolic candlelighting, from the trainer to the staff to the participants. And many LGATs include a surprise at the end: family and friends appear unexpectedly to congratulate the graduate.

But the weekend is not yet over. The "Guest Night" follows a few days later, when the graduate has invited his or her friends to a reunion to learn more about this wonderful weekend experience. At the guest night, the graduates are led off to a separate room where they are given the sales pitch for the advanced courses. Their "guests" are sold on the benefits of the initial weekend. The pitch may include instruction in pop psychology, simple awareness games, and especially testimonials of recent graduates of the advanced courses who describe the powerful difference the course has made on their lives. And the cycle is repeated again and again.

What is most remarkable to me is the number of similarities between the LGATs and the Cursillo weekend. The only real dis-similarities are in the belligerent attitude of the trainer and the New Age/ pop psychology orientation of the content. These are absent in the Cursillo (though Cursillo clearly has an aspect that is strongly psychological).

But the similarities are overwhelming:

---

[393] Ibid.
[394] Ibid.

Chapter 8: Other Forms of Cathartic Experiences

- the unquestioned authority of the leader
- the regression caused by the childlike (childish) behavior
- the secret "plants" at each table who have already experienced the weekend and who are able to guide the candidates into the proper responses
- seating participants with strangers so they are isolated from usual supports
- the lack of sleep and physical weariness
- the completely controlled environment
- the uncertain and unannounced schedule
- the format of the weekend (breaking down, catharsis, rebuilding)
- the emotional intensity, suspense and tension
- the sharing or confessing of painful secrets or shameful memories
- the hugging and group building techniques
- the shift from the serious and somber to the light and celebrative
- the closing surprise of having family/friends unexpectedly appear to congratulate and solidify the changes
- the vow of secrecy of not revealing the "surprises" to the uninitiated
- the warning that the feelings will wear off unless further steps are taken
- the graduates' sponsoring or inviting their friends to attend another weekend so they can have the same powerful experience

With such striking similarities one might be tempted to suspect a connection between LGATs and the Cursillo initiation weekend. To my knowledge this is not the case. I think they probably did have common ancestors, however, both being born out of the same psychotherapeutic orientation and milieu.

But do they work? Do LGATs produce lasting, positive change? Dr. Singer writes on the impact of such weekends:

What can be upsetting to certain people in such LGAT sessions is that, in these four or five intense, exhausting days, they become flooded with more emotion and conflict than they can handle all at once. Up until this time, they've handled their lives in their own way, but at these training sessions they've had to look at their entire past, in a brief but enforced way. This is quite different from psychotherapy, for instance, where the therapist and the patient progress more slowly in order to allow the patient to deal with whatever she or he wants or needs to at a manageable pace.³⁹⁵

And the effects can be dramatic and damaging.

> Religious issues aside, the pronounced psychological nature of many of the exercises within many of these programs is of concern. We cannot deny the fact that they grew out of the highly confrontational group therapy techniques introduced by the encounter, sensitivity, and large group awareness training movements. And in many ways, these psychological techniques are little different from the influence processes used in today's cults to achieve attitudinal change. This is apparent in the psychological and behavioral effects produced, and in the appearance of a certain number of psychological casualties during and after participation in some of these training programs.
>
> A further result is that the majority of participants experience varying degrees of alienation and instability because they are urged to give up old norms, goals, and ideals. They also suffer a type of culture shock as they try to reconcile pretraining values with what they learn in the training and with the realities of their posttraining existence. Importantly, *a certain number of participants will be seriously harmed as these stresses precipitate a handful of psychological conditions, such as brief psychotic episodes, posttraumatic stress disorder syndrome, a variety of dissociative disorders, relaxation-induced anxiety, and other miscellaneous reactions including phobias, cognitive difficulties, and stress-related illnesses.*³⁹⁶

Conclusion

It should be evident that relying upon catharsis alone for significant growth or positive change is inadequate. Catharsis is for the most part pleasurable, but the release of pent-up emotions as a major change agent is a woefully deficient view of human personality, of the effects of sin and the redemptive work of God in Christ, as applied by the Holy Spirit through the means of grace. In each of the above (Encounter Groups, Primal Therapy and LGATs) the cathartic experience may be enjoyable, but it has little demonstrable value in creating positive change or in teaching new behaviors. And this coupled with the observable, negative side-effects would indicate that such experiences though pleasing certainly appear to offer little lasting benefit and may create significant harm.

---

[395] Singer with Lalich, *Cults in Our Midst*, 195.
[396] Ibid., 211, emphasis added.

Chapter 8: Other Forms of Cathartic Experiences

The fact that encounter groups, primal therapy and LGATs share similar techniques with the Cursillo and achieve quite similar results does not conclusively establish a link between them, nor does it prove that the Cursillo is nothing more than a cathartic event, though it should raise significant concern. Therefore applying these conclusions to the Cursillo must be done tentatively. I would add that the content of the Cursillo is clearly (though generically) Christian. I would be reluctant completely to rule out the positive work of the Holy Spirit in such a Christian context, in spite of the questionable tactics employed. Nevertheless, these conclusions should be taken to heart and would prevent a ringing endorsement of the Cursillo without further investigation.

Of serious concern, however, are other factors about the Cursillo which will require more exploration.

1) The Cursillo certainly appears to be a psychological phenomenon, yet it is billed as a spiritual experience, perhaps *the* spiritual experience. The catharsis event in Cursillo which includes the pleasant, sometimes powerful relief and euphoria is attributed to the action of the Holy Spirit. And so one's spiritual experience is equated with deep and moving feelings, which should be highly suspect for biblical Christians. When the feelings wear off, as they inevitably do, the cursillista is left in a quandary. Has the reality of one's spiritual experience or relationship with God likewise evaporated? At this point begins the fruitless quest to recapture the feeling, and the result can be a spiritual roller coaster. This is what often attracts people to continued participation in the Cursillo in order to recapture the evaporated feelings.

2) The Cursillo is promoted as a truly Christian experience, perhaps *the* Christian experience. Its intense impact is offered as proof of its validity. Yet, the claim that the Cursillo must be a genuinely religious or spiritual experience because it is "deeply felt," "moving," or "impactful" is a *non-sequitur*, a logical fallacy in which the conclusion does not necessarily follow from the premises. The logic of the argument is as follows:

Meeting God is an emotionally powerful experience.
I had an emotionally powerful experience at Cursillo.
   Therefore: I MET GOD AT CURSILLO.

The flaw in this logic is the assumption that all emotionally powerful experiences are experiences with God, or that emotionally powerful experiences in a religious context are experiences with God. By the same, faulty logic one could arrive at the following absurd conclusions:

All men have two legs.
A crow has two legs.
   Therefore: A CROW IS A MAN.

Bears growl.
My stomach growls.
   Therefore: MY STOMACH IS A BEAR.

As previously demonstrated, Encounter Groups, Primal Therapy and LGATs also provide emotionally powerful experiences through various techniques. If the Cursillo uses the same or similar techniques to achieve the same or similar results, then one would be forced to question whether the techniques themselves produced the effect and not the religious content of the weekend.

Consider the following table:

Type of Therapy	Methodology +	Philosophy =	Result
Encounter Groups	Disorienting Techniques +	Various forms of Pop Psychology =	Catharsis
Primal Therapy	Disorienting Techniques +	Theories of Early Childhood Trauma =	Catharsis
LGATs	Disorienting Techniques +	New Age Philosophy & Pop Psychology =	Catharsis
The Cursillo Weekend	Disorienting Techniques +	Christian Teaching from Various Traditions =	Catharsis

Notice in the above that the constants are the methodologies and the results. The philosophy is virtually irrelevant to the outcome. It would be reasonable to assume, therefore, that in the Cursillo it is the technique and not the content or message that produces the cathartic effect.

3) Each of the other cathartic experiences demonstrates a certain amount of risk to the participants. Encounter Groups evidence a certain level of psychological harm. Janov warns that Primal Therapy is "dangerous in untrained hands." Large Group Awareness Trainings cause psychological harm to a certain percentage of participants as the stresses involved precipitate various psychological conditions. Indeed, with respect to the Roman Catholic Cursillo, as previously noted, some Cursillo participants have been "institutionalized following their initiation,"[397] and "persons assessed as mentally unstable"[398] are regularly weeded out of consideration. This should give great pause to the continuation of the Cursillo without further study into

---

[397] Marcoux, *Cursillo, Anatomy of a Movement: the Experience of Spiritual Renewal*, 39.
[398] Ibid., 38.

Chapter 8: Other Forms of Cathartic Experiences

the effect of such highly-charged, catharsis-oriented weekends, or at the very least, psychological screening of potential candidates.

4) Finally, no one to my knowledge has ever produced a definitive study of those who participate the in the Cursillo, assessing the enduring effects, if any, on such Christian practices as Church attendance/involvement, Christian disciplines including sacrifice and stewardship, Bible study and prayer, and the growth in Christian virtues such as love, humility, honesty, sexual purity, holiness in thought and speech, and the like. One would readily stipulate that the Cursillo can be a powerful, emotional experience and relief from tension, alienation and/or boredom. But so can be Encounter Groups, Primal Therapy and Large Group Awareness Trainings, which are decidedly non-Christian.

What if the Cursillo weekend is nothing more than a pleasant emotional experience? So what? What is so wrong with that? The same question was addressed regarding a similar kind of weekend renewal experience:

> Is it wise to offer people a big enthusiastic weekend that some term an emotional jag?
>
> Assuming for a moment that it was only a weekend jag, would there be anything awful about that? Don't we go to a basketball tournament involving our team and have a big emotional time? Does it destroy our love for a basketball game between our team and the traditional rival? Does this big emotion-ridden spree cure us of basketball fever? Then why not afford the same privilege to the lay witness mission?[399]

The answer, of course, is that the basketball tournament is billed as a basketball tournament and not something else. If the lay witness mission or Cursillo weekend is just an emotional jag, BUT IT IS MADE OUT TO BE the most significant spiritual experience of your life, or a genuine encounter with the Holy Spirit, or true Christianity, then we should expect problems to arise. Everybody expects the emotion of a basketball tournament to wear off. But what if one's perception of the Christian faith is equated with this emotional weekend and the emotion inevitably wears off? The person may then be left with the mistaken notion that his or her Christian faith has likewise evaporated.

---

[399] Robert L. Main, *Encountering Christ: Lay Witness, One Key to Renewal* (Nashville: Tidings, 1970), 79.

9. *In Their Own Words: Sharing Cursillo Stories*

In my formal research of Cursillo[400], I was most interested in the long-term effects of the initiation weekend. I limited my study to the Reformed Cursillo in Northwest Iowa. Proponents of the Cursillo will regularly cite the immediate results in the form of testimonials. My concern was to consider the more lasting effects, if any, of the Cursillo initiation weekend and further involvement. In this study, I interviewed in depth eight people who participated in the Reformed Cursillo weekend in Northwest Iowa at least eight years ago.[401] I pre-selected candidates for interviewing using a simple screening tool asking three questions:

1. In the month or so after I attended the Cursillo weekend, my attitude toward Cursillo was:
   _____ Generally positive
   _____ Generally neutral
   _____ Generally negative

2. Currently (and at least eight years after the Cursillo weekend) my attitude toward Cursillo could best be described as:
   _____ Generally positive
   _____ Generally neutral
   _____ Generally negative

---

[400] The substance of this chapter was previously published in Brian V. Janssen, "After the Weekend is Over: The Long-Term Effects of the Reformed Cursillo in Northwest Iowa" (D.Min. diss., Covenant Theological Seminary, 2007).
[401] The study was designed using a *qualitative* rather than a *quantitative* approach as described in Sharan B. Merriam, *Qualitative Research and Case Study Applications in Education* (San Francisco: Jossey-Bass Publishers, 1998).

Chapter 9: In Their Own Words: Sharing Cursillo Stories

3. I would agree to a confidential interview about my Cursillo experience lasting 30-45 minutes.

_____ Yes

_____ No

I was particularly interested in interviewing those who had changed their attitude or perspective. If possible, I wanted to find two who remained positive, two who remained negative, two who moved from positive to neutral or negative and two who moved from negative to neutral or positive in their perspectives toward Cursillo.

I mailed out eighty-eight invitation letters to forty-nine addresses. Of these, three envelopes (four letters) were returned as "no such address," not surprising since all addresses were over eight years old. Twenty-six invitations were returned (29.5%). Of these, one was deceased, four declined to be interviewed, two answered with a simple question mark, and one with a completely blank sheet. Of the nineteen (21.6%) remaining, fourteen indicated that they were generally positive about the Cursillo experience both immediately after the weekend and now, some eight or more years later.

Of these latter I chose to interview three: Barb, Ed and Fred. Scott and Sheila, a married couple, indicated that they were initially positive about the weekend, but now were generally neutral, and I chose to interview them as a couple. I also chose to interview Doris, who indicated that she was initially positive but now was between generally neutral and generally negative. I interviewed Gus who was generally positive both immediately after the weekend and at the present, but who noted on his screening survey that he had had some difficulties during the weekend itself. And I chose to interview Marlys, who noted that she was generally positive both then and now, but in between was a bit negative toward the Cursillo. This brought the total to eight, four women and four men, three (one man and two women) of whom were now only neutral or less than neutral toward the Cursillo.

IN THEIR OWN WORDS

BARB: *"It felt like I was going home spiritually."*

General Background

Barb responded on the screening survey that she was generally positive toward the Cursillo both immediately after attending and at the present, some 8-10 years later. She reports that though she did not grow up in Northwest Iowa, she and her parents had been active in a Reformed denomination in another state. Through her periodic attendance at churches of other denominations and through having friends from other, non-Reformed churches, she had "a lot of interfaith experiences" and came to a more inclusive understanding of her faith and how it could be expressed. "And so, when I came here to Northwest Iowa I felt extremely stifled in my Christian life and how I could express it. And so going to Cursillo, just like 'Ah!' it felt so good. It was like a spiritual spa for me."

She knew very little about the Cursillo before she attended. "I knew it was a spiritual renewal retreat. I knew the basics that when you go, you are divided into groups and sit around tables with these groups and listen to different talks and then have discussion times afterwards." She was attracted to the Cursillo because she felt "spiritually very isolated" in Northwest Iowa, and because she had heard "very positive responses" from people who had attended. "And, yeah, that was just something I thought, 'I want to try that, I want to see what it's like. Why are these people so excited about this? Is this a place where I could find what I grew up with? Are there people there that think more like me and express their faith more like me?' So that was why I was very curious and wanted to go." Barb has also remained very active in the Cursillo movement in Northwest Iowa and has participated in various serving and leadership roles.

The Immediate Impact of the Cursillo

When she attended the weekend, she found herself growing "more and more excited, and more and more thankful that I was there." She remembers having no concerns, doubts or questions whatsoever; for her the weekend was entirely positive. Most meaningful to her was the message of grace: "grace for myself, because of the grace Christ had extended to me, and grace for other people whom I had been hurt by, a lot of healing with wounds that I had, and the atmosphere of grace and Christ's grace that he extends to us provided an environment that allowed me to be open to that healing, allowing me to allow myself to forgive myself for different things, to forgive other people who had hurt me."

But Barb also found a new set of like-minded friends with whom she shared great affinity. "It brought me into a world of relating, of finally knowing and meeting other Christians in this area who I felt like I could relate to, and so felt like a whole new world had been opened to me." These were "people who were willing to talk about their relationship with the Lord, that their relationship was personal, that it was in their heart, not just in their head." This was something she had not really experienced much of before in Northwest Iowa, as she had when she was growing up.

The weekend did not immediately affect her relationship with her local church. That's because very few from her church had attended the Cursillo, and she felt that they would not be interested. "The makeup of our church is not one that people are interested in this kind of thing. And so, it wasn't something I even bothered sharing with people there. I knew that they had no interest in it, wouldn't understand it, didn't care to understand it, so I didn't even bother." She says that she felt little affinity with the people in her church, but "definitely" felt this with the people she had met at the Cursillo. But this affinity extended to the people in her church who had previously attended Cursillo. "We had an automatic bond," one that she did not feel with other members of her church.

The Cursillo also had a positive effect on her marriage and family. She reports that it was "part of the catalyst" that brought greater peace, forgiveness and communication to her relationship with her husband. Her children also reaped the benefits since she had "more peace inside" and their parents were "getting along better." She also found "a whole new body of friends," which she considered "a huge blessing" since she had "felt isolated for years living in (Northwest Iowa)."

The Purpose of the Cursillo

Barb understands the purpose of the Cursillo to be centered in teaching people how to live in God's grace in the context of Christian community. "Cursillo is about really knowing and learning what God's grace is all about. Really what it is. And to me Cursillo is also the best picture I have ever had about what Christian community should be, and I know it can be that kind of picture because it's isolated from the real world, you know: every care, everything else is set aside, and you come together, and you really experience Christian community. So in a way it's false…in a sense, because there's nothing else vying for your time. But yet, still at the same time I feel like, every time I go, I think, 'This really is what Christian community should be! This really is what it should be like, that we are accepting each other where we're at, for who we are, with whatever hurts, problems, sins, whatever it is we've got, we're accepting each other. We're trying to walk with each other, we're trying to build each other up, this is what it should be like; this is a picture of that.' And it's helped me to take that from there and try harder, every time I go, to try harder to live that kind of community out here, in this community. It's not easy, but it's helped me to try to do that."

The Means That Achieve the Impact of the Cursillo

Barb gives the credit for the effects of the Cursillo to the work of the Holy Spirit. "What brings about the results? Well, I would say the Holy Spirit." She is willing to acknowledge, however, that the Cursillo does allow the proper "setting" as well. She gives an analogy of a busy married couple struggling with the demands of careers and children, who then take a weeklong vacation alone. "They have just each other now to concentrate on, to interact with. It's just the two of them all of a sudden. The atmosphere is conducive for them alone to build their relationship, OK? I think that Cursillo provides that atmosphere, for them, for a person, however they want, to relate to God, if they want to relate to him in 'I hate You', 'I'm angry with You', it's there, that environment is there because they have the freedom to do that. Or if they want to say, 'I want to know who you are, but I don't,' they can say that. If they, you know, want to say, 'I love you, and I want to know you more,' whatever, wherever they're at, that environment is provided for them. The distractions are removed."

And while the Cursillo temporarily removes the distractions, it also focuses exclusively on Christ. "It's not about, 'OK, now we're all together and we're going to talk (about our families)' Well, you do talk about your families, etc., but that is not the focus. The focus is on Christ. It's on Him, at least at all the ones I've been to, that is continually the focus. Everything is brought to Him."

So if the means are so effective, then why does the sense of spiritual renewal from the Cursillo tend to wear off? Barb laughs. "Why does romance wear off? Cause we're sinners, cause we're human beings, we're fickle people, cause we're not easily satisfied. It doesn't from God! It doesn't wear off from Him. You know, he's not the one walking away. It's me."

Barb seemed unconcerned that, according to a survey of Cursillo participants, over one-quarter of those responding said that they had been subjected to emotional manipulation during the weekend. She would believe it to be very possible that they felt that way. "We are all very different people. We all come at things with who we are, our background. We come to things with our personalities. No, I wouldn't say I totally disagree with that. I would say, 'Yeah, probably.'"

When she was told that those who felt manipulated mentioned things like "not knowing the schedule ahead of time," some of the "shocks and surprises" that take place on the weekend, and that they found these to be disruptive, Barb replied, "Okay, and see, and I found that the exact opposite." She loved the spontaneity, the open-endedness, not knowing what was coming next and all the surprises. "I loved it! You know why? Cause I had no control over myself. It wasn't about me. It was like, 'Here, Lord, here, here I am. What are you going to do, what are you going to show me? I've got nothing. I've got nothing here. I can't control a thing.' And I loved being in that position. So, see, it's me, that's me, and other people aren't like that. So then they would probably take some of those things as 'You're controlling me. You're telling me what to do or not to do.'"

The Lasting Effects of the Cursillo

Barb cites several lasting benefits related to her participation in the Cursillo. For one thing, she enjoys a much-improved, healthy relationship with her husband, even though he has only remained marginally involved in the Cursillo, while she has stayed quite active.

But she also enjoys a growing group of like-minded friends. "I'm a lot happier just because I have a group that I belong to, that's like me, and I'm like

Chapter 9: In Their Own Words: Sharing Cursillo Stories

them." A lot of these new friends have attended the Cursillo. "When you start associating with other people who are like-minded and they're associating you with people who are like-minded but those people might not have attended Cursillo, but yet it brought me into a world where I felt more of an affinity with other people."

Her continued involvement with the Cursillo has been extensive, participating at least annually in service and/or leadership in the Cursillo work. But, at the same time, her involvement with her local church has declined. She has become more active in a new church. "I actually have withdrawn more from my church and joined a small group" with the new church. Why? "Because I feel like I'm a part of them, and…I don't feel an affinity (with my own church). I don't know, I feel a part of these people (in the new church)." At her own church "people don't expect you to do anything or ask you to do anything, but (the new church) is so small that everybody has to."

Barb struggles with the normal difficulties with family, work and some health issues. And she experiences some "ups and downs" in her spiritual life as well. "You know, I struggle in my relationship with God sometimes, you know I feel sometimes, I feel like, you know 'Where are You, not listening to me?' I don't know how much to go into it. Sometimes I feel like David in the Psalms, you know, up and down, and, you know, sometimes I feel so close to Him, and I'm filled with joy and I know that joy is from Him, and then sometimes I think, 'You're so far away! Where are you?'"

But Barb seems most animated about her work with the Cursillo. After relating a story of how God gave her just the right words to say to a fellow-worker, she later received a letter of affirmation from her co-worker that said, "It was what I was asking the Lord for. It was exactly what I needed to hear." Barb continued: "And I know that was the Spirit speaking through me, and, you know what? There's no high like watching God work, like seeing him work, nothing. Nothing on this earth compares to that. That this woman was spoken to by the Lord, was just like 'Thank you, Lord, for meeting her there. Thank you, Lord, for letting me be an agent of that.' It's wonderful; that fills me; that is what brings joy to my life. And Cursillo gives me that opportunity to do that. It's a means for me to be able to do that, and I don't have that in any other part of my life."

Question: "Not in your local church?"
Barb: "No. No. Not at all."
Question: "Nothing even close to it?"
Barb: "Nothing even close, no, no."

SCOTT AND SHEILA: *"It was a nice weekend, and I agree with 97% of what was presented."* (Scott)   *"It's one more thing in my suitcase of things that makes me look forward to heaven."* (Sheila)

General Background

Scott and Sheila were the only married couple both of whom were included in the interview process, so they were interviewed together. Both indicated on the screening survey that their immediate reaction to the Cursillo weekend was "generally positive," but that now, several years later they were both "generally neutral." Scott and Sheila had been committed Christians for many years, very active in church leadership, though, at the time they attended Cursillo they had been relative newcomers to Northwest Iowa.

Before Scott attended the Cursillo weekend, he only knew that "it was designed to be a short course in Christianity designed to deepen our walk with the Lord and to help us experience the teachings rather than just have a head-knowledge, and that people were excited about this." But he also knew that there was "this kind of mysterious thing, like, you know, 'We really want you to go, can't tell you too much, but you're welcome to go.'" Sheila did not know as much about it beforehand as Scott did. She did feel that it had been overly promoted as something bigger than a "salvation experience." She was told that "it was just this mountaintop experience that nothing could ever match, nothing before and nothing after would ever match." She was convinced "it was going to be a good thing because it was based on Scripture," but she was bothered by the dramatic buildup beforehand.

Scott thought the weekend would offer "the same kind of thing I would get from going to a weekend retreat or a church weekend at camp." And he admits that he was hoping "to gain some credibility as somebody who'd gone through the Cursillo weekend" since he had felt some pressure to attend. For Sheila, it was largely this pressure that motivated her. "Looking back on it, I was just doing it because people were saying, you know, how good it was....I don't know if I was hoping to get much out of it other than (to get people to stop bugging her to go)." She was not afraid to go, but was concerned about the time commitment it required. "I knew it wasn't anything bad, but, you know it's a huge commitment of time and energy....I knew it was going to be something good, you know, just because I knew it was something about the Lord, and I knew it wasn't a cult...."

The Immediate Impact of the Cursillo

Scott had "generally positive memories of the Cursillo weekend." He was immediately impressed with the amount of preparation that people did to "make this happen." And he thought the "prayer support" was very positive.

Chapter 9: In Their Own Words: Sharing Cursillo Stories

"They'd done a lot of creative activities and, you know, a pretty significant attempt not just to have a teaching session, but worship times and make it really a meaningful time of meeting with the Lord. You know, fellowship with other Christians. So, my reaction to the weekend was pretty positive." The teaching times were good. And he enjoyed the "positive interaction with other Christians." It was an enjoyable weekend: "nice, meaningful times of worship, and all that." But Scott said that he didn't really learn anything: "It was more of an experience for me of things I already knew."

Sheila was also impressed with the amount of work people had done for the weekend. She had helped with similar events and knew the prayer and preparations involved. She "thought all of the events were very powerful, especially...the culmination supper." She also appreciated the number of people who "were supporting me in prayer and through their cards and gifts and notes." She did not think she learned anything new, either. Rather, "it seemed to be a real emotional experience, very emotional" which she was not so sure was altogether helpful.

But both Scott and Sheila had some concerns with the weekend. Scott was troubled with "the secrecy about the events." He specifically mentioned the appearance of being disorganized because no schedule was posted. "Somebody knew what was going to happen next, but I didn't." "Not going outside" also concerned him. He could understand to some degree not wearing his watch, but he thought that covering the windows "so we're not distracted by whether the sun's up or not, that seemed kind of extreme." The secrecy about what would happen during the weekend was explained to him in terms of: "We want to do some things that will be a surprise, that is supposed to be a learning event, so we want to keep things secret to not take away the surprise." He could accept this rationale.

Scott also questioned the qualifications of some of the people giving the talks. One of the presenters who introduced himself and his talk spoke about struggles in his life. "I remember people introducing themselves as just not giving a talk but they were introducing themselves, which was real, very good. But he talked about some struggles he had in his life, and they were quite recent. And I thought, 'Is this guy really walking with the Lord, and does he know what it means to depend on God for these issues? And is he spiritually qualified to be giving this talk?' And I got that impression especially one time but other times it came up, you know. I kind of wondered (about their spiritual maturity). And then they went on to say good things, but I thought, 'Are you really walking the talk?' So, I had some questions."

Scott mentioned some "expectations" that went along with the weekend. For example, he felt the expectation of others that this should be the greatest spiritual experience of his life, that he would have this "mountaintop emotional experience" or "that it's going to be a mind-boggling experience" or that this was going to be "the new high-water mark" for his Christian experience. "It was subtle. It wasn't stated that overtly. And so I felt somewhat uncomfortable of having a 'nice' weekend when everybody was expecting me to have an awesome, earth-shattering weekend." And Scott said that he felt the "subtle expectation that I was going to be part of the leadership, or get more involved with Cursillo." He said it felt like "now that you've gone, you now know how wonderful it is. Wouldn't you like to be a part of this?"

Sheila was bothered by some of the teaching with which she did not agree. She was even more bothered by the fact that her questions or concerns seemed unwelcome to her table leadership. She did not feel at liberty to discuss her disagreements at the table. "I brought it up...but, no, I didn't feel like there was time or desire to deal with that." Instead, "It was more like, 'Well, we don't really want to emphasize that.' Or, 'We don't want this to be a time of disagreement.'" It was just "pushed aside."

Sheila was also troubled by the secrecy. "I appreciated the whole idea of why they want the whole secrecy thing and why they weren't telling you about certain things because it would have spoiled the surprise. It was a good surprise, but I was uncomfortable with the secrecy. Just, before we knew anything about Cursillo, when we were first told about Cursillo, I mean there was just a lot of secrecy around it, and when I think of secrecy, I think of the devil. You know, things that cults, or you know, I just don't like that kind of stuff." To Sheila, the secrecy seemed to involve a "controlling factor" that made her uncomfortable, "kind of like, 'if you don't know what's going on, you don't know what time it is, you don't know anything, we're in control,' and that was a little uncomfortable." She found the secrecy to be "distracting." "But," she said, "the events themselves and how they were put together were very powerful."

Sheila voiced another concern. During the weekend "the feeling that's trying to be created is, 'You are loved and accepted for who you are' in a kind of 'showering of love'." But, she said, she found herself disappointed after the weekend, when that "showering of love" didn't seem to be transferred to "people who aren't in the church," to "the non-Christian or the Hispanic on the street who doesn't experience that." For her it was the feeling of "a dissociation between Cursillo and real life, feeling like not all of that is overlapping to what I see going on in our community at large."

So how did the weekend impact their lives? For Scott, it was "a positive weekend, an enjoyable review of the basics of the Christian life, and meaningful times of worship and fellowship." For Sheila, it was an "awesome experience." "It was wonderful to see so many believers who were being supported in prayer as well as those who were supporting in prayer." But after the weekend, she had a lot of questions "about how all these people that I saw, who seemed to be real, solid believers, were responding afterwards." It was like a lot of things in life, "where you go and you have this great experience, and then there's things that don't mesh afterwards," like "someone who served as a

Chapter 9: In Their Own Words: Sharing Cursillo Stories

leader on the weekend, and then afterward was divorcing his wife." She realized that this was true of other Christian experiences, and not just the Cursillo.

Neither Scott nor Sheila felt that the Cursillo had created any significant, immediate change in their lives. With respect to the Cursillo affecting their church involvement, Scott noted that there was an undercurrent of controversy in his church regarding the Cursillo. He explained: "There were some people in our local church that were really glad that we were going to the Cursillo weekend and wanted to see us get more involved. There were other people in our church that felt like Cursillo was competing with their local church, and that I was getting sucked into this thing…. Our Sunday evening service would typically be very slimly attended on Cursillo weekends because some people were candidates and other people were going to the closing, so there was a mixed reaction, a mixed effect on the local church. So, some were really happy about it, and others were fearful."

It was controversial, Scott reported, but "not that there was … a lot of open controversy or discussion, but, you know, in a committee meeting it would come up, or someone would say, "Cursillo is depopulating our church.""

Sheila did not think that the Cursillo had any affect on their relationship with their local church. And neither Scott nor Sheila thought it affected their marriage or their relationship with their children.

It did, however, change their relationships with their friends. Sheila explained, "(For) some of the people who had gone to Cursillo, it was like now we were in the club." Scott agreed: "That was subtle, but it was real." Sheila likened it to attending a "Women of Faith" or "Promise Keepers" event. "It's like, 'If you haven't been to Cursillo, you've got to go' and 'If you haven't been to Women of Faith, you've got to go.' It's that whole dynamic."

The Purpose of the Cursillo

When it comes to the purpose for the Cursillo, Scott and Sheila differed on the perspective they gained. For Sheila the purpose of the Cursillo was one of spiritual growth and practical understanding of grace. "I feel like the purpose was for people to get closer to the Lord and to experience grace without conditions, and to know that they are purely and fully loved for who they are."

Scott's understanding is that the Cursillo seeks to provide a more encompassing knowledge of the faith and a stimulus for Christians to integrate faith and practice. "I thought it was to introduce people to the basics of Christianity, and…solidify that, like, you've got the whole package now, instead of just a bit or piece." Its purpose is not exactly evangelistic, but "to get people who are nominal church-goers to understand how important the gospel is and how important it is that Christ died for us, and that there's a life, a significantly different lifestyle to be lived, or to let the Lord change your heart, maybe that's a good way to say it."

The Means That Achieve the Impact of the Cursillo

So what produces the powerful effect? For Scott, it's the work of the Lord and his people. It is "Jesus Christ and Christians who intentionally want to bring people close to the Lord. The power's in the Word, and the power is in prayer, but the power is basically, these are a means to an end. The power is in meeting with the Lord."

Sheila thinks that the secrecy and the surprises play a role in the effect. "Even though I don't like the secrecy, secrecy adds power to things, whether it's a good power or a bad power. It usually adds power." And she thinks that the Cursillo could do with a little less "hype" and a little more humility. She compares the Cursillo "sales pitch" to that of "Amway." "Amway says, 'If you do this, then you'll get to go on all these vacations, and do this and this.' And there's some truth to that, if you build a business, and you work hard in it. There's some truth to the Cursillo, you know, if you go it's going to be this mountaintop experience. But some people, for one, don't have that experience. What about just saying, 'If you just really want to learn a little more about Scripture and just to really get to know the Lord a little better, this would be a great, great thing for you'? Cursillo isn't that poorly attended that they need to do this big sales trick. I just feel like if there was a little more focus on God instead of on what a great experience you're going to have. Sometimes when we go with these big expectations, we're either greatly disappointed, or we fall into the trap of almost making ourselves feel that way and then afterwards, 'poof,' it's gone."

Why do the powerful effects wear off? Scott thinks this is not unusual: "I don't know if that's different for Cursillo weekend as compared to any other spiritual retreat....We live in a fallen world; we aren't in heaven yet; 'the world the flesh and the devil': that's a very natural human tendency." Sheila similarly sees it as a failure to live our discipleship on a daily basis. "I think God calls us to meet fresh with him each day....If we could just have a big feast and not have to do it again for three months, he wouldn't tell us in his Word that we need to meet with him every day." In fact, Sheila challenges the notion that the real effects "wear off." "I think that the real fruit that I got from that weekend is still with me. There's lots of peripheral stuff and that emotional stuff that doesn't stick with you, but the meat of it sticks with you.... That would be like saying that God's Word comes back void, and I don't believe that."

What about the feeling on the part of some that that they were subjected to emotional manipulation? Scott was surprised, and disappointed. He thought that the Cursillo leaders were very well-intentioned and simply wanted the participants to have a "mountaintop experience." "If the subtle expectation that this is going to be a wonderful thing, if that's emotional manipulation, if that's what people are calling it, I guess I felt that, but I tend to tune that out or not pay attention to that." He also mentioned the implied sense that "you're not permitted to leave" and having his watch and cell phone

Chapter 9: In Their Own Words: Sharing Cursillo Stories

taken without prior notice. He suggested that people be told these things beforehand, a kind of "informed consent."

Sheila wondered if people were responding negatively to the secrecy of the weekend. She agreed that some of the rules and restrictions should be published beforehand, that this might "help to resolve some of that feeling of being manipulated." "People are adults. They want to be treated like adults. And when they're not, they feel disrespected, and maybe that's some of what goes on."

The Lasting Effects of the Cursillo

Neither Scott nor Sheila would attribute much to the Cursillo by way of lasting impact. Neither of them went back to work at a Cursillo, though they did attend a closing once or twice. They never attended an ultreya meeting and cannot recall if they were invited to a small cell group. In fact, Scott wouldn't have been interested even if he had been invited. "The idea of establishing a supportive Christian community seemed to me to be what the local church was supposed to do, and so I didn't feel the need to be looking for another avenue."

What lasting effect did the Cursillo have? Scott reflects: "I don't think I can look at where I'm at spiritually and say that it has much connection with the Cursillo weekend....Yeah, it was a nice weekend, and I agree with 97% of what was presented. God is using Cursillo. Is it something where I want to stay involved...?" (Scott did not remain involved).

Sheila considers it to be one of many great, spiritual experiences in which to participate. "It was a great weekend, and there were a lot of really neat things that happened." Particularly powerful was the "supper." She liked "the feeling I felt when I walked in and all the glory of it...I haven't forgotten that." But "I don't know how much that has affected me spiritually, you know, except that it's one more thing in my suitcase of things that makes me look forward to heaven."

DORIS: *"Full of surprises, but very emotional."*

General Background

Doris is a woman of retirement age, a life-long church member. On her screening survey she indicated that she was generally positive toward the Cursillo immediately following the weekend, but that now she was somewhere between generally neutral and generally negative. She reports that she knew "absolutely nothing" about the weekend before she went, though she had heard that there was "quite a discussion" about it in the Pella area a few years ago, and that some were "very negative on the thing." After she had been invited by a friend, she even asked her pastor whether or not he thought she should go, and he thought "it would be worthwhile." She was not sure how much he knew about the Cursillo: "maybe he knew more than he let out."

Doris could not say what she was expecting to get out of the weekend, because she didn't know what to expect. "I had no idea what it was going to be." She explains: "A friend of mine asked me to go, and she was my sponsor....'Someone would pick you up', that's all I knew."

The Immediate Impact of the Cursillo

Doris described the weekend as "full of surprises, but very emotional." She called it "a mountaintop experience." She was "quite amazed at some of the things that went on." She specifically mentioned surprise at "the letters you received and those kinds of things." She was caught off guard, because she "wasn't aware they were going to do anything like that." As the weekend progressed, "it really made me think about what heaven would be like." Yet the only thing she found particularly helpful about the weekend was that "it really taught me what it means to be a servant to others."

She did have some concerns about the weekend, however. She mentioned the emphasis on emotions: "It was a very emotional thing, sitting around the table and everybody has a sad story, and I had had several in my own life...." Did this discussion help her? "Well, it makes you very emotional, but to say that it was beneficial to bring that up, no, I don't know. I guess I'm not a real emotional person that really likes to dwell on this." She wasn't searching for an answer. Doris is a woman who accepts life's hardships as God's plan for her life. She does not "keep asking why, why, why." "It's really quite an emotional thing, and I don't think our religion or Christianity is based on feelings, emotions...." "It (the weekend) is all emotions."

And she noticed that some church members would become very enthusiastic about the Cursillo, while not showing much interest in their church. "I see people who will pay money to go work there (at the Cursillo weekend), where, if they had to do the same work in the church, they would say, 'No way.'" "If they're willing to pay a hundred dollars or whatever to go and clean toilets for a ...weekend, and you ask them to do something in church (they won't do it)." Why would someone pay to clean toilets at the Cursillo, but not help out at church? Doris was not sure. She suggested that "they maybe feel more useful there, and they really feel it's for a good cause, and maybe the church hasn't asked them to do certain things, or they don't feel comfortable." But she wasn't suggesting this was true of all Cursillo participants. "And I don't mean that I'm really opposed to Cursillo. I'm not saying that either."

A final concern was that the Cursillo retained some Spanish (she called it "Catholic") terms. She wasn't sure it was offensive, but still she wondered why it was necessary.

So what did it mean to her? "It was a very emotional thing," but she would not say that it was a very meaningful, life-changing event. In fact, she

Chapter 9: In Their Own Words: Sharing Cursillo Stories

cannot say that her life really changed in any way as a result of the Cursillo weekend. It did not really affect her relationship with her local church. "My church has always meant a lot to me, and I feel I have a close walk with God, and so, I don't know that it really enriched that part of it."

Nor did it really change her relationships with family members or friends. Even though some of her friends attended the same Cursillo weekend that she did, she didn't notice any differences in her relationships with those friends, or with any others.

The Purpose of the Cursillo

Doris was not sure about the purpose of the Cursillo. She thought that the emotional sharing might help some people, though it was not all that helpful for her. "I know God will take care of me, not that I don't have worries or anything like that. But I think there are people who don't have that, and maybe when they hear other peoples' stories and the part that faith has played in their lives, maybe that is beneficial to them."

The Means that Achieve the Impact of the Cursillo

When asked about what she thought tended to bring about the "mountaintop experience," Doris replied, "Because it's very emotional." She also cited "the way it's conducted." She specifically mentioned "the way they wait on you hand and foot." "It makes you humble." And she spoke of the "final banquet." "Well, I wasn't expecting all those people to come in there, and then you come into this hall, and you're invited to the banquet, just as Christ invites us to the banquet. And that really made an impression on me."

So why does the emotion tend to wear off? "Well, I think that's just part of life." She referred to other "mountaintop experiences" such as hearing inspiring speakers. For her, it is normal to have such experiences whose intensity fades with time.

But is all this emphasis on emotion tantamount to "emotional manipulation"? Doris would agree that it is. "I think that's very true." In fact, she said that she felt that way herself. She found herself sharing more than she really wanted to, that the emotion swept her along. "You get caught up in the emotion of the thing, and I don't think I would have told my whole story (or) said different things if it hadn't been that way. Not that I had anything to hide or anything like that. But I really didn't feel it necessary to bring out my whole story, but it's just set up that way. So I guess it is manipulation."

The Lasting Effects of the Cursillo

Doris had no further involvement with the Cursillo after the initial weekend. She never worked at a Cursillo weekend and did not attend any further meetings or closings. Since then, she has not experienced any extraordinary highs or lows in her Christian life. And Doris did not think the

Cursillo weekend changed her relationship with her local church any more than any other powerful experience would. "I think anytime that you have a mountaintop experience like that, whether it's Cursillo or some other thing, you're drawn closer, it's more meaningful to you, I think."

ED: *"It's kind of been our mission."*

General Background

A close relative had been trying to get Ed and his wife to go to the Cursillo for some time. Ed and his wife "kind of drug our feet because we just felt uncomfortable about it, cause we didn't know what it was." He admits to being "nervous the week before and even trying to get out of it a little bit," but his sponsor was insistent. "I had no idea what to expect. I knew it was a bunch of men that were going to be on a retreat weekend....All my (sponsor) told me was that you don't have to go up and talk, and you don't have to say too much if you don't want to, and it was good food, and that's about all he said." So since Ed didn't know what to expect, he had no particular expectations for the weekend. "I guess I just wanted to get it out of the way, cause he kept asking me to go. So I think I just went, just so he wouldn't ask me any more, to be honest."

The Immediate Impact of the Cursillo

Ed had a "delayed reaction" to the Cursillo weekend. "For me, the weekend was good. You heard good talks, and it was just a retreat. But the weekend didn't really take hold while I was there. I thought, 'Well, it's just a weekend.'" But a couple of weeks later, Ed found himself thinking about the subject of grace as he was driving. "I'm sure there have been pastors who have had sermons on grace, but it never really took hold, what grace really is, that God just forgives and forgives. And then, all at once, I was crying. I was going down the road, and it just happened." Ed says that this experience happened to him only once, and stresses that it was after the weekend, after a week had passed. "I can't explain it, it just started, grace came into my head, cause there were talks of grace, some of the speakers talked on grace, and I think God put that into my head at that moment."

In fact, Ed profited more from working subsequent weekends than from attending the initial weekend as a candidate. "A lot of my growing came afterwards, and it came after I worked a lot of Cursillo weekends. I probably got more out of working than actually going through it." He did not want to criticize the weekend: "It's just kind of a stepping stone, that's just where you start....Some men who go through there, and women, they just get their lives changed right there, but that didn't happen to me. Some have just real big testimonies on that it really hit them, but it wasn't the case with me."

Chapter 9: In Their Own Words: Sharing Cursillo Stories

Though Ed was nervous the week before he attended, he cannot recall having any doubts or concerns about what was going on during the weekend. It did stretch him at times, however. "You get out of your comfort zone a little bit.... A lot of these men that go, ...they've never been in situations like that where you have to go up front and say, 'John Smith from Sioux Falls, I go to First Church.' That was a stretch; it's just out of your comfort zone." Ed felt the same way occasionally. "At times I'm sure I thought, boy I'd sure like to be back home. Some of that stuff you're just not used to, but it was really good....I don't think I ever felt that I didn't want to be there. Just certain things that maybe we were doing that I felt uncomfortable with, but they were good. And after it was all over, you knew it was good."

Ed reported a mixed effect of the Cursillo on his relationship with his local church. On the one hand, during worship at the Cursillo he would "think back about how I was when I would sit in the pew." But at the Cursillo, "you just got more out of the service and you got fired up more. You wanted more. We would sing contemporary songs and we'd raise our hands, and it would just come in you more, and sometimes in the church it just seemed dead. I don't want to say that our church dead, but it is kinda.... (compared to the weekend)."

Ed indicated a greater kinship with the members of his church who have attended the Cursillo. But he recognized a danger. "We're close, we're like brothers and sisters, you know with a couple, and you have to watch that because you don't want it to be cliquish, because pretty soon, everybody thinks, you know that, 'Well, they went there'. So you've really got to watch that." Still, he enjoys the closeness: "Sometimes we'll have people come down here and listen to music and do things like that. But sometimes at church it seems a little bit dead."

Ed continues to work at Cursillo weekends: But "it kind of wears off like everything, and maybe it shouldn't but it does. When you get out of the weekend your highs are real high and slowly you come down. And after six weeks or so, you kind of come down again and everything levels off, and good or bad, that's the way it is with me. It would be nice to stay on that high all the time, but I can't, I mean, I do if I could meet with those couples all the time." Does his local church ever put him on a "high" like the Cursillo? Ed's answer is "No, no, nope. Not like, nope." Question: "Not even close?" Ed: "No."

Ed saw a dramatic effect on his family as a result of the Cursillo. "After my wife and I got back from Cursillo...then the kids started going to TEC and YATEC. So they went through TEC and YATEC, and it was just great. We were so much closer." Ed did not enjoy that kind of closeness in the home in which he grew up. "I was raised where my Dad never showed much emotion, a real hard worker. Love was never mentioned in my family, and through this I got to tell my sons that I loved them, which I never did, I never would have thought of."

"When my youngest son got out of YATEC, and then on the way home from that, he was really touched, and we got out and gave each other hugs, and said, 'Love you, Dad.' Maybe a lot of families do that, but we didn't. It was just kind of a big circle there with Cursillo, and YATEC and TEC, and it was just really a blessing to my family."

The immediate impact on Ed's friendships was that Ed began to recruit his friends to attend the Cursillo. Shortly after the weekend, Ed says, "I wanted to have other people go. And so then we started asking our friends….I couldn't wait, I was fired up get other people to go." And the Cursillo involvement brought new friendships. These new friends shared an immediate intimacy. "You'll see them now, and wherever you see them, most of the time you will embrace. There's just a bond there that you just, it's just a bond like a brother or sister." Ed says that it's a bond that is not really shared with other people, not even members of his own church who have not attended the Cursillo." And yet it would be possible: "Maybe you would if you would have a special something to do with them." He mentions a special, home Bible study from their church that met on a series of evenings. "We built a bond there, and that was special. But I just think that you've got to do something out of the ordinary, and you've got to do something…that makes you not comfortable, that lets you kind of bond with other people."

The Purpose of the Cursillo

For Ed, the purpose of the Cursillo is quite simple. It is to evangelize non-Christians, and to bring renewal to those who are Christians. "I would say (the Cursillo is about) changing lives. That's what I think it's about: helping people find the Lord, and if you know the Lord when you get there, the you just renew, you just get renewed, you just get fired up."

The Means that Achieve the Lasting Impact of the Cursillo

Ed thinks that the effects of the Cursillo are largely produced by the gradual bonding with others that takes place at the table groups. "When you walk in the doors the person who walks beside you is just like you are. I mean, you don't know what's going on. You know God, but you don't know to what extent you know God, and slowly together you grow together. You're sitting at a table and every talk, you learn a little bit, you discuss it, and every talk, you grow. You grow a little bit toward God, and there's a bonding there. When you grow with somebody toward God, there's a bond there." Near the beginning of the interview, Ed indicated that the "growth" that occurred, or at least a part of the process of that growth, involved becoming more willing to talk about your faith and your feelings. He describes his own experience: "You think being a Christian is going to church and stuff like that, but there's so much more than that, and I guess I learned that, that there's a lot more than just going to church. It was just good to see men come closer to God."

By coming "closer to God," Ed meant that men would "open up," that is, give up their reluctance to talk about personal issues, a reluctance he called "pride," or perhaps an unwillingness to share. "And it was slow, it was day by day and talk by talk, and our table would talk, and through sharing, you could just tell that men would kind of start to open up, because a lot of us have pride, and they would slowly, slowly, slowly start opening up and they would forget about their pride, and would start, and God would slowly come in and pride would go out. And at the end, it was mostly all God."

Apparently for Ed, the main benefit or work of God resulting from the Cursillo is an "opening up" that results in a more relaxed ability to talk about God and personal issues. "Before this weekend, it was hard for me to talk about certain things about God and stuff, and once you start to share, and you see how the sharing helps people and helps me, then you do it more." The mechanism by which men would "open up," by which "pride would go out and God would come in" is through men practicing and modeling such sharing at table groups.

So why does the effect wear off? According to Ed, it is due to distractions and a lack of practicing Christian disciplines. "I could sit down and read the Bible more, and if I wanted to I could go and pray with my pastor more, and then I would stay on more of a high that way. I get too busy, I get too involved with what's going on in the world, and that's why. So then you get these weekends, or if you meet with a Bible study, so then you get built up and fired up again. And why you don't keep that day by day, maybe some people do; I don't, I lose it."

Do the techniques used on the Cursillo weekend amount to emotional manipulation? Ed, at first, seemed completely surprised by the question. He did admit that during the weekend the organizers take participants' watches, cover the windows, publish no schedules, strand candidates at the retreat center by not permitting them to bring their own cars, and they do create "surprises." He also indicated that the weekend could make a candidate emotionally vulnerable.

Ed even volunteered some stories of people who were bothered by some of these peculiarities: a woman who refused to stay overnight at the retreat center, two men who actually walked away from the center. But all of these were brought back and had positive experiences in the end. "You know everybody's different. And some people are going to feel that way....You talk to those guys (who had walked away) now, and you can't believe how strong a weekend they had. It's just unbelievable. I mean, they didn't want to be there, they wanted out. And they didn't even know where they were walking, they were just going to walk and find a ride and get back home, but somehow God touched them."

The Lasting Effects of the Cursillo

Ed would say that he found a whole new mission in life through the Cursillo: sponsoring more people to attend Cursillo weekends. "We try to sponsor as many as we can I guess." He explains: "It's just that it's such a good weekend, that you just get blessed so much out of that. It's kind of been our mission, a different kind of a mission in a little way. You know, when you sponsor people, there is a cost, and I just feel that it's so good to spend money that way." "I love the closings cause people share what it meant to them, and that makes you feel really good, to see people that it touches their lives like that, changed lives, because some people have such hard lives, and to know that they can leave that life and be real happy is just great."

But it's not just adults attending the Cursillo: "We sponsored a lot of kids to go to TEC and YATEC, and it's just so good to go to the closings on the weekends and just see the change, even just the change that night." Sponsorship has brought him many close relationships: "So that's become a very important part of life, a mission, because all the people that we've sponsored, we're just close.... It just seems like there's something that you find a closeness to God through that weekend, with me. I found some kind of a closeness that I have, and it just seems like whoever goes has that same thing, it just bonds us together with something, it's something that, that kind of feeling that I don't have with people in our church, and other people don't have it either."

And speaking of the church, Ed has remained active in his local church even with his increased participation in the Cursillo. "I think (my church participation's) been stronger. I think I step forward a little more. I still get real nervous. But you make an effort to praise God more." He still participates in various forms of service: "Like now, putting on contemporary services, a while back did children's service, just different things in the groups and stuff, getting more involved, not for the reason to be involved, but just to serve God."

Still, he has some frustrations. "Our church is an old (he mentions an ethnic group) church, and to stand in the front row, if you're singing a hymn and God touches you all at once and you raise your hands, they'd probably want to commit you. It's just something that they don't understand. And sometimes you just really feel God that way."

Ed cherishes his walk with God: "I always ask for help. I always ask God for help, cause I know I'm not perfect and that I'm going to sin. But I just pray that I can serve him, and always try to serve him, always trying to do whatever he put in my brain that I can do....God's got to tell me what to do, to help somebody. I'm glad to help anybody, I love the Lord and he protects me and my family."

Chapter 9: In Their Own Words: Sharing Cursillo Stories

MARLYS: *"Just another piece of the puzzle that put my life together a bit."*

General Background

At the time she attended the Cursillo weekend, Marlys was a busy mom with young kids. She had experienced a loss and was suffering some mild depression. Marlys is a life-long Christian, very active in her local church. On her screening survey she marked that she was generally positive toward the Cursillo both immediately following and at the present. But she also wrote the following comment on the survey: "In between I was a bit negative, now back to positive." She said that her initial reaction to the weekend was that it was "very beneficial, a nurturing time probably, a growing time."

Some of her friends had been talking to Marlys and her husband about attending the Cursillo for a few years. Marlys states that she "always wanted to go, cause this stuff appeals to me," but her husband was "hesitant." Eventually he was convinced as well, and he enjoyed the weekend. All she knew about the Cursillo before attending was that "it was supposed to be very secretive....I knew that it would only be women there, and I knew that we'd probably be listening to speakers, and beyond that I was basically clueless." She also had spoken to friends who had attended and who enjoyed the weekend, but understood that they were instructed not to share very much because "there were lots of surprises" and "it's just more enjoyable if you don't have a lot of information." She did not attend with some great expectations, "just a little bit of spiritual renewal....I'd heard that people had good experiences."

The Immediate Impact of the Cursillo

Marlys' experience of the weekend began with some hesitancy. "I'm always that way if I leave home. It's like I just want to be back home again; I don't want to have to go through that two or three days or whatever when I'm going to be gone. I look forward to it, but when it actually comes.... So I remember my friend picking me up on Thursday night and me thinking, 'Ugh, I just wish it was Sunday and I was back here', and I didn't really want to go so much."

Her feeling of discomfort actually increased at first. "I remember feeling, when they take your watches away and everything, feeling a little bit trapped to a degree, I mean, not seriously, but 'OK, I'm not in control' and I like control sometimes, so that bothered me maybe a little bit. And it was a little bit uncomfortable at first just meeting the people, although I am pretty much a people person. I love meeting people; I love talking to people and stuff, but because you don't know them, you don't know where people are coming from and stuff. So maybe it was a little uncomfortable."

But for Marlys, the uneasiness dissipated quickly. As the weekend progresses "you just continue to grow closer to the people at your table, and I really like that. I felt like throughout the weekend that by the end of the time I felt pretty attached to some of the people, more some than others, but it was sort of like you come in feeling a little bit scared and hesitant, but you leave feeling very glad that you have done it."

What Marlys found particularly helpful was establishing some new friendships and the availability of the table leaders "if you wanted to talk about something." She appreciated "feeling the unity among not only your own table group but with the whole group" and "times where you could feel united with Christians of other backgrounds." But she also benefited from "realizing the depth a little bit more of God's grace." She understood that serving others was not "to get God's approval," but "because you want to do these things...because the Spirit is just working in you and you feel responsible to do them."

Marlys did have some concerns about the Cursillo, both before attending and during the weekend. Some friends who had attended voiced some doctrinal objections. "I do remember thinking that a little bit, 'Was this going to be theologically correct?'" And she was a bit uncomfortable with the "liturgies and things like that." "I thought, 'Ooo, this feels pretty Catholic or Lutheran.'"

And after the weekend, some matters concerned her as well. When she worked a weekend as a team member, she noticed that some fellow team members shirked their responsibilities. "I had one or two people on my team that just would go to sleep in their bunks instead of working, and I thought, 'We're hardly required to do anything!'....And so that frustrated me." But Marlys eventually discovered that one of these women must have been having problems because she later ended up going through a divorce.

She felt most discouraged, though, by the attitudes of some of the leaders "who were very intimidating to a lot of us." These leaders stressed their outward appearance and exhibited an attitude of superiority. "They just seemed to be the type of people that had it all together, and they're trying to lead us, and I'm thinking, 'We're not here to show off; we're here to serve.' So I guess that attitude bothered me, and I knew that they were very involved in it, and that discouraged me from getting more involved in it."

Another red flag was the fact that a good friend later attended the Cursillo and did not have a positive experience. "I think she kind of felt misplaced or displaced or something. She felt like she wasn't going through so much of the junk that the majority of the people at her table were. And so she almost felt like she was sort of counseling some of the people at her table, and sort of like she didn't really fit there, and part of it is her personality. But because of that, that kind of gave me, I tried not to feel negative, but it kind of discouraged us...."

Chapter 9: In Their Own Words: Sharing Cursillo Stories

At the conclusion of the weekend, Marlys thought it had been beneficial, but she quickly grew in her appreciation for it. "Since then I've really gained a sense more of God's grace and acceptance and just another awareness of the broadness and the depth of God's family. I think we can so often just get involved our own schools and churches, and just awareness again of how big His family really is. And just truly feeling that it's nothing that we do, it's God's love to us, and of course we do it out of our thanks, but, I think just a freedom, a sense of freedom that way, I think. That's probably what I'd say I gained most."

The Cursillo did not greatly change Marlys' life in the short run. The most immediate effect was "just feeling a little bit more connected to people who had gone through Cursillo. Having that spiritual connection more." For example, at the closing she discovered that people she already knew had attended the Cursillo before. And a co-worker who had attended the Cursillo before greeted her warmly on the Monday morning after the weekend. "So, feeling more spiritually united with some people I would say was the first benefit that I felt from it."

It had little impact on her relationship with her local church, however. She felt a bond with some fellow church members who had attended the closing. With respect to her family, she supposed it helped her and her husband to share "a little bit more spiritually" by "discussing some of the things that happened there." But she could not really say that it greatly affected her relationship with her children or extended family members. And it did not really affect her friendships very much, either, except the new friendships she had formed with her table group. With her other friends, she said, "I guess it just gave another source of conversation or a little bit more depth in a couple of areas."

The Purpose of the Cursillo

Marlys understands the purpose of the Cursillo to be both informational and practical. It involves deepening knowledge about "who God is" and "understanding the grace that we are given through him." But it also involves "taking it out." And she means this in two ways. First, by "not just staying there" in the Cursillo world, but taking the newfound truths and attitudes back to regular life, "the fourth day": facing questions, living as Christians in the world and engaging the same struggles as before the Cursillo weekend, "but hopefully with a whole different attitude about it."

But second, the Cursillo involves "taking it out" in the form of serving others, "to help people serve others." Apparently Marlys means "service" through participation in the Cursillo weekends. She spoke of a couple she was thinking of sponsoring, a couple that already exhibits skill and desire to serve. To her, the point of getting them involved in the Cursillo movement would be to allow them "to help others in their walk for Christ" by working at subsequent Cursillos.

The Means that Achieve the Impact of the Cursillo

When asked about the cause of the "mountaintop experience" of the Cursillo weekend, Marlys at first jokingly said, "Some people would say 'lack of sleep.'" She was referring to a common critique of the teenage version of Cursillo called TEC (Teens Encounter Christ): "Well, they're not sleeping well, and they're so emotional and stuff." Marlys discounts this appraisal: "I'm convinced it's the power of the Holy Spirit. I'm very convinced of that. And it's coming to the realization that it's about God and not about us. I think that is what produces it." Marlys did not define any specific way that the Cursillo weekend brings people to this "realization." And she would not describe her initiation as a "mountaintop experience." "I would say it was a good experience," not as powerful as something she has perhaps known at a Christian conference with her husband or with close Christian friends.

Why does it tend to wear off? Marlys chalked it up mainly to other distractions and responsibilities, and a separation from like-minded people. "You head back to your regular life, and you can't focus totally on it. You begin to focus on so many other things. And I think that on that weekend you're allowed to just focus totally on God, and I think any time you do that (it) is a very spiritual time of renewal....But you're not going to keep feeling that way because God gives you all kinds of other responsibilities. I think that's why it wears off, and a little bit because you're not around those people any more."

Marlys rejected the idea that she might have been subjected to emotional manipulation. She did not like some of the methods of taking the watches, covering the windows, lack of schedule, but she said that her distaste came more from "our independent society more than anything else." She saw it not so much in terms of manipulation but as "we have to give up control." For this reason, she did not think the Cursillo was for everyone. "I think you have to get to the point where you are willing to submit to the authority of somebody else a little bit." She did feel that her friend who reacted negatively to the weekend did mention something about not feeling she was as emotionally involved in it as were other people, and that this bothered her because she felt that she was not on "the same page" as everybody else, so that she could not relate, "or that she was just at a whole different stage on her spiritual journey...compared to the other people, and so she felt out of place."

The Lasting Effects of the Cursillo

Marlys does not think the Cursillo has had much of a long-term affect on her. She mentioned the immediacy she enjoys with some of her close friends who have attended Cursillo. She also mentioned the continuing feeling of grace and freedom, "like that was a part of the puzzle that God used in my

Chapter 9: In Their Own Words: Sharing Cursillo Stories

life, or a chapter in my life, or a page of a chapter." She and her husband have had some minimal continued involvement in the Cursillo, sponsoring a couple and attending a few closings. She felt it had little impact, if any, on her church involvement, which has "basically stayed the same," except that she has cut back to some extent in her volunteer work for the church.

She jotted down a note in preparation for the interview: "I felt very accepted, pampered, challenged, prepared, connected and nourished." "I guess as I look at my life, Cursillo has been one of the things that has helped me grow spiritually, and it helped me realize the grace of God. But I would say it's maybe one of several things that have done that in my life, probably equal to maybe four or five....I think it's just one of the factors, one of the puzzle pieces."

GUS: *"Not a mountaintop, but it was a good experience."*

General Background

Gus is a busy man, very involved in church leadership, in business and with his family. Finding time to attend the Cursillo weekend was difficult. In his screening survey, Gus indicated that he was generally positive about the Cursillo both immediately after the weekend and at the present. His relatives invited him and his wife to attend and were quite persistent. Gus thought he was too busy to go since he perceived that it might involve further time commitment beyond the initial weekend. But he and his wife finally agreed to attend, some six months before the weekend. Gus reported that he knew nothing at all about the weekend before it began.

"Whenever you ask them a question, it was a secret. 'Can't tell you. Can't tell you. Can't tell you.'" Gus would have appreciated it if they had simply said, "There's some really neat stuff that goes on and you're really going to like it, but eventually you'll know (what happens there)." The secrecy "Just didn't work good for me."

As the time approached, Gus announced that he was too busy to attend, but relented at the last minute. It was only then that he found out that he would not be able to have his car, mobile phone or even wristwatch at the retreat center. Gus arrived "just wound up, pretty tight." And he had no specific expectations for the weekend: "I was (only) appeasing my (relatives)...truthfully!"

The Immediate Impact of the Cursillo

Because he was so "tight" as the weekend started, he felt that he quickly became a special project by the leadership to help him loosen up. "I sat in the back row, and then they could see that this guy needs a little work." So they asked him to lead a prayer, which he said was a very truthful one: "(Lord), I don't really know what I'm doing here." As the weekend went on, he was surprised to see some men there that he knew, but was unaware of their connection with the Cursillo. And he was amused and somewhat bemused to find some of those very men dressed up as farmers and singing a "goofy" "chicken song."

Gus found the Stations of the Cross to be quite meaningful. And he learned to appreciate the table meal: "I was enjoying it, you know, once I got into it." Gus thought the weekend was good, but for various reasons he did not feel completely a part of the group. "I didn't get as heavily involved, (though) I did get involved. But I still probably had that 'observer' feeling a bit." During the interview, Gus got choked up as he recalled the encouragement letters he received during the weekend (he reported that it was not unusual for him to become emotional).

"That was something that just blew me away. The first day, the first afternoon when they kind of send you back to your bunk to relax a bit, and here you've got this whole pile of mail. It so amazed me, how many people knew about this deal; 'were praying for you.'" He mentioned being touched by receiving a letter from a man he had known for many years and had done business with. This was a side to him that Gus had never known. During the weekend, Gus had no concerns, doubts or questions it, beyond his objection to the absolute secrecy.

The weekend had little immediate impact on Gus' life. It did not significantly change his church involvement since he was already heavily involved with his church, nor did it have much effect on his relationship with family. He did not really find any new friends or begin to associate with any new people, though he was aware that men who attended the Cursillo would often remain close with their table group members.

The Purpose of the Cursillo

What did Gus understand the purpose of the Cursillo to be? His answer was succinct: "I think (it is about) deepening your relationship to the Lord, (a) deepening commitment-type thing. I think that's the bottom line of it."

The Means that Achieve the Impact of the Cursillo

And how are people brought to the point of this "deepened commitment?" Gus listed several factors. "I think the speakers that you have can say some really challenging things." The table group was also a factor. Even though Gus was a busy man, he could appreciate the power of the protracted length of time: "You pretty much set everything aside and you get pretty deeply involved with it so you really concentrate on what you're doing." And he mentioned the communal spirit and direction of the weekend: "Everybody's pretty much, well theoretically, doing the same thing." He mentioned the power of the candlelight at the end: "I think that's part of the mountaintop thing that people will say."

The Cursillo weekend was not all that powerfully moving for Gus. He explains: "I've had an awful lot of experiences ahead (of the Cursillo weekend) that were pretty neat, too, that were mountaintoppers in different things." And for various reasons Gus felt like he missed out on part of the weekend. "So, you know, for me to say it was a mountaintop experience, no, you know, it really wasn't. But it was a good experience."

So why does the "mountaintop experience" tend to fade away? It's like anything else: "Any experience that you have, you know, you have a memory of it, and you know, the memory lessens. There's emotion involved in there, too, especially emotion involved. And the longer it is, you know, it gets frittered away and then the emotion of it isn't there any more." If "especially emotion" is involved in the Cursillo weekend, did Gus think it includes emotional manipulation? He did: "That probably is true to a point, because the talks, usually there's some emotion in those, because somebody's talking about their experience and stuff, a lot of times, personal experience things, and so from what I heard and what I remember, yeah, you know, there's some emotional things said and some emotional things happen."

But Gus defended the emotional aspects: "If you can get someone emotionally involved, that they're not just sitting there as an observer, but they're emotionally involved, it's gonna click with them better, they're gonna remember it better. That's part of where that mountaintop thing is coming from also. But if you sit back and you do it as an observer and you're just kind of watching, then that's not as helpful. And that's kind of where I was, so that's not as helpful. And when I think about it, you know, there was a bunch of these things that did get me emotionally involved."

What would he say about other aspects of the weekend that might seem manipulative, such as taking participants' watches and masking the windows and the surprises? Gus thought the surprises were good. He didn't understand why they covered the windows, but he felt it didn't affect him. He was concerned about giving up his watch, "but once it was started it didn't make any difference." And he did not care about not having a schedule. "That didn't bother me at all." He thought churches might be better off if their worship services were not so tied to a schedule (i.e. bulletin).

The Lasting Effects of the Cursillo

Since the Cursillo weekend, Gus has remained a busy man with expanding family, community and business responsibilities. Aside from attending several closings, he has not had any further involvement in the Cursillo. He has remained very active in his local church. "I've always been heavily involved in the work of our local church. And that was part of why I didn't (become more involved with the Cursillo). I had enough stuff going on that I didn't need one more thing. All that stuff I was doing took a lot of time away from the family."

Gus did voice one concern about the lasting effects of the Cursillo, at least the lasting effect on some others, some he called "the strong Cursillo guys." Hesitantly he said, "I almost think that some of the guys, they almost set themselves a notch above the other local parishioners just because they did have this experience. And it's like, 'Well those guys back there, they don't know what they're doing' and stuff. I don't know; that's something that I don't think is a good thing. And, I don't know, as you listen to guys talk, you hear some of that sometimes. I don't think that's a good thing. And they preach against that, you know, when they wind that deal up. (At the closings) they talk hard against that, you know, to NOT you know, not go home and telling your pastor how to do everything, like you know all the answers. . . ."

And Gus thinks the Cursillo can be helpful: "You learn some really good things that will help you to serve better, and if you are a (church leader), if you're a past Cursillo person, you know, whatever, our job is to serve the Lord and to serve other people also. That's what I think. And if we're keeping our eyes open, if we're a leadership person, you know, you've got to be paying attention to the other folks around you. If you're serving them, that's going to help bond (you) to them also."

FRED: *"God opened my heart at Cursillo."*

General Background

Fred capably described himself and his initial interest in the Cursillo: "I was born and raised in the church and attended church regularly, but a lot of people go to Cursillo as seekers. I am the curious type, the adventurous one, and a friend at church asked me if I'd be interested in going. And I had heard of Cursillo, and didn't know what it was at all (about). It was kind of like, 'It's a big secret, and I want to find out what it is.' So I agreed to go. I also agreed for my wife, without asking her. But in any case, we went, and I found out that I had a fair amount of head knowledge, but I didn't have it in my heart. So God opened my heart at Cursillo. And, I don't know, I'm not certain to this day if I made a commitment or a recommitment, but I fully committed my life there at Cursillo. Whereas before, I think there were some strings attached."

Fred knew "almost nothing" about the Cursillo before going. "Cursillo is secret." He now understands that this is so as "not to spoil the surprise of things that happen there." The secrecy served to pique his interest: "You ask a few questions, and you get short, little, trite answers that were not enough, and it was a curiosity." He had heard it referred to many times and had often heard in church requests to "pray for the upcoming Cursillo." So when "a good friend of ours at church" asked if he and his wife would be interested, they agreed to go. He views the timing as "a God thing." And he got more than he expected from the weekend: "I was expecting to hear, if I may say, a bunch of good sermons, and having a good time with other people like myself, Christian people, just enjoying their company, and praise and worship, that sort of thing. I guess I didn't expect God to get in my head the way he did."

The Immediate Impact of the Cursillo

Fred looks back on the weekend as "a wonderful experience," so much so that he wishes he could get more and more people to go. He realizes that the goal of Cursillo is not simply to get people to go to the weekends, but "it's given us so much joy that you'd like to see the same joy revealed in others." He does recall having a few questions and concerns during the weekend: "At the beginning, you have doubts. You wonder if, they're doing some strange things here. I'm not allowed to wear a watch, and now we're going to have silent time where nobody talks to nobody, and you just have that time with God, and you view it all as kind of funky. See, you have some of those little doubts, but to say that I have some distressing doubts, no, pretty much go with the flow. At first, I think probably everybody puts some shield up, some barriers, some defenses." But the experience of the weekend was so altogether positive that his suggestion to the Cursillo leadership is: "Keep it up. As is."

He describes the impact it had on him: "(Early in the weekend) I came to this great awareness of how great my sins and miseries were, you know, how I was not really walking the walk. That's the fore-part. And as time progressed it was revealed to me that, you know, my biggest enemy was not what wrongs people had done to me and my resentment of that, but my biggest enemy was me and my inability to forgive people and my inability to forgive myself. You know, I knew God could forgive, but I couldn't let go of my past sins, like a stone in my leg or my arms full of luggage."

He felt himself opening up emotionally: "It all climaxes with being part of a Christian community where you feel this burden lifted from hiding from others." He mentions his ethnic heritage: "We were born and raised to be very into ourselves, not outgoing, not wearing our feelings or anything on the outside, you know, keeping them to ourselves, just grin and bear it, very closed people, opposed to other nationalities. And, you know, that's a struggle for many of us today yet. But when we're there, and even when we're not there at the meeting place of Cursillo, when we're gathered together as a body of Christ, a Christian community, we don't have that burden. We can be open, we can wear it on our shirtsleeve, what our sorrows, joys, concerns, everything is."

After the weekend, he noticed an immediate change in his attitude, especially at work. His business occasionally involves dealing with angry people, and he found that he could now get "somebody very angry to mellow out on the phone before he's done." He felt himself grow in relationships with other people, with new compassion, even a growing generosity with respect to money and giving.

How did it affect his relationship with his local church? He felt drawn to lend a hand to his pastor: "I'm a lot more supportive of my pastor... prayerfully supportive and publicly supportive and willing to go to him and work with him, and pick up some of the work load that he can't get around to. I've been on church boards, not currently serving, so I know, being a man of God, called by God, they need some help, too."

But it had a surprising effect on his family. For a time, it pushed one of his children away from the church. This child had "had some issues" with Fred, of which Fred was not aware. This child did not really believe that Fred was a changed man. But this has been resolved now for several years. He and his child are reconciled, and the child is back in church.

Fred was quite frank about the changes it made with some friendships: "You know, some friends you lose because of it. You've got a new life, and you don't sit around and have a few beers and revel in somebody else's (that you don't care for) misfortune, and talk down about other people. And so when you withdraw from that kind of walk, then you're not accepted any more. You can sit there and witness, and unless there's a heart-change on that person's part, unless there's a heart change on their part, they just view you as 'goody-two-shoes' or on a different plateau, or 'Jesus freak', or whatever you want to call it. And so you do annihilate some friends; you make some new ones. And the new ones you make are truly friends, where if you fall down, they pick you up."

The Purpose of the Cursillo

So what is the purpose of the Cursillo? For Fred, its purpose is to lead Christians into a greater personal authenticity, which, in turn, creates a more genuine Christian community. "It's building up the body of Christ through community, Christian community. And it's not about us, although we as people are the body of Christ. We have to be reflections of that, so people see that in us; they don't just see us going to church. That they see Christ in us, and so that is what Cursillo is. It's 'a short course in Christian living'. I know that's the short answer, but it's also a simple answer that says it all. It opens your mind, it opens your heart, grace is revealed, and that is building up the body."

The Means that Achieve the Impact of the Cursillo

So how does it work? What causes the changes? What creates the "mountaintop experience"? Fred seemed perplexed. "I can't explain that." He pointed to the methodology: "One would think that it's all orchestrated. It is so meticulously, carefully planned, you know, the talks and the program. And one would think, you know, everything's orchestrated to climax with this mountaintop experience, this emotional high, if you will." He was aware of criticism that would consider it nothing but "orchestration." "Some nay-sayers would say, 'Well, it's due to lack of sleep, you know, this is kind of like the pajama party, the dorm room, the out of-your-norm type thing, you know, you're sleeping in a bunk bed, and you're not getting good rest and you're putting in long days due to the discussion and worship and visiting, and so you get worn down, and that's how the emotions are (created). But I believe, and I firmly believe this, that you're all gathered together, your concentration is away from time, it's away from work, your focus is on Christ Jesus our Lord, and you're all of a common focus. And I believe the whole building is surrounded by God's grace. And the devil is outside of that force field, and I think that's what makes it all come together."

But it does not "all come together" for some. Fred knows some react unfavorably to the weekend: "And not that the devil doesn't seep in, you know, because we've had people already that have walked. They asked their sponsor to take them home, and their sponsor kind of gave them the hem-haw, and 'We'll see once; give it a little more time.' And they got just dissed about the whole thing and started walking down the road. And, you know, one of those guys that did that here a few years back, he's a good friend of mine today, and he is probably one of the most vocal witnesses for walking two miles down the road and having God turn his butt around and send him right back. And he does not know why. And he got back and he gave it just a little bit of time, and (it was) just like God split his melon and got in his head. And today he's a powerful witness. And it's kind of like 'Wow! This is Wow!' The guy was so mad that he'd walk, and all of a sudden get turned around on a gravel road and sent back."

So why does the sense of spiritual renewal tend to wear off? Fred thinks it is the neglect of persevering discipline. He likens it to the person who resolves to get into better physical condition. "It's like the dieter that watches the diet, does the good exercise. It gets to be summertime and food tastes a little bit better, there's barbeques and what not. We're busy and we don't do the running, or the walking or whatever. And I think the same thing is true with maintaining your spiritual life."

But does the fact that the weekend is "orchestrated" amount to emotional manipulation? How would Fred answer those who would say it felt like it to them? Fred appeared to grow defensive: "I would say, 'I'm sorry you feel that way, but, if it makes you feel any better, that never was the intent. There was no intention there... to manipulate your emotions.' There is no intention to mess with your emotions. Matter of fact, if there's a person who's having deep emotional trials, we encourage them to wait with going to Cursillo, because..., you know, it can put them into an overload, I know, where...it's possible that they could have a breakdown. I'm sure it is. So, you've got to be careful a little bit in your selection process."

When pressed on the use of disorienting techniques like taking people's watches or covering the windows so they do not know if it is night or day, Fred defended at least some of these methods. "Um, there is a time where we do paper windows, just to, we want to have the night time effect, rather than the daytime. You know, the day is still too long for the setting (for the banquet). And I guess they do paper a bit in the conference room. They're allowed to go outside, in breaks....It's just, like in a school setting, we don't want them gazing out the window thinking about that tractor driving in that cornfield, or whatever. Keep the focus where we want the focus to be. To eliminate the distractions."

"And the watch thing, I found that to be very refreshing, to tell you the truth. Cause in our busy lives, it seems like we're always fighting the clock, we're always out of time, you know. At Cursillo, time stands still....You don't have this conscious thing of time, time, time. It's just another distraction taken away from you. And that's good, it's good."

The Lasting Effects of the Cursillo

Fred has not experienced many disruptive life changes since attending the Cursillo weekend. He still works at the same job and lives in the same residence. Fred and his wife are "very, very involved" in their local church. "Sometimes, we think, too much. You know, because, like most churches, you've got 10% of the people doing 90% of the work. But, yeah, we're very active in the church: Sunday School, catechism, youth leaders, been elder, been deacon, been Sunday School superintendent, and call on the sick, and house visitation, visit families throughout the church and, yeah, been carpenter, been plumber, did the hands-on grunt work and, yeah, all those things."

He has become quite involved in the Cursillo movement. Of all the people interviewed, Fred is the only one who mentioned continuing participation in a "Fourth Day" small group. "It involves four couples who meet together twice a month. Though not involved in every Cursillo weekend, he relishes them: "Only so many people can come, and...I still want to leave the opportunity open (to others). I don't want to be hogging. There's a number of people that... hardly ever miss one."

But Fred and his wife continue to attend many of the closings: "Not all of them...(b)ecause they get quite full. We've gone to closings already, when you read the list, (you think) 'Boy, those people are really bad!' (But they) went through as candidates, and (at the) closing...they're just in awe by the community that shows up for that, and the faces in the community. They can't (believe it): 'You've gone?! You know about this?!' And they become part of the (Cursillo) community. And they know that they can rely on their community."

10. *Thinking Through the Stories*

Out of the eighty-three invited to participate (originally eighty-eight, but four came back with "no such address" and one was deceased), only nineteen (less than 25%) agreed to be interviewed, and five of these were something less than fully enthusiastic about the Cursillo.[402]

There was general agreement among those interviewed with regards to the emotional nature of the weekend and their appreciation for the hard work, servant attitude, and earnestness of the leadership. There was, however, less concurrence on the issues which most concerned me, namely: 1) the purpose of the movement, 2) the means that achieve the impact, or 3) the long-term personal effect of the Cursillo weekend.

1. How do past participants in the Cursillo weekend presently understand the purpose of the movement?

Some understood the purpose of the weekend in terms of personal, spiritual growth. Doris thought that the emotional sharing might help some people, though she was not much affected by it. Gus saw the purpose as deepening one's relationship with and commitment to the Lord. Scott and Sheila also understood it in individualistic terms. For Sheila it meant people getting closer to the Lord and experiencing unconditional grace. Scott saw it as an attempt to integrate beliefs with practice.

Others appreciated more the community aspect of the Cursillo weekend. Marlys pointed to the practical impact it might have on others.

---

[402] I was surprised by the relatively small number of past Cursillo participants who wanted to talk about their experience some eight years later. The retired RCA pastor who served in Cursillo leadership in Northwest Iowa had called the weekend "this king of revival and miracles and movement of the Holy Spirit." Early Roman Catholic Cursillo promoter Bishop Juan Hervás claimed a success rate of almost 100% of those who persevere after the weekend (*Questions and Problems Concerning Cursillos in Christianity*, 328).

Deepened knowledge about God was to be implemented in everyday life, especially in a life of serving others. Barb focused on the experience of Christian community during the weekend itself as "the best picture I have ever had about what Christian community should be." It was intended to equip her to live that same kind of community outside of and beyond the weekend. For Fred the Christian community experienced during the weekend helped build up the body of Christ, so that Christians could then be more effective models of Christ to others.

However, none of the participants understood the true purpose of the Cursillo as intended by its Roman Catholic founders. As Cursillo historian, Ivan Rohloff noted, "the (weekend) Cursillo exercise is the least important component of the method."[403] Rather, the ultimate goal is 1) locating the people who are the "backbone" of various "environments," 2) "converting" them into leaders during the Cursillo weekend, and 3) turning them back to evangelize their environments, all the while connecting them and supporting them through continued group reunions and ultreya meetings.

2. What is their understanding of the means that were used to achieve the impact?

When it came to the means employed to create the effect, the participants also differed in their understanding. Some pointed exclusively to the means used. For Doris, for example, the experience was largely, if not exclusively emotional. Being waited on "hand and foot" was humbling. The final banquet "made an impression" on her. Sheila attributed much to the "secrecy and surprises." "Secrecy adds power to things, whether it's a good power or a bad power." And the "hype" before the weekend built up expectations and emotional fervor. Gus likewise pointed to the techniques employed: the speakers said "some really challenging things." The length of the weekend, lack of distractions and the communal spirit helped focus and raise emotion, as did the symbolic candlelight service.

On the other hand, Scott attributed the whole effect to the power of meeting with God. The Word and prayer were the means to this end. But if the effect was entirely due to God's work through the Word and prayer, then Scott failed to explain why the techniques were necessary.

Marlys and Fred acknowledged the common allegations that the effects were due to manipulative techniques. Marlys admitted discomfort at some of the aspects of the weekend. And she joked that some would say the effects were all due to "lack of sleep" and becoming emotional as a result. But she rejects this notion and is convinced it is all due to the power of the Holy Spirit.

---

[403] Rohloff, *The Origins and Development of Cursillo (1939-1973)*, 55.

Fred noted that as the weekend begins "everybody puts some shield up, some barriers, some defenses...." And he admitted that it all seemed very "orchestrated....It is so meticulously, carefully planned...." He pointed to the charge of the sleep deprivation, the "pajama party, the dorm room, the out-of-your-norm thing." But he discounted these and attributed the effect to the common focus on Christ and the grace of God. Yet both Marlys and Fred failed to answer the very criticisms they raised. If in other situations such as "pajama parties" lack of sleep produces emotionalism, why should the emotional high experienced by the worn-out Cursillo participants be attributed entirely to God's work and not at all to sleep deprivation?

Ed and Barb were willing to acknowledge a cooperation between human means and God's grace. For Ed, the results came from the gradual bonding with others that took place at the table groups. The "growth" that took place, according to Ed, was opening up emotionally, so that you were more willing to talk about personal issues and struggles. As men "opened up" and let go of their "pride," or reluctance to share, God would come in. And the mechanism that achieved this opening up was through observing other men who were already opened up emotionally and who modeled sharing at table groups. Barb gave credit for the results to the Holy Spirit and to the relaxed, unhurried, and non-judgmental "setting" of the weekend. But both Ed and Barb then face Dragostin's knotty question:

> Finally, there is the extent to which one emphasizes that the effects of the *cursillo* are the result of divine grace or the natural outcome of well-known social psychological techniques. This is not a question that lends itself to empirical evidence. If you insist that the effects of the *cursillo* are entirely the effect of Divine grace, then to whom do you attribute the non-random instances of fanaticism and the rare instances of complete personality disorganization? I would also like to know why God's grace habitually stops short with whole classes of people for whom the *cursillo* is not "a fitting means." The maximalists will answer that only the good effects are to be attributed to the Holy Spirit. When things go wrong, the human element is to blame. As I said, the question does not lend itself to empirical evidence.[404]

If the effects of the Cursillo weekend are attributed to the work of the Holy Spirit, then how does one account for the fact that the effects invariably fade over time, often quite rapidly? Scott, Doris and Gus suggest that this is quite natural, part of the emotional ebb and flow of the ordinary Christian life.

---

[404] Dragostin, "The Cursillo as a Social Movement," 489.

Scott acknowledges this to be true of any other "spiritual retreat." "We live in a fallen world; we aren't in heaven yet." Doris agrees: it is just "part of life," as when you have other "mountaintop experiences." Gus thinks that it is especially the "memory" and the "emotion" of the event that naturally fade with time, as do all memories and emotions.

But the other participants point to some kind of failing on our part to explain why the power of the experience fades. Barb states flatly, "Cause we're sinners." It is not that God walks away from us, but that we walk away from him. Fred thinks it is due to a lack of persevering discipline, much like the dieter who eventually falls back into old, unhealthy eating habits. Ed confesses a lack of practicing Christian disciplines: "I could sit down and read the Bible more, and, if I wanted to, I could go and pray with my pastor more, and then I would stay on more of a high that way." Sheila sees it as a failure to live out our discipleship on a daily basis. Marlys agrees: "You head back to your regular life, and you can't focus totally on it....I think that's why it wears off, and a little bit because you're not around those people any more."

What's interesting is that none of the participants clearly perceives the obvious. On the weekend several methods are employed which produce the "high." After the weekend, the means are discontinued, and so the high is not sustained.

And some of the participants also seem to share several unspoken assumptions:

1. This emotional "high" is desirable and valuable and is to be retained.
2. This emotional "high" is closely identified with, if not identical to true Christianity.
3. This emotional "high" should be our normal experience, but it gets stifled by the demands of "regular life."
4. Vital Christianity is experienced or recaptured on these weekends, only to be gradually diminished in the "real world."

But do the techniques of the Cursillo weekend amount to emotional manipulation? The answers here also varied widely. Doris agreed that the strong emotional component was manipulative. She found herself sharing more than she intended, swept away with the emotion, and it made her uncomfortable (though she said she did not have anything to hide). Both Scott and Sheila said they felt elements of emotional pressure, especially through the secrecy and surprises, but would not consider it manipulation. Marlys denied that manipulation took place. She thought that people who felt uncomfortable were having trouble relinquishing control to others, due to "our independent society more than anything else." And that meant that Cursillo might not be for everyone.

Chapter 10: Thinking Through the Stories 183

Barb thought it very possible that people might feel manipulated during the weekend but was unconcerned. She felt delighted by the very elements that others might consider manipulative. "We are all very different people," and some might not respond well to the Cursillo weekend.

Ed and Gus agreed that elements of the weekend might involve emotional manipulation, but excused it for the positive results that were achieved. Ed noted some who reacted unfavorably at first, but "had positive experiences in the end." Gus noted that these elements helped people "get emotionally involved" so that they were no longer observers but participants.

Fred reacted most strongly to the allegations of manipulation. He insisted that there was no intention to "mess with your emotions." Fred noted that if a person was having "deep emotional trials" they were encouraged "to wait with going to Cursillo," because "it can put them into an overload…. It's possible that they could have a breakdown." He defended the techniques of masking the windows and taking away watches as simply eliminating distractions.

Notice that all of the participants acknowledged that the Cursillo weekend employed emotionally manipulative (or at least pressuring) techniques. Only one, Doris, objected strongly to this. The rest either downplayed their effect or excused their use either because they personally enjoyed them or felt that they accomplished a greater good.

3. What do past participants perceive to be the long-term personal effects (especially with regards to their relationship with their local church) and how have these effects either deepened or diminished over time?

Once again, the participants expressed widely divergent responses. Over eight years after their initiation, five of these eight participants reported very little lasting value from the weekend. Not surprisingly, none of these five remained active in Cursillo work. And for all five, it was the initial impact of the weekend that seemed to be the greatest factor in determining both continued involvement and long-term impact.

Gus said that he had an enjoyable weekend, but not a mountaintop experience. He had had other more powerful spiritual experiences before attending the weekend. And he was too busy to remain involved. Marlys likewise had a positive weekend, though not a great emotional high. She even worked a weekend or two afterward, but was soured by some of the attitudes exhibited by her co-workers on the Cursillo team. Scott and Sheila had enjoyable weekends, especially Sheila. But they sensed nothing special or unique that would make them want to continue, and neither would consider the Cursillo weekend as having any significant connection to their present spiritual life. Both were troubled by some of the aspects of the weekend or attitudes of those in leadership. Doris acknowledged that it was a mountaintop experience for her, but found parts of the weekend so troubling that she had no further involvement.

Ed, however, did have a deeply emotional experience, albeit delayed by about a week. He has remained very involved in the Cursillo ever since. "A lot of my growing came afterwards, and it came after I worked a lot of Cursillo weekends. I probably got more out of working than actually going through it." In fact, he found "a new mission in life": sponsoring many others to attend, working many weekends, and gaining new friendships with those he has sponsored. Fred, likewise, was deeply impacted by the weekend, and this also led to regular involvement: sponsoring others and working weekends. Fred alone said that he had participated faithfully in a monthly small group of Cursillo participants ever since the initial weekend over eight years ago. And Barb had been involved faithfully with the Cursillo since her initial weekend, which was very positive. "It felt like I was going home spiritually." She has served in various leadership roles in the Cursillo movement and has gained many like-minded friends.

Not surprisingly, the participants' relationship with their local church has mirrored their response to the Cursillo. Those who had only a mild experience on the Cursillo weekend and so had no further participation with it, also tended to see the least impact on their church involvement. Doris never attended another Cursillo event and remained quite active in her local church. Gus attended a few closings but elected to continue serving in his church. Sheila reports no impact at all in her church involvement. Scott came to perceive the Cursillo as competing with the local church. He had no desire to join a Cursillo small group: "The idea of establishing a supportive Christian community seemed to me to be what the local church was supposed to do, and so I didn't feel the need to be looking for another avenue." Marlys was only minimally involved with post-weekend Cursillo work and remained active in her local church, though she says that she does not volunteer at church as much as she did before.

Ed became very involved with Cursillo but also remained active in his local church. He did, however, become critical of his church when he compared it to his Cursillo work. He said he "got fired up more" on Cursillo weekends. But "sometimes in the church it just seemed dead. I don't want to say that our church is dead, but it is, kinda," compared to the weekend. The local church never creates the emotional "high" experience as does the Cursillo weekend. "Not even close." He admits to feeling a greater kinship with those in his church who have attended the Cursillo. He enjoys the closeness with them, but knows it can become a problem: "You don't want to be cliquish." He still attends church and serves faithfully, but he has frustrations: "It's just something that they don't understand."

Chapter 10: Thinking Through the Stories

Barb has experienced a withdrawal from her local church proportional to her growing participation with the Cursillo. She said she felt little affinity with those in her church, assuming they would not be interested in her Cursillo experiences, though she did feel "an automatic bond" with those few in her church who had attended Cursillo. In fact, through the Cursillo she found "a whole new body of friends," something she had been longing for, having "felt isolated for years." What's more, she has become active in a new, smaller church, having "withdrawn" from her original church.

Fred alone has managed to remain deeply involved in both Cursillo work and in his local church, "very, very involved." "Sometimes we think (involved) too much" in church. It is perhaps significant that his church is apparently favorable toward the Cursillo. Before he attended the weekend he said his interest was piqued by "prayer requests" in church to "pray for the upcoming Cursillo," and that he and his wife had been sponsored by friends "from church." Unlike Scott, Fred has apparently perceived no competition between the Cursillo and the local church.

11. *The Unpaid Bills of the Church*

In his book, *The Four Major Cults*, Anthony A. Hoekema begins with a familiar expression: "The cults are the unpaid bills of the church." He explains:

> Though this statement does not tell the whole story, there is a great deal of truth in it. Cults have sometimes arisen because the established churches have failed to emphasize certain important aspects of religious life, or have neglected certain techniques. Though one may assign many reasons for the rapid growth of the cults, one reason we may be sure of: people often find in the cults emphases and practices which they miss in the established churches.[405]

He hastens to add, though, that "This is not to suggest that where the cults differ from the churches, the cults are invariably right and the churches are always wrong."[406]

Though I insist once again that the Cursillo is not a cult, perhaps we could say the same is true about the popularity of the many expressions of the Cursillo method. The Cursillo was born in the context of a dead and formalistic Roman Catholic Church in Spain. Though I suspect that many of the enthusiastic promoters of the Protestant Cursillo expressions today are unrealistic in their demands of the church, perhaps the Cursillo does touch some nerves that reveal areas of neglect in contemporary Protestant churches. While certainly not endorsing or participating in Cursillo events, church leaders today might be wise humbly to listen and learn from those who appreciate the Cursillo.

Several comments by the past Cursillo participants I interviewed indicated that in some ways the Cursillo movement is attempting to do what the local church should be and may not be doing. Ed compared the Cursillo

---

[405] Anthony A. Hoekema, *The Four Major Cults* (Grand Rapids, Michigan: William B. Eerdmans Publishing Co., 1963), 1.
[406] Ibid.

weekend to his local church, and the church was found wanting. Barb found that her Cursillo work gave her a spiritual high far superior to anything she experienced in church. She found herself withdrawing more and more from her local church because she felt a greater affinity with the new community she found at Cursillo. Perhaps Scott's perspective was most perceptive. He noted controversy in his church. There was a clear sense that Cursillo was in competition with the local church's ministry. Scott himself could not recall if he was invited to join a Cursillo small group after the weekend, but he did note that he would not be interested even if asked: *"The idea of establishing a supportive Christian community seemed to me to be what the local church was supposed to do*, and so I didn't feel the need to be looking for another avenue." (emphasis added)

From the participants' comments it is clear that the Cursillo is attempting to compensate for some perceived lack in the life and worship of the local church. Not surprisingly, the Cursillo weekend incorporates several aspects of the church's regular program, though often in a modified form. And the continued program of small groups and "working" Cursillo weekends is expressly intended to provide "a supportive Christian community" for those involved. This might account for some of the acknowledged disaffection with the local church.

The Cursillo apparently seeks to revitalize the church. In the original context of mid-twentieth-century, Roman Catholic Spain, this revitalization was thought to be necessary. Perhaps the Reformed Cursillo in Northwest Iowa which I studied is also responding to a perceived need for church revitalization. In some cases the Cursillo "becomes" the church for some participants. This may be due to the fact that the Cursillo weekend imitates or employs portions of the church's regular ministry, but often in a modified or truncated form. I suggest that the Cursillo tries to provide 1) the ministry of the Word, 2) the sacraments, 3) prayer, 4) Christian community, 5) Sabbath, and 6) a heart on fire.

1. The Ministry of the Word in Cursillo.

The Word of God is certainly the primary means of grace. According to the Westminster Shorter Catechism, the Word, along with the sacraments and prayer, is among "the outward and ordinary means whereby Christ communicateth to us the benefits of the redemption" (Q. 88). Specifically, "(t)he Spirit of God maketh the reading, but especially the preaching, of the Word an effectual means of convincing and converting sinners, and of building them up in holiness and comfort, through faith unto salvation" (Q. 89).

The Cursillo weekend features several "talks." What is interesting is that none of the participants I interviewed mentioned any specific Scripture that they heard or that became meaningful to them. Scott and Sheila specifically stated that they did not learn anything new during the weekend. Gus mentioned the impact of speakers who "say some really challenging things," but much of the teaching he cited was in the form of emotional sharing and storytelling. Scott had questions about some of the speakers' qualifications, whether or not they were really "walking the talk." Sheila disagreed with some of the teachings and found that her table leaders were not open to questions or discussion/debate.

The specific teaching that was mentioned by several participants was the message of "grace" which apparently means "forgiveness." Ed was impacted by hearing "what grace really is, *that God just forgives and forgives*" (emphasis added). Marlys defined this grace in terms of serving others not "to get God's approval," but "because you want to do these things." Barb mentioned that the grace of Christ extended to her so that she said she could "forgive (her)self for different things" and "forgive other people who had hurt (her)." Fred described how early in the weekend he became aware of "how great my sins and miseries were," but later came to understand that "my biggest enemy was me and my inability to forgive people and my inability to forgive myself." Grace certainly is a central message in God's Word, a worthy subject for discussion. But these participants reflect a truncated view of grace as mere forgiveness ("God just forgives and forgives") and largely "forgiving myself."

The notion of grace as self-forgiveness is a recent, psychological innovation, unknown in Scripture. Forgiveness presupposes an offense. An offense is a violation of God's Law, a trespass against another that incurs a debt and fractures a relationship. It causes a right sense of moral outrage, and it requires punishment as an act of divine justice. For this reason, self-forgiveness is unnecessary, because any offense is not really against us but against God and/or another person. Those interviewed may simply have meant that they needed to accept Christ's forgiveness for past failures, but to speak of a need for "self-forgiveness" would be biblically and theologically inaccurate.[407]

2. The Sacraments in Cursillo.

During the Cursillo weekend, participants are invited to share in the Lord's Supper. Communion is also one of the primary means of grace. The sacraments are "an effectual means of salvation" (Westminster Shorter Catechism Q. 91). The Lord's Supper is "a holy ordinance instituted by Christ, wherein, by sensible signs, Christ and the benefits of the new covenant are represented, sealed, and applied to believers" (Q. 92).

Interestingly, none of the participants mentioned sharing in the Lord's Supper as having any particular impact on them. In fact, none of them

---

[407] For a critique of "self-forgiveness" see Robert D. Jones, *Forgiveness: "I Just Can't Forgive Myself!"* (Phillipsburg, NJ: P & R Publishing, 1999).

mentioned it at all. What several did speak of, often in glowing terms, were other symbolic actions and rituals that did create a powerful influence. Gus mentioned the "stations of the cross" as quite meaningful to him. He also pointed to the "candlelight service at the end." Doris was humbled by "the way they wait on you hand and foot" and was impressed by the "banquet." Sheila also pointed to the "supper," especially "the feeling I felt when I walked in and all the glory of it;...I haven't forgotten that." Most all reflected on the power of the "secrecy and surprises."

It is ironic, even troubling, that the beauty and simplicity of the Lord's Supper, which has been instituted by the Lord himself, becomes obscured or overshadowed by the more emotionally powerful rituals of the stations or the banquet or the candlelighting, none of which has been authorized by Christ.

3. Prayer in Cursillo.

Who could question the central importance of prayer in the ministry of the church? The Westminster Shorter Catechism defines prayer as "an offering up of our desires unto God, for things agreeable to his will, in the name of Christ, with confession of our sins, and thankful acknowledgment of his mercies" (Q. 98). James declares: "Therefore, confess your sins to one another and pray for one another, that you may be healed. The prayer of a righteous person has great power as it is working" (James 5:16). Our Lord Jesus specifically called his people to "secret" prayer as opposed to outward and announced prayer (Matt. 6:4-6).

But once again the participants seldom mentioned prayer as a significant factor during the weekend, even though it is one of the primary means of grace. What they did mention was "palanca," letters and notes from people who said they were praying for them. It appears that what impacted many of the participants was not necessarily prayer but the explicit communication that others were praying for them. Doris was surprised at "the letters you received," notes which stated that close friends or complete strangers were praying for her. Sheila also appreciated the many people who "were supporting me in prayer and through their cares and gifts and notes." Perhaps most impressed was Gus, who, when he recalled receiving his palanca notes (promises of prayer) during the interview was moved to tears: "That was something that just blew me away. The first day, the first afternoon when they kind of send you back to your bunk to relax a bit, and here you've got this whole pile of mail....It so amazed me, how many people knew about this deal, were praying for you."

Undoubtedly during the Cursillo weekend there is much genuine prayer offered for candidates and their families. Prayer honors God. It acknowledges what only God can do and what we cannot do. And for this reason secret, unannounced prayer is most honoring to God. But because it is announced through notes and letters at critical times during the weekend, prayer in the Cursillo seems calculated to provide its most potent psychological effect. It becomes "palanca" (Spanish for "lever"), a "lever" to move the stubborn or emotionless candidate, used to impress him or her with the message: "someone is praying for you." To be assured of the prayers of others can bring great comfort. The Apostle Paul often reported his prayers for the churches to which he wrote (see Eph. 1:15ff., Philip. 1:9ff., Col. 1:9ff., etc.). One suspects, however, that in the Cursillo method, the psychological pressure of the announcement of this sacrificial prayer is calculated to impress or move the candidate.

4. Christian Community in the Cursillo.

Christian community or fellowship is essential to the life of the church. The New Testament term for church requires a community, for it literally means "assembly" or "congregation." And God's people are to come together frequently, "not neglecting to meet together, as is the habit of some, but encouraging one another, and all the more as you see the Day drawing near" (Heb. 10:25).

The Cursillo weekend seeks to give Christians an experience of Christian community. But it does so in a context that is separated from the day-to-day pressures and responsibilities of life. Perhaps Barb said it best: "...Cursillo is also the best picture I have ever had about what Christian community should be. And I know it can be that kind of picture because it's isolated from the real world, you know: every care, everything else is set aside, and you come together, and you really experience Christian community. So in a way it's false...in a sense, because there's nothing else vying for your time." Marlys likewise notes the effect of the cloistered life at Cursillo and the difficulty that comes afterward: "You head back to your regular life, and you can't focus totally on it."

And this Christian community at Cursillo is based on unconditional love. Barb states: "Every time I go, I think, 'This really is what Christian community should be! This really is what it should be like, that we are accepting each other where we're at, for who we are, with whatever hurts, problems, sins, whatever it is we've got, we're accepting each other." She describes it as a freedom: "I think that Cursillo provides that atmosphere, for them, for a person, however they want, to relate to God, if they want to relate to him in 'I hate You', 'I'm angry with You', it's there, that environment is there because they have the freedom to do that."

Fred describes it as a burden being lifted: "It all climaxes with being part of Christian community where you feel this burden lifted from hiding from others. We were born and raised to be very into ourselves, not outgoing, not wearing our feelings or anything on the outside, you know, keeping them to ourselves, just grin and bear it, very closed people, opposed to other nationalities. And, you know, that's a struggle for many of us today yet. But when we're there, and even when we're not there at the meeting place of Cursillo, when we're gathered together as a body of Christ, a Christian community, we don't have that burden. We can be open, we can wear it on our shirtsleeve, what our sorrows, joys, concerns, everything is."

During the weekend experience, "unconditional love" is offered freely and in great abundance. This is crucial to develop the unity and family feeling essential to a successful weekend. For many reasons, our culture produces lonely people. Marital breakups, impersonal workplaces, busy lives, passive forms of entertainment, as well as the general self-centeredness of contemporary life combine to produce people starving for affection and care. In such weekends, these are offered in great measure. People are often told they are loved unconditionally. Participants are taken seriously and are listened to with interest. In the small group sharing there are "no wrong answers."

As noted before, all of this is reminiscent of the "unconditional positive regard" used in the "non-directive, client-centered" psychotherapy approach championed by Carl Rogers. There as well, the purpose of the "unconditional positive regard" is to "break down psychological defense mechanisms." According to Rogers, the problem is that clients have internalized their parents' "conditional positive regard."

> If the therapist can demonstrate unconditional positive regard for the client, then the client can begin to become more accurately aware of the experiences that were previously distorted or denied because they threatened a loss of positive regard from significant others. When clients perceive such unconditional positive regard, existing conditions of worth are weakened or dissolved and are replaced by a stronger unconditional positive self-regard. If the therapist who matters is able to prize and consistently care about clients no matter what the clients are experiencing or expressing, then the clients become free to accept all that they are with love and caring.[408]

In the paragraph above, one could easily substitute the words, "Cursillo leader" for "therapist," and "candidate" for "client." The goal of this therapy is a "catharsis" in which a client gets in touch with his or her feelings and is able to "fully express the feelings of the moment." At the same time, "emotional experiences that were previously denied are bubbling up." "The release and acceptance of such feelings are frequently vivid, intense and dramatic for the

---

[408] Prochaska, *Systems of Psychotherapy: A Transtheoretical Analysis)*, 117-118.

clients...."[409] The emotional release described here as a result of psychotherapy is remarkably similar to the catharsis and high experienced on the weekend renewal experience.

But this wonderful experience of "Christian community" often backfires. For one thing, it is (in Barb's words) "false." It cannot be sustained beyond the weekend because the same dynamics do not exist in the world outside of the retreat center, the very world in which we are called to live out our discipleship and Christian community. Sheila noted this problem: during the weekend "the feeling that's trying to be created is, 'You are loved and accepted for who you are' in a kind of 'showering of love'." But, she says, she found herself disappointed after the weekend, when that "showering of love" did not seem to be transferred to "people who aren't in the church," to "the non-Christian or the Hispanic on the street who doesn't experience that." For her it was the feeling of "a dissociation between Cursillo and real life, feeling like not all of that is overlapping to what I see going on in our community at large."

For another thing, ordinary church life must pale by comparison. In the church, where we are not "isolated from real life" we cannot practice this "unconditional love" or "non-judgmental, blanket acceptance." Certainly Scripture teaches that we are "accept one another" (Rom. 15:7), but we must also "submit to one another" (Eph. 5:21), "admonish one another" (Col. 3:16), "exhort one another" (Heb. 3:13) and "stir up one another" (Heb. 10:24).[410] Such an unreal, distorted view of "Christian community" cannot help but create disappointment with the local church.

But there is a further concern with the Cursillo's variety of Christian community. Both Barb and Marlys mentioned the need to relinquish control to the Cursillo leaders. When Barb was asked about some of the aspects of the weekend that others perceived as manipulation, she replied, "I loved it! You know why? Cause I had no control over myself. It wasn't about me. It was like, 'Here, Lord, here, here I am. What are you going to do, what are you going to show me? I've got nothing. I've got nothing here. I can't control a thing.' And I loved being in that position. So, see, it's me, that's me, and other people aren't like that. So then they would probably take some of those things as 'You're controlling me. You're telling me what to do or not to do.'" Similarly, Marlys stated, "We have to give up control....I think you have to get to the point where you are willing to submit to the authority of somebody else a little bit."

In the God-ordained institutions of family, church, and government, we are called by the fifth commandment to submit in the Lord to lawful

---

[409] Ibid., 122.
[410] For a critique of the use of "unconditional" to describe God's love see David Powlison, *God's Love: Better Than Unconditional* (P & R Publishing: Phillipsburg, NJ, 2001).

authority. But the Cursillo weekend is neither family, church, nor government. Submitting one's will to the control of others, especially those who refuse to inform participants of what they are going to do, and who require symbolic capitulation through surrendering watch and cell phone, is not only unwise, it can be dangerous. This is an aspect of the Cursillo movement that is most chilling, perhaps even cult-like.

5. The Sabbath in the Cursillo.

Several of the participants seemed to be expressing an appreciation for the "Sabbath" aspect of the weekend. Barb spoke of the Cursillo allowing a proper "setting." She gave an analogy of the hassled married couple finding renewal in the relaxed atmosphere of a weeklong vacation, just the two of them, with no distractions. In defending the confiscation of watches and masking the windows, Fred observed: "in our busy lives, it seems like we're always fighting the clock, we're always out of time, you know. At Cursillo, time stands still….You don't have this conscious thing of time, time, time. It's just another distraction taken away from you. And that's good, it's good." Gus suggested that not having a published schedule as at the Cursillo weekend might be a good practice for church worship services, so they would not be so tied to a schedule/bulletin.

Perhaps the reason why the weekend is attractive to many is that so few Christians practice a weekly Sabbath on the Lord's Day. The Westminster Shorter Catechism declares that the "Sabbath is to be sanctified by a holy resting all that day, even from such worldly employments and recreations as are lawful on other days; and spending the whole time in the public and private exercises of God's worship, except so much as is to be taken up in the works of necessity and mercy." (Q. 60) But the typical Lord's Day experience for many involves rushing off to a cramped worship service that must not exceed sixty minutes, perhaps teaching Sunday School to a class of ill-prepared and ungrateful youngsters, a hasty meal before the kickoff or during halftime, followed by homework or housework or more prime time TV. No wonder a Cursillo weekend with no responsibilities can seem so inviting. Practicing the Lord's Day Sabbath, "spending the whole time in the public and private exercises of God's worship," would undoubtedly bring renewal and refreshment to many a beleaguered saint.

6. The *"Heart on Fire"* in the Cursillo.

Certainly the most striking aspect of the whole Cursillo experience is emotion. All of the participants mentioned it. Doris thought the weekend was "all emotions." Sheila did not think the strong emphasis on emotions was altogether helpful. Fred confessed to a "fair amount of head knowledge" before the weekend, but that he did not "have it in my heart." Barb said she met people at Cursillo whose relationship with the Lord was "personal, that it was in their heart, not just in their head." Gus talked about getting "emotionally involved" as helpful, though it was not a mountaintop experience for him. Ed experienced a great emotional crisis, though it had been delayed. He spoke several times about experiencing a "high" on the weekend or getting "fired up."

And we should become emotional about our faith. Jesus said that we should love the Lord with all our heart and soul (Matt. 22:37) which certainly must include our emotions. Paul commands in Romans 12:11: "Do not be slothful in zeal, be fervent in spirit, serve the Lord." In commenting on Hebrews 2:1-4, the Puritan John Owen writes: "The apostle uses the incomparable excellency of the Author of the Gospel as the basis of his argument. He reminds them, and us, in general, that in handling the doctrines of the Gospel about the person and work of Jesus Christ, we should not be satisfied with mere intellectual assent, but should endeavor to have our hearts set on fire by them through faith, love, obedience, and perseverance."[411]

Likewise Jonathan Edwards could go so far as to say "True religion, in great part, consists in holy affections."[412] He noted that the "Holy Scriptures do everywhere place religion very much in the affections; such as fear, hope, love, hatred, desire, joy, sorrow, gratitude, compassion and zeal,"[413] and "hence we may learn, what great cause we have to be ashamed and confounded before God, that we are not more affected with the great things of religion. It appears...that this arises from our having so little true religion."[414]

Here is the danger of the so-called "dead orthodoxy" which is content only with the intellectual, giving the right answers, while being unconcerned, even suspicious of the enflamed heart. We need to seek to become emotionally involved with the truth. And if we really believed what we profess, how could we help but become emotionally involved? Who in his right mind would not love a Savior so glorious, or be horrified by the hideousness of sin? Who would not recoil from the terrors of hell and pour out ardent prayer that all might escape such everlasting torment? Who would not soar with joy at every hint of the hope of heaven and its eternal glory and delight?

The goal is "truth on fire," an earnestness enflamed at the magnitude of what is declared in the Gospel. This is not emotionalism, which is mere "fire on fire,"[415] nor is it simply getting "pumped up" like a crowd at a basketball

---

[411] John Owen, *Hebrews* (repr., Wheaton, IL: Crossway Classic Commentaries, 1998), 31.
[412] Jonathan Edwards, *A Treatise Concerning Religious Affections in Three Parts*, ed. John E. Smith, vol. 2 of *The Works of Jonathan Edwards,* ed. Perry Miller (New Haven: Yale University Press, 1959), 95.
[413] Ibid., 102.
[414] Ibid., 122.
[415] While a great champion of religious affections, Edwards also warned: "Indeed there may be such means, as may have a great tendency to stir up the passions of weak and ignorant persons, and yet have no great tendency to benefit their souls. For though they may have a tendency to

Chapter 11: The Unpaid Bills of the Church

game. Rather, it is a steady, growing blaze feeding on the solid fuel of the glory of God in the Gospel.

However, one suspects that much of the Cursillo effect is merely "fire on fire." The "truth" component seems largely lacking in the weekend experience, and because the Cursillo effect is largely not truth-driven, it must be emotionalism. Doris reported, "It was a very emotional thing, sitting around the table and everybody has a sad story...." In fact, for both Ed and Fred, the power of the weekend was largely in getting in touch with their feelings or gaining the freedom to express their feelings.

Ed explains: "I was raised where my Dad never showed much emotion, a real hard worker. Love was never mentioned in my family, and through this I got to tell my sons that I loved them, which I never did, I never would have thought of." "When my youngest son got out of YATEC, and then on the way home from that he was really touched, and we got out and gave each other hugs, and said, 'Love you, Dad.' Maybe a lot of families do that, but we didn't. It was just kind of a big circle there with Cursillo, and YATEC and TEC, and it was just really a blessing to my family." He talks about the benefits of the Cursillo in terms of men "opening up," that is becoming less reluctant to talk about personal issues. "Before this weekend, it was hard for me to talk about certain things about God and stuff, and once you start to share, and you see how the sharing helps people and helps me, then you do it more."

Fred described a similar experience: "We were born and raised to be very into ourselves, not outgoing, not wearing our feelings or anything on the outside, you know, keeping them to ourselves, just grin and bear it, very closed people, opposed to other nationalities. And, you know, that's a struggle for many of us today yet. But when we're there, and even when we're not there at the meeting place of Cursillo, when we're gathered together as a body of Christ, a Christian community, we don't have that burden. We can be open, we can wear it on our shirtsleeve, what our sorrows, joys, concerns, everything is."

It is certainly positive and commendable when men can become emotionally open to talk about their faith and feelings, to tell their sons that they love them. But is opening up emotionally the same thing as conversion to Christ? What might we say about specifically non-Christian religions and organizations that can accomplish the same? (See Chapter 8.)

In his daunting study *Revival and Revivalism*,[416] Iain Murray distinguishes sharply between "revival," which is solely a work of God, and "revivalism," which is a human attempt to employ special means in order to stir people up. He is careful to note that no special means are employed to promote true revival. "...God has appointed the means of prayer and preaching for the

---

excite affections, they may have little or none to excite gracious affections, or any affections tending to grace." Ibid.

[416] Murray, *Revival and Revivalism: The Making and Marring of American Evangelicalism 1750-1858*.

spread of the gospel and ...these are *the great means* in the use of which he requires the churches to be faithful. There are no greater means which may be employed at special times to secure supposedly greater results. It is therefore the Spirit of God who makes the same means more effective at some seasons than at others."[417] "Thus what characterizes a revival is not the employment of unusual or special means but rather the extraordinary degree of blessing attending the normal means of grace."[418]

Revivalism, on the other hand, "*aims* to produce excitement."[419] Murray quotes Gardiner Spring's affirmation, "Revivals are always spurious when they are *got up* by man's device and not *brought down* by the Spirit of God."[420] Until the 1820s this distinction was carefully observed in American Protestantism. Christian leaders welcomed true revival when God gave it, but did not employ extraordinary practices to try to create it. All this changed under a new variety of preacher, most notably Charles G. Finney and his "new measures."

> It was a question of being for or against, not emotion, but rather the adoption of means in addition to preaching and prayer, to *promote* emotion. There was no disagreement over whether or not hearers under the power of the truth ought to feel and be disturbed and moved, but should methods not mentioned in Scripture be employed to induce a response in those hearing the gospel? Most of the new measures were deliberately calculated to have that effect. They included such things as denunciatory language designed to alarm, pointed remarks to particular individuals delivered in public, naming unconverted people in prayer, using inquiry meetings to make individuals pray or 'submit,' and other similar practices.[421]

In these terms, the Cursillo is unmistakably revivalism. None of its "secrets and surprises" or "shocks and jolts" has Scriptural warrant. In fact, "the great means" of preaching and prayer are largely absent from the Cursillo weekend, having been replaced by emotional sharing and storytelling and the palanca-prayer offered for psychological effect. And the Cursillo will undoubtedly suffer from the same problems as all revivalistic emotionalism.

In the 1820s these "new measures" were introduced in revivals that were already taking place in America during the Second Great Awakening. Murray points out the drawback of the "new measures":

---

[417] Ibid., 127 (emphasis original).
[418] Ibid., 129.
[419] Ibid., 201 (emphasis original).
[420] Ibid. (emphasis original).
[421] Ibid., 243 (emphasis original).

(W)hile they succeeded in heightening excitement, they inevitably confused the feeling that attends the powerful preaching of the truth in a revival with the excitement that can be worked up where there is no revival.... What (the older revival leaders) deplored was the deliberate use of emotion to increase the number of converts without regard to the danger of counting as converts the spurious as well as the true. As Weeks later wrote: "We complain that the whole system of measures seems to be adapted to promote false conversions, to cherish false hopes, and to propagate a false religion; and thus, ultimately not only destroy the souls of those who are deceived by it, but to bring revivals and experimental religion itself into discredit."[422]

This caution should be heeded by those who promote all forms of revivalism, especially the Cursillo.

Recommendations

My recommendation for church leaders or individuals considering the Cursillo or for Cursillo leaders is not to become or remain involved with the Cursillo in any form. They should not attempt to modify, reform, or fix the Cursillo as Boyd and Rydholm suggest. The Cursillo is fatally flawed from the outset. Its theology is incompatible with Reformed (biblical) doctrine, not simply tangentially but at the very core. Its methods are inexcusable, offensive to human dignity and freedom, and potentially dangerous, as even Cursillo leaders will admit. The ends certainly do not justify these means. And the results, especially the long-term results are unclear, but certainly nowhere near the overblown rates of success Cursillo promotional literature often claims. And it certainly has the potential of the unwelcome side effects of disaffection with or even division in the local church.

Church leaders would be far wiser and faithful if they work to reform and vitalize the church according to the biblical pattern.

1. Churches should return to Christ-centered, expository preaching, proclaiming the whole counsel of God, and always pointing to Christ, with appropriate passion and urgency.

Those churches which have abandoned the second or evening preaching or teaching service for the sake of music concerts, small groups or nothing at all should return to the commitment to preaching as the primary means of grace. This should be done as an act of trusting God to honor his

---

[422] Ibid.

message (the Gospel), method (preaching) and means (the power of the Holy Spirit).[423]

2. Churches should consider the "frequent" use of the sacrament of the Lord's Supper in worship as a means of grace.

This is not for its symbolic or emotive value but for its efficaciousness as God's appointed means to signify the Gospel and seal it to his people, lifting us up to true, mystical, corporate communion with and in the presence our Lord Jesus.

3. Churches should promote private, urgent prayer and give themselves to public prayer as the full body and in smaller prayer groups.

Asking God honors God, and God has promised to hear the prayers of his people. Iain Murray highlights the importance of prayer in sustaining God's work:

> As with the truth that is preached, prayer has no inherent power in itself. On the contrary, true prayer is bound up with a persuasion of our inability and our complete dependence on God. Prayer, considered as a human activity, whether offered by few or many, can guarantee no results. But prayer that throws believers in heartfelt need on God, with true concern for the salvation of sinners, will not go unanswered. Prayer of this kind precedes blessing, not because of any necessary cause and effect, but because such prayer secures an acknowledgement of the true Author of the blessing.[424]

4. Churches should ensure and promote ample opportunity for protracted Christian community and fellowship.

Every effort should be made to connect God's people in some form of small group, be it a Sunday school class, Bible study group, fellowship group, choir, or even a well-functioning committee. Churches should promote and engage in healthy and positive church discipline to assist members in overcoming conflicts and prevent the growth of bitterness or division.

---

[423] See Arturo Azurdia's excellent study *Spirit Empowered Preaching* (Fearn, Ross-shire, Great Britain: Mentor/Christian Focus Publications, 1998).
[424] Murray, *Revival and Revivalism: The Making and Marring of American Evangelicalism 1750-1858*, 129.

Churches would be wise to provide periodic services of confession, repentance, and reconciliation in order to neutralize stumbling blocks and break down walls that keep members apart.

5. Churches should promote a healthy practice of the weekly Lord's Day Sabbath.

Members should be encouraged to prepare for the Lord's Day on Saturday, as far as possible finishing all housework and homework on Saturday, and avoiding the late night out. The Christian life is a struggle. The Lord's Day Sabbath should be reserved for glad repentance, renewal, rearmament, and refreshment through the blessed means of worship and fellowship in God's presence. Reserving the whole day as the Lord's Day, not a "play day," "recreation day," "catch-up day," or even "family day" (least of all a "TV day"), will do much to strengthen, encourage and equip God's people.

6. Churches should encourage members to live passionately for Christ.

The church has often fallen into one or the other of two deadly errors: "dead orthodoxy" or a "warm heresy." Dead orthodoxy means settling for a cold, lifeless doctrinal correctness that does not impact true holiness of life. Dead orthodoxy says that as long as we affirm the right beliefs, we are doing well. It might also be called "formalism" or "Phariseeism." Warm heresy, on the other hand, is an emotional religion that denies central truths of the faith, but pretends to be warm and loving and alive. Protestant liberalism is an example of warm heresy. (Of course you can also have the worst of these, a dead heresy, a cold and lifeless religion that also denies the faith. The Sadducees both denied the faith and were quite dead and formal in their religious practice.) But there is no reason, with God's help, why the church cannot be fully alive with a warm and vital orthodoxy. The true church both loves God's truth passionately, and lives her faith joyfully.[425]

---

[425] For examples of emotionalism mistakenly interpreted as true religion, see Arnold Dallimore, *Forerunner of the Charismatic Movement: The Life of Edward Irving* (Chicago: Moody Press, 1983) and Iain H. Murray, *Pentecost—Today? The Biblical Basis for Understanding Revival* (Cape Coral, FL: Founders Press, 1998), especially pages 134-169. For a positive study of the place of emotions in the Christian life, see Benjamin Breckinridge Warfield, *The Person and Work of Christ* (Philadelphia: The Presbyterian and Reformed Publishing Company, 1950) especially his essay, "The Emotional Life of Our Lord," pages 93-145.

12. *After the Weekend is Over*

On the wall of my study I keep a poster sent out by the organizers of a local Christian conference, advertising their yearly theme and schedule. I keep it for the picture. It features a barefoot, young woman dressed in blue jeans and a sleeveless, off-white top. Her shoulder-length brown hair is windblown. She is apparently standing on the top of some peak or cliff with a cloudy sky in the backdrop. Her head is poised slightly upward, eyes closed with her arms at her side, a little away from her body, her open palms facing forwards. She appears to be in a dreamy trance or some kind of altered state of consciousness.

If the captions from the poster were removed so that the picture alone remained, one could imagine numerous scenarios. She might be a jilted girlfriend trying to muster the courage to jump off the cliff and end her misery. She might be intoxicated by hallucinogenic drugs, in danger of unwittingly falling to her death. She could perhaps be the practitioner of some eastern religion, up on the mountaintop under her guru's guidance in a self-induced trance communing with the cosmos. She could simply be enjoying the sunrise.

But, in fact, this is an advertisement for a Christian conference because this is the ideal for much of what passes for Christianity today. She is apparently in ecstasy. She has somehow achieved an altered state of consciousness that is quite pleasurable. She is able to tune out her problems and enjoy some solitary, deep experience. Apparently this conference is in the business of providing extraordinary, mystical, perhaps even out-of-the-body experiences. This is the proposed goal, the ideal Christian experience: a high that is produced without medication or mantra, but a high nonetheless.

This is what we are up against in the church of Jesus Christ today. Cursillo is but one of many forms of achieving this individualistic dream-state. But what will be the lasting effect on people who pursue this mystical religion? The long-term consequences of continual Cursillo participation, the lasting effects which take place "after the weekend," help to highlight the serious results of the pursuit of this false religion.

One of the consistent failures of our age is our chronic short-sightedness. Popular slogans such as "live for the moment," "you only go around once," and "if it feels good, do it" betray our inability or refusal to take the longer view. This same mindset has been carried over into the church. After describing the tendency for many churches to adapt themselves to the felt needs of their congregations, "much as a business might adapt its product to a market," David F. Wells writes:

> However, what people who are coming in these church doors today are thinking about, and what they want, is not primarily personal salvation. What they want is a sense of *personal well-being*, however momentary and fragmentary that personal sense of well-being is, and our churches are beginning to cater to this. I have no doubt at all that they are going to become very successful. Indeed, some are successful already and they are going to become more successful because marketing in America is what makes the wheels go around.[426]

Indeed, what's wrong with success? Everyone wants to be successful, especially in the church. But, as Wells points out, "The answer is that marketing will produce success but not necessarily the kind that has much to do with the Kingdom of God."[427]

I would be the first to admit that the Cursillo initiation weekend and its counterparts are successful and even growing in success. But it is not the kind of success that has much to do with the Kingdom of God. It produces wonderful experiences and warm feelings, as the numerous testimonials will indicate. But at what cost? Beyond the compromised integrity of resorting to the questionable tactics and techniques of mind control in order to achieve the success (to get the desired results), there are other long-term effects (mostly negative) that far outweigh the immediate and temporary sense of contentment and happiness.

THE LONG-TERM EFFECTS: THE LONG AND LONELY ROAD

In the short run, right after the emotional catharsis, the participant is left with a strong feeling of resolution and peace, a sense of personal well-being, a euphoria that may last for weeks, occasionally months, and usually a close bonding with other members of the group. This feeling inevitably wears off. But unbeknownst to the participant, there are several long-term, unhelpful consequences.

---

[426] David F. Wells, *The Bleeding of the Evangelical Church*. (Carlisle, PA: The Banner of Truth Trust), 3, emphasis original.
[427] Ibid.

1. The Emotional Letdown and Desire for Repeated Experiences.

The first long-term effect that will be noticed is that the high wears off. The cathartic experience that seemed to be the solution to so many problems, that brought peace and a strong sense of personal well-being, begins to slip away. This may be quite gradual or almost immediate depending on the problems and resistance faced after the weekend is over and the degree of continued contact with fellow participants. This might explain why the effects of all-church weekend renewal experiences tend to last longer than the effects of Cursillo weekends where participants are largely strangers to one another. If the whole church has the experience together, the effects are reviewed and recalled together week after week, prolonging the interval before it wears off.

But even though at the time the experience seems to be the solution to the participant's problems, it is not. As the effects fade away the problems remain or return. It is even possible that the problems have worsened due to inattention. A shaky marriage is still shaky: nothing has really changed; a selfish personality is still selfish; a substance-abuser still gravitates toward the substance; legal troubles are still pending; poor financial habits remain uncorrected as the bills continue to pile up; and so forth.

And as the high wears off, the participant is faced with a dilemma, the same question addressed to me by those three young people: "Is this for real?" If the answer is "no," then the person may at this point write off the faith completely and dispatch it to the "been there, done that" file. This is truly tragic. This person then has little interest in the faith, and is turned off to subsequent attempts at evangelism. "Hardened" might be the correct term.

If the participant decides that the experience was "for real," then he or she must explain why it has worn off. Often an attempt is made to recapture the fading glow by repeating the experience. So the desperate seeker will become a lay witness and attend more weekends or volunteer to "work a Cursillo:" anything to try to feel again the power of the cathartic experience. We all want to feel better. Or the participant may try new and more exciting experiences: "There's got to be more." This may lead them to other retreats, or weekend experiences, or into the charismatic movement or even more bizarre "experiences."

Once begun, this quest for emotional experiences runs directly into the next long-term effect.

2. The Law of Diminishing Returns.

A powerful experience, if it is repeated, will not be as powerful the next time around. This principle is well-known among those who treat substance abusers. As with drugs or alcohol, the first "high" is the most powerful. But in time it will take more and more of the drug to achieve the same effect. This "diminishing return" continues until no amount of the substance can produce

Chapter 12: After the Weekend is Over

the high. The same, sad law is in effect for emotional experiences as well.

Pastor and professor Art Azurdia explains the diminishing returns of these experiences:

> From a *pastoral* perspective, we need to be concerned that the spiritual development of well-meaning Christians can become vulnerable to the law of diminishing returns. That is to say, the maturing of a Christian will be consistently impaired if devotion to Jesus Christ is determined by fresh experiences of spiritual ecstasy. Why is this the case? Because one's sensation of being overpowered by God will need to steadily intensify. The ordinary will give way to the unusual. The unusual will surrender to the extreme. The extreme will topple to the ridiculous. Often the inevitable consequence is spiritual emptiness. [428]

Azurdia quotes the former-pentecostal George Gardiner with respect to charismatic emotional experience:

> So the seeker for experience goes back through the ritual again and again, but begins to discover something; ecstatic experience, like drug-addiction, requires larger and larger doses to satisfy. Sometimes the bizarre is introduced. I have seen people run around a room until they were exhausted, climb tent poles, laugh hysterically, go into trances for days and do other weird things as the 'high' sought became more elusive. Eventually there is a crisis and a decision is made; he will sit on the back seats and be a spectator, 'fake it', or go on in the hope that everything will eventually be as it was. The most tragic decision is to quit and in the quitting abandon all things spiritual as fraudulent. The spectators are frustrated, the fakers suffer guilt, the hoping are pitiable and the quitters are a tragedy. [429]

This "law of diminishing returns" may help to explain why Cursillo leaders will not permit a participant or candidate to repeat the initiation experience. The techniques will not work as well, and this will lead to greater disillusionment. Instead the recapturing of the effect is sought through "reunions" or through volunteering to be a Lay Witness or to work at subsequent Cursillos or YATEC weekends. Some of the original passion can be re-captured, but it will continue to dwindle.

---

[428] Azurdia, *Spirit Empowered Preaching*, 49.
[429] Ibid.

3. The Spoiling.

Another long-term effect of the weekend renewal experiences is that of "spoiling." The intensity of the emotional catharsis experience is to such a degree that nothing else will compare. This is why the participants experience a longing for the weekend feeling. It could be likened to being allowed to watch high-definition, digital television for a few days, and then being sentenced to watching grainy, black-and-white, analog television for the rest of your life.

Compared to the weekend high, "regular life" can only be dissatisfying. From a weekend of being praised and pampered and "unconditionally loved," the participant is then dropped back into regular life with all of its problems: bills, hassles at work, crabby kids and dirty diapers, laundry, vacuuming, cantankerous neighbors, etc. The person is effectively "spoiled," pining away for excitement, acceptance, and a carefree life that does not exist in the real world.

4. Dissatisfaction with the Local Church.

Comparing the weekend renewal experience to the local church also finds "regular life" falling far short. The artificially-generated, emotional high produces an unrealistic expectation for spirituality, and especially for the local church. Returning home to "church as usual," the "spoiled" participant looks to the church and thinks, "There's got to be more than this. Why do I not feel as excited in church as I did on the weekend experience?" The reason is simple: the two have different goals. The weekend renewal experience has as its goal the precipitation of a cathartic experience that produces a powerful emotional "high." The church service has as its goal the worship of almighty God, and the declaration of the Word of God. One focuses on feelings; the other focuses on God. No wonder there is no comparing the "feeling" generated by the two.

Another dissatisfaction frequently felt toward their local church by the weekend renewal experience participant is with respect to feelings of warmth and unity. "Why can't we experience such 'unconditional love' in our church?" At this point, you can probably understand that the "unconditional love" of the weekend experience is an artificial, distorted and therefore, temporary "love," which cannot be sustained. That's why the weekend must end. No one can continually generate this so-called "unconditional love." In fact, such "unconditional love" tends toward escapism and avoidance. If "there are no wrong answers" (and so I cannot challenge your incorrect answer in a small group) then we cannot deal with significant problems or conflicts that may arise.[430]

People returning from weekend renewal experiences tend to be less committed to their local church. One couple I know worked a YATEC

---

[430] For a critique of "unconditional love" in the Cursillo weekend, see chapter 11.

weekend, so they obviously missed worship that Sunday. But the next Sunday, they missed Sunday school and the evening worship service, uncharacteristic for them. Another man came home very enthused about his Cursillo weekend experience. But the next weekend, when his wife was at Cursillo, he elected to stay home from church with his family. This couple, which had been attending church regularly, never returned and still remains apart from the church.

Graduates of weekend renewal experiences tend to have great energy for things related to the weekend experience, but become detached from their local congregation. I have known some Cursillo veterans to host "home Bible studies" with fellow veterans at the same time their local church is holding worship services for the rest of the congregation. The net effect is that the powerful weekend experience leads to dissatisfaction and detachment from the local church.

5. Elitism.

The weekend renewal experience leads toward an inescapable feeling of superiority. Graduates are assured that they have attained a higher spiritual level, that they are now a part of an elite group that exists covertly in the midst of the larger church. Part of this elitism undoubtedly stems from the terminology. For example, before the weekend, one is merely a "candidate." After the weekend, the graduate is now a "Cursillista" or a "TECie" or a "YATECie." The groups that hosts the weekends are called the "Cursillista Community," the "TEC Community," and the "YATEC Community" (the United Methodist version of Cursillo, called "Walk to Emmaus" is sponsored by—you guessed it— "the Emmaus Community"). So now within the church, or even among the churches, there is a "Cursillista Community." The only way to join is to become a "Cursillista."

This elitist attitude is exacerbated by the secrecy to which each graduate is sworn. The expressed purpose is to maintain the surprises necessary for potential candidates to experience the full effect of the weekend. And yet the secrecy is another part of the mysterious bond that unites all members. There is likewise a new vocabulary associated with the Cursillo weekend, the effect of which is to unify the group, but also to distinguish group members from the non-initiates. And due to the intense bonding and the power of the catharsis experience, veterans of these weekend experiences find themselves quite naturally drawn to one another, and drawn away from outsiders. The elitism is quite understandable, though no less disruptive to the life of the local church community.

6. The Regression.

Part of my growing discomfort with the weekend renewal experiences came from an unplanned meeting some years ago with a psychotherapist who had an office in our community. I was waiting for an appointment with my tax accountant when we struck up a conversation.

This therapist worked mainly with recovering substance abusers. His approach was of the "Twelve Steps" variety, helping the person work away from the chemically induced quick fix into a more responsible and disciplined life. At one point he asked me if I knew anything about Cursillo. I honestly told him, "Not much." And he volunteered an observation. He noted that when someone he was treating returned from a Cursillo weekend, he found that they had regressed, sometimes significantly. "They were right back to step one," he said. "They were more emotional, more irresponsible, and more undisciplined. All the progress we had made was undone in a weekend. *It was like they were back on drugs."*

In truth, the weekends encourage a regression, a recapturing of childhood. Remember Alan's comment on the Moonie retreat: "It was like being a kid again."[431] The pampered, "get away from it all," "not a care in the world" atmosphere encourages a regression back to immaturity. This undoubtedly contributes to the intensity of the catharsis. Children are allowed to be more emotional than "big boys" who "don't cry." The silly songs and the (encouraged) immature behavior help to produce the emotional regression.

Unfortunately, the regression frequently lingers after the weekend. The biblical virtue of being "childlike," (i.e. helpless and humble) is confused with the undesirable quality of being "childish," (i.e. immature and irresponsible). Because of the overwhelmingly pleasurable and satisfying feeling of the catharsis, the participant is misled to think that all is well. For some time the person continues to bask in the glow, perhaps tuning out concerns of the "real world" by remembering, rehearsing, and re-living the high of the weekend: "All will be well if I only maintain my child-like faith." But often the translation of this is, "All will be well as long as I refuse to face my responsibilities."

And yet there is a more serious down side to this regression as well. The participant may become utterly "feeling-oriented" so that emotions become the basis for making choices, and even the test for truth: "If it feels good, do it." Remarkably, this feeling-oriented way of life is a desired result of the client-centered psychotherapy of Carl Rogers: "Clients are discovering that experiencing feelings with immediacy and intensity is a possible guide for living. They begin to trust their feelings and base more of their valuing on what they like or dislike, what makes them happy or sad, what produces joy or anger."[432] This is regress, not progress.

The Bible continually points us away from childishness toward maturity. For example, Ephesians 4:11-14 states:

---

[431] See chapter 1.
[432] Prochaska, *Systems of Psychotherapy: A Transtheoretical Analysis*, 122.

And he gave the apostles, the prophets, the evangelists, the pastors and teachers, to equip the saints for the work of ministry, for building up the body of Christ, until we all attain to the unity of the faith and of the knowledge of the Son of God, *to mature manhood*, to the measure of the stature of the fullness of Christ, *so that we may no longer be children*, tossed to and fro by the waves and carried about by every wind of doctrine, by human cunning, by craftiness in deceitful schemes. (Emphasis added)

Note that it is through the ordinary ministry of the church, through pastors and teachers, and not through mystical weekend adventures, that God's people are to grow into "the unity of the faith and of the knowledge of the Son of God" and "to mature manhood." The result is a spiritual resilience that is impervious to the deceits and pleadings of false teachers.

7. The Emotional Roller Coaster.

The "weekend high" is invariably followed by the "real life low." When the techniques are discontinued and the "unconditional love" is no longer available, the high wears off. As pleasurable as the high feeling may be, the "low" is distressing and unpleasant. And here the weekend has a particularly nasty side-effect. What can explain the "low"? If the participant were honestly told to expect an emotional high due to the particular techniques employed, then the low could be explained as the natural result of the discontinued techniques. But instead, the weekend teaching identifies the high with the participant's closeness to Christ or the measure of his or her Christian commitment. And when the high wears off, the only logical conclusion is that the participant is no longer "close to Christ," or that the fire of his or her Christian commitment has chilled, or that "Satan has stolen away their joy."

And so the options are rather limited: reject the experience and maybe the faith that went with it, accept a "second-class" Christian status, or try to recapture the feeling of being close to Christ. From firsthand experience, I know this third option to be particularly heartbreaking. One will bounce on a roller coaster ride from weekend experience to weekend experience, in desperate search for the lost "it" (the catharsis). From time to time "it" will be temporarily recharged, but never to full potency. Because of the aforementioned "law of diminishing returns," the effect will be less and less satisfying until the weekend experience will have little or no effect at all. And this leads to the end of the quest, a dead end.

8. The Depression.

When the high is no longer available due to the diminishing returns, the participant is left emotionally spent and empty. And this is the final result of the quest for emotional experience. I repeat the words quoted by Azurdia:

Eventually there is a crisis and a decision is made; he will sit on the back seats and be a spectator, 'fake it,' or go on in the hope that everything will eventually be as it was. The most tragic decision is to quit and in the quitting abandon all things spiritual as fraudulent. The spectators are frustrated, the fakers suffer guilt, the hoping are pitiable and the quitters are a tragedy.[433]

THE REAL FRUIT OF THE WEEKEND RENEWAL EXPERIENCE

This is often the ultimate fruit of the weekend renewal experience lifestyle, the quest for "it," for emotional experience: a disappointing letdown that initiates a futile quest for more and more experience; a spoiling of the participant's expectations so that "real life," and especially the local church, pale by comparison; the production an elitist "community" existing secretively in the midst of the churches; a regression to spiritual and emotional immaturity that makes one ill-equipped for the hard life of genuine discipleship; and, at the end of the road, a despairing dead end. Obviously, these are serious concerns.

Objection #1: *"But it must be good—it works!"*

A careful examination of these long-term effects is crucial. The main defense for these weekend experiences is that they "work." This evidence is offered in the form of testimonials. Critique of the weekend movements is usually met with a "don't knock it unless you try it" response. And if the critique comes from those of us who have "tried it," the response is that "it helps many people, so it must be good."

But the fact of the matter is that while the cathartic experience helps many people feel better in the short run, the long-term effects are largely negative. The weekend experiences indeed do *not* "work," not in the long run. This is a fatal flaw with the Cursillo method. And there are numerous "testimonials" to this side as well.

If a person of mature faith and an emotionally stable personality experiences one of these weekends, the effect is often less intense. Since it will not have the same strong "high" component, the person may leave the weekend merely feeling refreshed. This will tend to mute the long-term effects. This person will be less likely to experience the severe let-down, will therefore not long to repeat the experience, will not be "spoiled" to regular life or to the local

---

[433] For a brief, clear introduction to the biblical faith, see John R. W. Stott, *Basic Christianity* (Downer's Grove, IL: InterVarsity Press, 1958).

church, etc. Remarkably, the weekend experience tends to have the greatest negative, long-term effect upon those on whom the techniques are most "successful," i.e., those who experience the emotional catharsis most strongly.

When the deleterious long-term effects of these weekend renewal experiences are coupled with the indefensible, manipulative techniques used to achieve the emotional high and the fact that these techniques are used either without the knowledge or the admission that they are "techniques," to my mind these weekend renewal experiences are beyond redemption.

Again, let me state the obvious. Without the techniques, the weekend renewal experiences would not "work." And when an atheistic psychotherapist or a non-Christian cult employs the same techniques without the Christian content, the techniques also "work." The effect is identical: the emotional catharsis and the bonding with the group. Therefore, it is primarily if not exclusively the techniques employed during the weekend which produce the effects and not the Christian content. If anything, the Christian content (emotional testimonials, graphic portrayals, or dramatic reenactments of the crucifixion or resurrection) merely support the techniques, and not the other way around.

By analogy, suppose a group of people were taken away on a weekend where, unbeknownst to the participants, all their food was spiked with time-release narcotics. And then when the effects of the narcotics became apparent, the leaders told the participants that they were having an experience with the Holy Spirit. The experience may be perceived by the participants to be very real, yet few outside observers would attribute the effects to the Spirit. Obviously the narcotics were producing the effects, and not the Holy Spirit, even though the experience would be deeply-felt, and the participants might even attach great meaning to them. Few Christians would accept this as genuine spiritual experience. Most would consider it merely to be a psychological phenomena induced by the chemical.[434]

By no means am I suggesting that narcotics are secretly being used on these weekends. And yet the principle is the same. The psychological techniques alter mood, the physiological techniques alter consciousness, and the combination produces the cathartic emotional release. The participant feels better, and deep meaning may then be attached to the religious words and symbols that are offered during the weekend. To the participant, the experience is "for real." But would the outside observer agree? I think not.

And this accounts for the "you can't explain it, you've got to experience it" mentality. Without experiencing it, that is, without undergoing the effects of the techniques, the weekend certainly will not "make sense" or be understood by the observer. The techniques, like the narcotics in the hypothetical situation,

---

[434] For a fuller discussion of this topic, please see Appendix B.

are what make the real difference. Without the techniques, the weekends cannot stand.

Objection #2: *"But surely some good comes out of these weekends."*

This point must be granted. Surely some lasting good, some genuine spiritual growth, perhaps even true conversions take place on these weekends. Not all of it is emotional hype. Sometimes a marriage is strengthened, a problem is solved, a strained friendship sees reconciliation, and growth in grace appears. But surely this is not as a result of the techniques. If anything, it is in spite of the techniques.

As an older friend used to say "a blind pig finds an acorn once in a while." On these weekends, or before the weekend, genuine prayer is offered up for the salvation or spiritual growth of participants. The Bible is usually read and explained to some extent. The sacrament of the Lord's Supper is offered and received. These and not the psychological techniques are the means of grace endorsed by God. And these means are effective if they are received by faith in Christ. So one would expect some genuine, positive effect, again, not because of the techniques, but in spite of the techniques.

But the ends do not justify the means. The few lasting and positive results really are vastly outweighed by the negative effects. And there is no credible justification for using the psychological techniques and attributing the effects to the "work of the Spirit." The few, lasting positive results can be achieved in other more noble and God-honoring ways that will not have the unwholesome and questionable baggage of the techniques.

As a pastor, I can certainly understand and empathize with the desire to "make things happen" for people. Even our best, God-honoring and biblical attempts at ministry sometimes meet with lackluster response, if any response at all. At this point, in the face of great spiritual apathy and deadness, it can become quite tempting to resort to techniques like Cursillo which are intended to "disorient," "shock," and "jolt" (that is, "wake up") people into a response. But this is God's responsibility and not ours. Only Divine power can accomplish this, and not human works or techniques. We must own up to the sinful arrogance of believing that we can "make things happen," and our unbiblical attempts to do so. Paul explains the proper order: "I planted, Apollos watered, *but God gave the growth.*" (1 Corinthians 3:6, emphasis added).

Objection #3: *"But the motives of the Cursillo leaders are pure and their intentions are good!"*

It is impossible for me or anyone else to know the motives of the weekend renewal leadership. "The LORD [alone] looks on the heart." (1 Samuel 16:7) And so it is impossible for me or anyone else to criticize motives. I freely assume that the real desire of the Cursillo leadership is to see others happy and growing in Christ. Don't forget that for years I was one of those weekend renewal experience leaders. And my motives were largely innocent and well-meaning. I knew that these weekends made me feel happy, and I simply wished the same for others.

And yet, in all honesty, speaking only for myself, I cannot say that my motives were completely pure. For example, as I admired the "witnesses" who came to my home church, so I did not mind being admired by others. And in my desire to help others find the "high," I also knew that I would get a bit of a buzz myself. And later, as a pastor who wanted to be "successful," who mistakenly (sinfully) believed himself responsible to "make things happen," I knew these techniques really could "make things happen." Surely the reader can sense my deep regret at "making things happen." So, while it is impossible for me to assess the motives of others, I can report that my motives were not absolutely pure.

A Final Plea

And so let me offer one final appeal to those who lead and sponsor these morally indefensible, spiritually distracting, perhaps even destructive weekends. Please go back to your local church, with all its flaws and failings, and rejoin the rest of us in serving Jesus Christ who is head of the *Church*. Please give up these shamefully manipulative practices, and regain integrity in Christian ministry which focuses on the ministry of the Word of God and not deceptive tricks. Take to heart the Apostle Paul's personal testimony of an honorable and upright service to Christ:

> For our appeal does not spring from error or impurity or any attempt to deceive, but just as we have been approved by God to be entrusted with the gospel, so we speak, not to please man, but to please God who tests our hearts. (1 Thessalonians 2:3-4)

> But we have renounced disgraceful, underhanded ways. We refuse to practice cunning or to tamper with God's word, but by the open statement of the truth we would commend ourselves to everyone's conscience in the sight of God. (2 Corinthians 4:2)

APPENDIX A: *THE PERSPECTIVE OF POST-CALVIN REFORMED CONFESSIONS AND CATECHISMS*

It is obvious that the root of the Reformed concepts of human inability and of preaching and prayer as the primary means of grace is firmly planted in John Calvin himself. But what about later Reformed documents? Do they share this perspective? Do they disagree or depart from these foundations? Do they run beyond them into speculation?

The Reformed confessions and catechisms in view are those accepted as doctrinal standards by the Reformed Church in America and the Christian Reformed Church (The Belgic Confession, the Heidelberg Catechism and the Canons of Dort) and those accepted by the Presbyterian Church (USA) (The Scots Confession, The Heidelberg Catechism [also], The Second Helvetic Confession, the Westminster Confession and the Westminster Catechism [Shorter and Larger]). Doctrinal standards of these three denominations were selected because of the relative size of the denominations, but also because of their substantive involvement in the Cursillo. Each of these documents will be consulted in chronological order with respect to our two key issues: human inability and preaching and prayer as the primary means of grace.

A. HUMAN INABILITY.

The Scots Confession (1560) [PCUSA]

(The Scots Confession was written mostly by Scottish Reformer John Knox. He was a student of John Calvin and the father of Reformed Christianity among those who speak English. It was written only one year after Calvin's definitive 1559 edition of the *Institutes*.)

The Scots Confession follows Calvin in noting that as created, humanity had free will.

We confess and acknowledge that our God has created man, i.e., our first father, Adam, after his own image and likeness, to whom he gave wisdom, lordship, justice, free will, and self-consciousness, so that in the whole nature of man no imperfection could be found. From this dignity and perfection man and woman both fell; the woman being deceived by the serpent and man obeying the voice of the woman, both conspiring against the sovereign majesty of God, who in clear words had previously threatened death if they presumed to eat of the forbidden tree. (Chapter II 3.02)

The Scots Confession likewise agrees with Calvin on the utter inability of humanity in sin with respect both to the mind and the will, and the absolute requirement of regeneration before anyone can respond to God. Such regeneration is dependent upon the free and undeserved grace of God. Even those good works performed after regeneration are due to God's grace and not unaided human effort.

Our faith and its assurance do not proceed from flesh and blood, that is to say, from natural powers within us, but are the inspiration of the Holy Ghost; whom we confess to be God, equal with the Father and with his Son, who sanctifies us, and brings us into all truth by his own working, without whom we should remain forever enemies to God and ignorant of his Son, Christ Jesus. For by nature we are so dead, blind, and perverse, that neither can we feel when we are pricked, see the light when it shines, nor assent to the will of God when it is revealed, unless the Spirit of the Lord Jesus quicken that which is dead, remove the darkness from our minds, and bow our stubborn hearts to the obedience of his blessed will. And so, as we confess that God the Father created us when we were not, as his Son our Lord Jesus redeemed us when we were enemies to him, so also do we confess that the Holy Ghost does sanctify and regenerate us, without respect to any merit proceeding from us, be it before or be it after our regeneration. To put this even more plainly; as we willingly disclaim any honor and glory for our own creation and redemption, so do we willingly also for our regeneration and sanctification; for by ourselves we are not capable of thinking one good thought, but he who has begun the work in us alone continues us in it, to the praise and glory of his undeserved grace. (Ch. XII)

The Belgic Confession (1561) (CRC, RCA)

(So-called because it was addressed to the Low Countries which include both the Netherlands and Belgium, the Belgic Confession was mainly written only two years after Calvin's 1559 *Institutes* by Guido de Bres, a Reformed itinerant pastor. The Reformed church was severely persecuted by the Roman Catholic Philip II of Spain. The Confession was an apology for the Reformed churches who wished to demonstrate that they were law-abiding, biblical Christians.)

In the Belgic Confession we find the same, clear unmistakable themes: humanity was created good, with the ability to conform to God's will. But through a "willing" subjection to sin they "corrupted their entire nature," having lost ability, plunging themselves into "darkness." They became "slaves of sin" with no understanding or will "apart from Christ's involvement" (Article 14).

The Belgic Confession–Article 14: The Creation and Fall of Humanity

We believe that God created human beings from the dust of the earth and made and formed them in the divine image and likeness— good, just, and holy; able by the divine will to conform in all things to the will of God. But when they were in honor they did not understand it and did not recognize their excellence. But they subjected themselves willingly to sin and consequently to death and the curse, lending their ear to the word of the devil. For they transgressed the commandment of life, which they had received, and by their sin they separated themselves from God, who was their true life, having corrupted their entire nature. So they made themselves guilty and subject to physical and spiritual death, having become wicked, perverse, and corrupt in all their ways. They lost all their excellent gifts which they had received from God, and retained none of them except for small traces which are enough to make them inexcusable. Moreover, all the light in us is turned to darkness, as the Scripture teaches us: "The light shines in the darkness, and the darkness did not overcome it." Here Saint John calls the human race "darkness."

Therefore we reject everything taught to the contrary concerning human free will, since humans are nothing but the slaves of sin and cannot do a thing unless it is given them from heaven. For who can boast of being able to do anything good by oneself, since Christ says, "No one can come to me unless drawn by the Father who sent me"? Who can glory in one's own will when they understand that "the mind that is set on the flesh is hostile to God"? Who can speak of one's own knowledge in view of the fact that "those who are unspiritual do not receive the gifts of God's Spirit"? In short, who can produce a single thought, since we know that we are "not able to think a thing" about ourselves, by ourselves, but that "our competence is from

God"? And therefore, what the apostle says ought rightly to stand fixed and firm: "For it is God who is at work in you both to will and to work for God's good pleasure." For there is no understanding nor will conforming to God's understanding and will apart from Christ's involvement, as he teaches us when he says, "Apart from me you can do nothing."

And this curse was passed on to the rest of the race, so that all share in this inability.

The Belgic Confession—Article 15: The Doctrine of Original Sin

We believe that by the disobedience of Adam and Eve original sin has been spread through the whole human race. It is a corruption of all human nature— an inherited depravity which even infects small infants in their mother's womb, and the root which produces in humanity every sort of sin. It is therefore so vile and enormous in God's sight that it is enough to condemn the human race, and it is not abolished or wholly uprooted even by baptism, seeing that sin constantly boils forth as though from a contaminated spring.

Nevertheless, it is not imputed to God's children for their condemnation but is forgiven by his grace and mercy— not to put them to sleep but so that the awareness of this corruption might often make believers groan as they long to be set free from the "body of this death."

Therefore we reject the error of the Pelagians who say that this sin is nothing else than a matter of imitation.

The cure for this condition is none other than receiving Christ's righteousness through a "true faith that embraces Jesus Christ." This faith does not justify us, properly speaking, but is "only the instrument by which we embrace Christ, our righteousness." We do not generate this true and saving faith ourselves, but rather "the Holy Spirit kindles (it) in our hearts."

The Belgic Confession—Article 22 The Righteousness of Faith

We believe that for us to acquire the true knowledge of this great mystery the Holy Spirit kindles in our hearts a true faith that embraces Jesus Christ, with all his merits, and makes him its own, and no longer looks for anything apart from him. For it must necessarily follow that either all that is required for our salvation is not in Christ or, if all is in him, then he who has Christ by faith has his salvation entirely. Therefore, to say that Christ is not enough but that something else is needed as well is a most enormous blasphemy against God— for it then would follow that Jesus Christ is only half a

Savior. And therefore we justly say with Paul that we are justified "by faith alone" or by faith "apart from works." However, we do not mean, properly speaking, that it is faith itself that justifies us— for faith is only the instrument by which we embrace Christ, our righteousness. But Jesus Christ is our righteousness in making available to us all his merits and all the holy works he has done for us and in our place. And faith is the instrument that keeps us in communion with him and with all his benefits. When those benefits are made ours they are more than enough to absolve us of our sins.

The Heidelberg Catechism (1563) [PCUSA, CRC, RCA]

(Appearing only four years after Calvin's 1559 *Institutes*, the German Heidelberg catechism is one of the most widely translated, circulated and accepted statements of the Reformed faith. Officially commissioned by Elector Frederick III, it was mainly composed by professor Zacharias Ursinus, with assistance from pastor Caspar Olevianus.)

In the first section of the catechism, titled, "Of Man's Misery," we discover our predicament before God. God's Law requires perfect obedience, expressed in love for God and neighbor. But we are unable to love as required because we are prone to the precise opposite: hatred of God and neighbor. God is not to blame for this condition because he created us good, with the ability to love and know God. But our first parents fell into disobedience and so "poisoned" all of human life that we are now "conceived and born in the state of sin." We are all "so perverted that we are altogether unable to do good and prone to do evil," that is "unless we are born again through the Spirit of God" (Q 4-8).

Q. 4. What does the Law of God require of us?
A. Jesus Christ teaches this in a summary in Matthew 22:37-40: "You shall love the Lord your God with all your heart, and with all your soul, and with all your mind. This is the great and first commandment. And a second is like it, you shall love your neighbor as yourself. On these two commandments depend all the law and the prophets." (Cf. Luke 10:27.)

Q. 5. Can you keep all this perfectly?
A. No, for by nature I am prone to hate God and my neighbor.

Q. 6. Did God create man evil and perverse like this?
A. No. On the contrary, God created man good and in his image, that is, in true righteousness and holiness, so that he might rightly know God his Creator, love him with his whole heart, and live with

him in eternal blessedness, praising and glorifying him.

Q. 7. Where, then, does this corruption of human nature come from?
A. From the fall and disobedience of our first parents, Adam and Eve, in the Garden of Eden; whereby our human life is so poisoned that we are all conceived and born in the state of sin.

Q. 8. But are we so perverted that we are altogether unable to do good and prone to do evil?
A. Yes, unless we are born again through the Spirit of God.

The Second Helvetic Confession (1566) [PCUSA]

(This Swiss confession is important because it represents the view of the Zwinglian branch of the Reformed faith. It was penned by Zwingli's successor in Zurich, Johann Heinrich Bullinger, as a personal confession and testimony. Asked by Frederick III to provide a declaration of the Reformed faith, Bullinger presented this personal statement. It was written only seven years after Calvin's 1559 *Institutes* and against the background of the Counter-Reformation Council of Trent [1545-1563].)

What we find from the Zwinglian Reformer is a seamless agreement with Calvin. In Chapter IX, entitled, "Of Free Will, and Thus of Human Powers," there is a clear distinction drawn between the powers of humanity before and after the fall, and in believers after regeneration. At creation, humanity was made "upright and free," but "declined to evil" and therefore has "involved himself and the whole human race in sin and death." In sin, the mind has been "darkened" and the will "enslaved" so that it now "serves sin, not unwillingly but willingly," and in no way forced to sin by God or the devil. What is required for salvation is a regeneration or rebirth. Nothing from our first birth in Adam contributes anything at all to our salvation. "Wherefore, man not yet regenerate has no free will for good, no strength to perform what is good." In this regeneration, the mind must be illumined by the Holy Spirit in order to understand the things of God, and the will must be changed and equipped by the Holy Spirit "so that it wills and is able to do the good of its own accord." The renewed mind and will actively cooperate with God, though the will is weak always in this life as the flesh continues to war against the Spirit, and believers take no pride in their (regenerated) free will because it is purely a gift from God.

CHAPTER IX Of Free Will, and Thus of Human Powers

In this matter, which has always produced many conflicts in the Church, we teach that a threefold condition or state of man is to be considered. WHAT MAN WAS BEFORE THE FALL. There is the state in which man was in the beginning before the fall, namely, upright and free, so that he could both continue in goodness and decline to evil. However, he declined to evil, and has involved himself and the whole human race in sin and death, as has been said already. WHAT MAN WAS AFTER THE FALL. Then we are to consider what man was after the fall. To be sure, his reason was not taken from him, nor was he deprived of will, and he was not entirely changed into a stone or a tree. But they were so altered and weakened that they no longer can do what they could before the fall. For the understanding is darkened, and the will which was free has become an enslaved will. Now it serves sin, not unwillingly but willingly. And indeed, it is called a will, not an unwill[ing].

MAN DOES EVIL BY HIS OWN FREE WILL. Therefore, in regard to evil or sin, man is not forced by God or by the devil but does evil by his own free will, and in this respect he has a most free will. But when we frequently see that the worst crimes and designs of men are prevented by God from reaching their purpose, this does not take away man's freedom in doing evil, but God by his own power prevents what man freely planned otherwise. Thus Joseph's brothers freely determined to get rid of him, but they were unable to do it because something else seemed good to the counsel of God.

MAN IS NOT CAPABLE OF GOOD Per Se. In regard to goodness and virtue man's reason does not judge rightly of itself concerning divine things. For the evangelical and apostolic Scripture requires regeneration of whoever among us wishes to be saved. Hence our first birth from Adam contributes nothing to our salvation. Paul says: "The unspiritual man does not receive the gifts of the Spirit of God," etc. (I Cor. 2:14). And in another place he denies that we of ourselves are capable of thinking anything good (II Cor. 3:5). Now it is known that the mind or intellect is the guide of the will, and when the guide is blind, it is obvious how far the will reaches. Wherefore, man not yet regenerate has no free will for good, no strength to perform what is good. The Lord says in the Gospel: "Truly, truly, I say to you, everyone who commits sin is a slave to sin" (John 8:34). And the apostle Paul says: "The mind that is set on the flesh is hostile to God; it does not submit to God's law, indeed it cannot" (Rom. 8:7). Yet in regard to earthly things, fallen man is not entirely lacking in understanding.

UNDERSTANDING OF THE ARTS. For God in his mercy

has permitted the powers of the intellect to remain, though differing greatly from what was in man before the fall. God commands us to cultivate our natural talents, and meanwhile adds both gifts and success. And it is obvious that we make no progress in all the arts without God's blessing. In any case, Scripture refers all the arts to God; and, indeed, the heathen trace the origin of the arts to the gods who invented them.

OF WHAT KIND ARE THE POWERS OF THE REGENERATE, AND IN WHAT WAY THEIR WILLS ARE FREE. Finally, we must see whether the regenerate have free wills, and to what extent. In regeneration the understanding is illumined by the Holy Spirit in order that it may understand both the mysteries and the will of God. And the will itself is not only changed by the Spirit, but it is also equipped with faculties so that it wills and is able to do the good of its own accord (Rom. 8:1 ff.). Unless we grant this, we will deny Christian liberty and introduce a legal bondage. But the prophet has God saying: "I will put my law within them, and I will write it upon their hearts" (Jer. 31:33; Ezek. 36:26 f.). The Lord also says in the Gospel: "If the Son makes you free, you will be free indeed" (John 8:36). Paul also writes to the Philippians: "It has been granted to you that for the sake of Christ you should not only believe in him but also suffer for his sake" (Phil. 1:29). Again: "I am sure that he who began a good work in you will bring it to completion at the day of Jesus Christ" (v. 6). Also: "God is at work in you, both to will and to work for his good pleasure" (ch. 2:13).

THE REGENERATE WORK NOT ONLY PASSIVELY BUT ACTIVELY. However, in this connection we teach that there are two things to be observed: First, that the regenerate, in choosing and doing good, work not only passively but actively. For they are moved by God that they may do themselves what they do. For Augustine rightly adduces the saying that "God is said to be our helper. But no one can be helped unless he does something." The Manichaeans robbed man of all activity and made him like a stone or a block of wood.

THE FREE WILL IS WEAK IN THE REGENERATE. Secondly, in the regenerate a weakness remains. For since sin dwells in us, and in the regenerate the flesh struggles against the Spirit till the end of our lives, they do not easily accomplish in all things what they had planned. These things are confirmed by the apostle in Rom., ch. 7, and Gal., ch. 5. Therefore that free will is weak in us on account of the remnants of the old Adam and of innate human corruption remaining in us until the end of our lives. Meanwhile, since the powers of the flesh and the remnants of the old man are not so efficacious that they wholly extinguish the work of the Spirit, for that reason the faithful are said to be free, yet so that they acknowledge their infirmity and do not glory at all in their free will. For believers ought always to keep in mind what St. Augustine so many times inculcated according to the apostle: "What have you that you did not receive? If then you received it, why do you boast as if it were not a gift?" To this he adds that what we have planned does not immediately come to pass. For the issue of things lies in the hand of God. This is the reason Paul prayed to the Lord to prosper his journey (Rom. 1:10). And this also is the reason the free will is weak.

IN EXTERNAL THINGS THERE IS LIBERTY. Moreover, no one denies that in external things both the regenerate and the unregenerate enjoy free will. For man has in common with other living creatures (to which he is not inferior) this nature to will some things and not to will others. Thus he is able to speak or to keep silent, to go out of his house or to remain at home, etc. However, even here God's power is always to be observed, for it was the cause that Balaam could not go as far as he wanted (Num., ch. 24), and Zacharias upon returning from the temple could not speak as he wanted (Luke, ch. 1).

HERESIES. In this matter we condemn the Manichaeans who deny that the beginning of evil was for man [created] good, from his free will. We also condemn the Pelagians who assert that an evil man has sufficient free will to do the good that is commanded. Both are refuted by Holy Scripture which says to the former, "God made man upright" and to the latter, "If the Son makes you free, you will be free indeed" (John 8:36).

The Canons of Dort (1619) [CRC, RCA]

(In some ways the Synod of Dort (1618-1619) was convened to address the very subject of this paper. It was held to settle a controversy in Dutch churches initiated by James Arminius, from whom we get the term "Arminianism." After his death, his followers presented their views called the Remonstrance of 1610, in which they asserted five main points including the freewill and only partial depravity of man, the resistability of grace, and the possibility of a falling away from grace of those who are truly converted. The Synod condemned these views as heretical and formulated a response to each of the five points called the Canons of Dort. From this response come the so-called "five points of Calvinism": unconditional election, limited atonement, total depravity, irresistible grace, and the perseverance of the saints.)

To demonstrate that Canons of Dort assert the complete inability of the fallen person to respond to Christ in saving faith is not difficult, for such assersion is most emphatic, especially in the joined Third and Fourth Heads of Doctrine. Simply reading through the seventeen Articles and nine Rejections leave no room whatsoever for doubt. Humanity was created with true knowledge of the mind and with a will that was good, upright and holy, and with affections that were pure. But by his own free will, at the instigation of the devil, he rebelled against God and so forfeited these gifts. The mind was darkened, the will became rebellious and wicked, and the affections became impure. This was passed along to all their children, not merely by imitation but by "propagation of a vicious nature." The result is that sinners are "neither able nor willing to return to God" nor even "to dispose themselves to such reform."

The light of nature could not bring fallen humanity to a saving knowledge of God, but merely renders humanity "inexcusable." Nor could the Law. Though it reveals sin, the Law offers no remedy nor strength against sin. Rather God alone can effect such salvation "by the operation of the Holy Spirit through the word or ministry of reconciliation" i.e. the Gospel. When God applies his salvation to the elect, he illumines their minds by the Holy Spirit so that they may believe, he opens closed hearts and "infuses new qualities to the will" making it alive, good, obedient and pliable. This is called in Scripture "regeneration," a work of God alone "without our aid," "a supernatural work, most powerful, and at the same time most delightful, astonishing, mysterious, and ineffable. Saving faith, therefore, is a gift, not merely an offer, which is conferred upon the elect, by God's most free election, by which he owes salvation to no one. Rather, the saved owe all things to God.

CANONS OF DORT: The Third and Fourth Main Points of Doctrine

Human Corruption, Conversion to God, and the Way It Occurs

Article 1 *The Effect of the Fall on Human Nature*
Man was originally created in the image of God and was furnished in his mind with a true and salutary knowledge of his Creator and things spiritual, in his will and heart with righteousness, and in all his emotions with purity; indeed, the whole man was holy. However, rebelling against God at the devil's instigation and by his own free will, he deprived himself of these outstanding gifts. Rather, in their place he brought upon himself blindness, terrible darkness, futility, and distortion of judgment in his mind; perversity, defiance, and hardness in his heart and will; and finally impurity in all his emotions.

Article 2 *The Spread of Corruption*

Man brought forth children of the same nature as himself after the fall. That is to say, being corrupt he brought forth corrupt children. The corruption spread, by God's just judgment, from Adam to all his descendants— except for Christ alone—not by way of imitation (as in former times the Pelagians would have it) but by way of the propagation of his perverted nature.

Article 3 *Total Inability*

Therefore, all people are conceived in sin and are born children of wrath, unfit for any saving good, inclined to evil, dead in their sins, and slaves to sin; without the grace of the regenerating Holy Spirit they are neither willing nor able to return to God, to reform their distorted nature, or even to dispose themselves to such reform.

Article 4 *The Inadequacy of the Light of Nature*

There is, to be sure, a certain light of nature remaining in man after the fall, by virtue of which he retains some notions about God, natural things, and the difference between what is moral and immoral, and demonstrates a certain eagerness for virtue and for good outward behavior. But this light of nature is far from enabling man to come to a saving knowledge of God and conversion to him—so far, in fact, that man does not use it rightly even in matters of nature and society. Instead, in various ways he completely distorts this light, whatever its precise character, and suppresses it in unrighteousness. In doing so he renders himself without excuse before God.

Article 5 *The Inadequacy of the Law*

In this respect, what is true of the light of nature is true also of the Ten Commandments given by God through Moses specifically to the Jews. For man cannot obtain saving grace through the Decalogue, because, although it does expose the magnitude of his sin and increasingly convict him of his guilt, yet it does not offer a remedy or enable him to escape from his misery, and, indeed, weakened as it is by the flesh, leaves the offender under the curse.

Article 6 *The Saving Power of the Gospel*

What, therefore, neither the light of nature nor the law can do, God accomplishes by the power of the Holy Spirit, through the Word or the ministry of reconciliation. This is the gospel about the Messiah, through which it has pleased God to save believers, in both the Old and the New Testament.

Article 7 *God's Freedom in Revealing the Gospel*

In the Old Testament, God revealed this secret of his will to a small number; in the New Testament (now without any distinction between peoples) he discloses it to a large number. The reason for this difference must not be ascribed to the greater worth of one nation over another, or to a better use of the light of nature, but to the free good pleasure and undeserved love of God. Therefore, those who receive so much grace, beyond and in spite of all they deserve, ought to acknowledge it with humble and thankful hearts; on the other hand, with the apostle they ought to adore (but certainly not inquisitively search into) the severity and justice of God's judgments on the others, who do not receive this grace.

Article 8 *The Serious Call of the Gospel*

Nevertheless, all who are called through the gospel are called seriously. For seriously and most genuinely God makes known in his Word what is pleasing to him: that those who are called should come to him. Seriously he also promises rest for their souls and eternal life to all who come to him and believe.

Article 9 *Human Responsibility for Rejecting the Gospel*

The fact that many who are called through the ministry of the gospel do not come and are not brought to conversion must not be blamed on the gospel, nor on Christ, who is offered through the gospel, nor on God, who calls them through the gospel and even bestows various gifts on them, but on the people themselves who are called. Some in self-assurance do not even entertain the Word of life; others do entertain it but do not take it to heart, and for that reason, after the fleeting joy of a temporary faith, they relapse; others choke the seed of the Word with the thorns of life's cares and with the pleasures of the world and bring forth no fruits. This our Savior teaches in the parable of the sower (Matt. 13).

Article 10 *Conversion as the Work of God*

The fact that others who are called through the ministry of the gospel do come and are brought to conversion must not be credited to man, as though one distinguishes himself by free choice from others who are furnished with equal or sufficient grace for faith and conversion (as the proud heresy of Pelagius maintains). No, it must be credited to God: just as from eternity he chose his own in Christ, so within time he effectively calls them, grants them faith and repentance, and, having rescued them from the dominion of darkness, brings them into the kingdom of his Son, in order that they may declare the wonderful deeds of him who called them out of darkness into this marvelous light, and may boast not in themselves, but in the Lord, as apostolic words frequently testify in Scripture.

Article 11 *The Holy Spirit's Work in Conversion*

Moreover, when God carries out this good pleasure in his chosen ones, or works true conversion in them, he not only sees to it that the gospel is proclaimed to them outwardly, and enlightens their minds powerfully by the Holy Spirit so that they may rightly understand and discern the things of the Spirit of God, but, by the effective operation of the same regenerating Spirit, he also penetrates into the inmost being of man, opens the closed heart, softens the hard heart, and circumcises the heart that is uncircumcised. He infuses new qualities into the will, making the dead will alive, the evil one good, the unwilling one willing, and the stubborn one compliant; he activates and strengthens the will so that, like a good tree, it may be enabled to produce the fruits of good deeds.

Article 12 *Regeneration a Supernatural Work*

And this is the regeneration, the new creation, the raising from the dead, and the making alive so clearly proclaimed in the Scriptures, which God works in us without our help. But this certainly does not happen only by outward teaching, by moral persuasion, or by such a way of working that, after God has done his work, it remains in man's power whether or not to be reborn or converted. Rather, it is an entirely supernatural work, one that is at the same time most powerful and most pleasing, a marvelous, hidden, and inexpressible work, which is not lesser than or inferior in power to that of creation or of raising the dead, as Scripture (inspired by the author of this work) teaches. As a result, all those in whose hearts God works in this marvelous way are certainly, unfailingly, and effectively reborn and do actually believe. And then the will, now renewed, is not only activated and motivated by God but in being activated by God is also itself active. For this reason, man himself, by that grace which he has received, is also rightly said to believe and to repent.

Article 13 *The Incomprehensible Way of Regeneration*

In this life believers cannot fully understand the way this work occurs; meanwhile, they rest content with knowing and experiencing that by this grace of God they do believe with the heart and love their Savior.

Article 14 *The Way God Gives Faith*

In this way, therefore, faith is a gift of God, not in the sense that it is offered by God for man to choose, but that it is in actual fact bestowed on man, breathed and infused into him. Nor is it a gift in the sense that God bestows only the potential to believe, but then awaits assent—the act of believing—from man's choice; rather, it is a gift in the sense that he who works both willing and acting and, indeed, works all things in all people produces in man both the will to believe and the belief itself.

Article 15 *Responses to God's Grace*

God does not owe this grace to anyone. For what could God owe to one who has nothing to give that can be paid back? Indeed, what could God owe to one who has nothing of his own to give but sin and falsehood? Therefore the person who receives this grace owes and gives eternal thanks to God alone; the person who does not receive it either does not care at all about these spiritual things and is satisfied with himself in his condition, or else in self-assurance foolishly boasts about having something which he lacks. Furthermore, following the example of the apostles, we are to think and to speak in the most favorable way about those who outwardly profess their faith and better their lives, for the inner chambers of the heart are unknown to us. But for others who have not yet been called, we are to pray to the God who calls things that do not exist as though they did. In no way, however, are we to pride ourselves as better than they, as though we had distinguished ourselves from them.

Article 16 *Regeneration's Effect*

However, just as by the fall man did not cease to be man, endowed with intellect and will, and just as sin, which has spread through the whole human race, did not abolish the nature of the human race but distorted and spiritually killed it, so also this divine grace of regeneration does not act in people as if they were blocks and stones; nor does it abolish the will and its properties or coerce a reluctant will by force, but spiritually revives, heals, reforms, and—in a manner at once pleasing and powerful—bends it back. As a result, a ready and sincere obedience of the Spirit now begins to prevail where before the rebellion and resistance of the flesh were completely dominant. It is in this that the true and spiritual restoration and freedom of our will consists. Thus, if the marvelous Maker of every good thing were not dealing with us, man would have no hope of getting up from his fall by his free choice, by which he plunged himself into ruin when still standing upright.

Article 17 *God's Use of Means in Regeneration*

Just as the almighty work of God by which he brings forth and sustains our natural life does not rule out but requires the use of means, by which God, according to his infinite wisdom and goodness, has wished to exercise his power, so also the aforementioned supernatural work of God by which he regenerates us in no way rules out or cancels the use of the gospel, which God in his great wisdom has appointed to be the seed of regeneration and the food of the soul. For this reason, the apostles and the teachers who followed them taught the people in a godly manner about this grace of God, to give him the glory and to humble all pride, and yet did not neglect meanwhile to keep the people, by means of the holy admonitions of the gospel, under the administration of the Word, the sacraments, and discipline. So even today it is out of the question that the teachers or those taught in the church should presume to test God by separating what he in his good pleasure has wished to be closely joined together. For grace is bestowed through admonitions, and the more readily we perform our duty, the more lustrous the benefit of God working in us usually is and the better his work advances. To him alone, both for the means and for their saving fruit and effectiveness, all glory is owed forever. Amen.

Rejection of Errors

Having set forth the orthodox teaching, the Synod rejects the errors of those

I. Who teach that, properly speaking, it cannot be said that original sin in itself is enough to condemn the whole human race or to warrant temporal and eternal punishments.

For they contradict the apostle when he says: *Sin entered the world through one man, and death through sin, and in this way death passed on to all men because all sinned* (Rom. 5:12); also: *The guilt followed one sin and brought condemnation* (Rom. 5:16); likewise: *The wages of sin is death* (Rom. 6:23).

II. Who teach that the spiritual gifts or the good dispositions and virtues such as goodness, holiness, and righteousness could not have resided in man's will when he was first created, and therefore could not have been separated from the will at the fall.

For this conflicts with the apostle's description of the image of God in Ephesians 4:24, where he portrays the image in terms of righteousness and holiness, which definitely reside in the will.

III. Who teach that in spiritual death the spiritual gifts have not been separated from man's will, since the will in itself has never been corrupted but only hindered by the darkness of the mind and the unruliness of the emotions, and since the will is able to exercise its innate free capacity once these hindrances are removed, which is to say, it is able of itself to will or choose whatever good is set before it— or else not to will or choose it.

This is a novel idea and an error and has the effect of elevating the power of free choice, contrary to the words of Jeremiah the prophet: *The heart itself is deceitful above all things and wicked* (Jer. 17:9); and of the words of the apostle: *All of us also lived among them* (the sons of disobedience) *at one time in the passions of our flesh, following the will of our flesh and thoughts* (Eph. 2:3).

IV. Who teach that unregenerate man is not strictly or totally dead in his sins or deprived of all capacity for spiritual good but is able to hunger and thirst for righteousness or life and to offer the sacrifice of a broken and contrite spirit which is pleasing to God.

For these views are opposed to the plain testimonies of Scripture: *You were dead in your transgressions and sins* (Eph. 2:1, 5); *The imagination of the thoughts of man's heart is only evil all the time* (Gen. 6:5; 8:21). Besides, to hunger and thirst for deliverance from misery and for life, and to offer God the sacrifice of a broken spirit is characteristic only of the regenerate and of those called blessed (Ps. 51:17; Matt. 5:6).

V. Who teach that corrupt and natural man can make such good use of common grace (by which they mean the light of nature)or of the gifts remaining after the fall that he is able thereby gradually to obtain a greater grace— evangelical or saving grace—as well as salvation itself; and that in this way God, for his part, shows himself ready to reveal Christ to all people, since he provides to all, to a sufficient extent and in an effective manner, the means necessary for the revealing of Christ, for faith, and for repentance.

For Scripture, not to mention the experience of all ages, testifies that this is false: *He makes known his words to Jacob, his statutes and his laws to Israel; he has done this for no other nation, and they do not know his laws (Ps. 147:19-20); In the past God let all nations go their own way (Acts 14:16); They(Paul and his companions)were kept by the Holy Spirit from speaking God's word in Asia; and When they had come to Mysia, they tried to go to Bithynia, but the Spirit would not allow them to(Acts 16:6-7).*

VI. *Who teach that in the true conversion of man new qualities, dispositions, or gifts cannot be infused or poured into his will by God, and indeed that the faith [or* *believing] by which we first come to conversion and from which we receive the name "believers" is not a quality or gift infused by God, but only an act of man, and that it cannot be called a gift except in respect to the power of attaining faith.*

For these views contradict the Holy Scriptures, which testify that God does infuse or pour into our hearts the new qualities of faith, obedience, and the experiencing of his love: *I will put my law in their minds, and write it on their hearts (Jer. 31:33); I will pour water on the thirsty land, and streams on the dry ground; I will pour out my Spirit on your offspring (Isa. 44:3); The love of God has been poured out in our hearts by the Holy Spirit, who has been given to us (Rom. 5:5).* They also conflict with the continuous practice of the Church, which prays with the prophet: *Convert me, Lord, and I shall be converted (Jer. 31:18).*

VII. *Who teach that the grace by which we are converted to God is nothing but a gentle persuasion, or (as others explain it) that the way of God's acting in man's conversion that is most noble and suited to human nature is that which happens by persuasion, and that nothing prevents this grace of moral suasion even by itself from making natural men spiritual; indeed, that God does not produce the assent of the will except in this manner of moral suasion, and that the effectiveness of God's work by which it surpasses the work of Satan consists in the fact that God promises eternal benefits while Satan promises temporal ones.*

For this teaching is entirely Pelagian and contrary to the whole of Scripture, which recognizes besides this persuasion also another, far more effective and divine way in which the Holy Spirit acts in man's conversion. As Ezekiel 36:26 puts it: *I will give you a new heart and put a new spirit in you; and I will remove your heart of stone and give you a heart of flesh....*

VIII. *Who teach that God in regenerating man does not bring to bear that power of his omnipotence whereby he may powerfully and unfailingly bend man's will to faith and conversion, but that even when God has accomplished all the works of grace which he uses for man's conversion, man nevertheless can, and in actual fact often does, so resist God and the Spirit in their intent and will to regenerate him, that man completely thwarts his own rebirth; and, indeed, that it remains in his own power whether or not to be reborn.*

For this does away with all effective functioning of God's grace in our conversion and subjects the activity of Almighty God to the will of man; it is contrary to the apostles, who teach that *"we believe by virtue of the effective working of God's mighty strength"* (Eph. 1:19), and that *"God fulfills the undeserved good will of his kindness and the work of faith in us with power"* (2 Thess. 1:11), and likewise that *"his divine power has given us everything we need for life and godliness"* (2 Pet. 1:3).

IX. Who teach that grace and free choice are concurrent partial causes which cooperate to initiate conversion, and that grace does not precede—in the order of causality—the effective influence of the will;that is to say, that God does not effectively help man's will to come to conversion before man's will itself motivates and determines itself.

For the early church already condemned this doctrine long ago in the Pelagians, on the basis of the words of the apostle: *It does not depend on man's willing or running but on God's mercy (Rom. 9:16); also: Who makes you different from anyone else? and What do you have that you did not receive?(1 Cor. 4:7); likewise: It is God who works in you to will and act according to his good pleasure (Phil. 2:13).*

(adopted by the 1986 Synod of the Christian Reformed Church.)

The Westminster Confession (1647) [PCUSA]

(Originally convened to bring greater unity and uniformity of faith and practice within the church in England by revising the Thirty-nine Articles, the Westminster Assembly was given a broader mandate with the signing of the Solemn League and Covenant. Its divines were charged with the responsibility of bringing the Church of England into line with the theology and practice of the Presbyterian Church in Scotland. The chief document it produced, the Westminster Confession, is a clear and carefully-worded statement of seventeenth-century Reformed doctrine, an enduring standard for English-speaking Presbyterians around the world and the pattern for other Reformed confessions which followed it.)

Chapter IX of the Westminster Confession is titled "Of Free Will." As it is precisely to our point and speaks with clarity and succinctness, it will be quoted in full:

1. God hath endued the will of man with that natural liberty, that it is neither forced, nor by any absolute necessity of nature determined to good or evil.
2. Man, in his state of innocency, had freedom and power to will and to do that which is good and well-pleasing to God; but yet mutably, so that he might fall from it.
3. Man, by his Fall into a state of sin, hath wholly lost all ability of will to any spiritual good accompanying salvation; so as a natural man, being altogether averse from that good, and dead in sin, is not able, by his own strength, to convert himself, or to prepare himself thereunto.
4. When God converteth a sinner and translateth him into the state of grace, he freeth him from his natural bondage under sin, and, by his grace alone, enableth him freely to will and to do that which is

spiritually good; yet so as that, by reason of his remaining corruption, he doth not perfectly, nor only, will that which is good, but doth also will that which is evil.

5. The will of man is made perfectly and immutably free to good alone, in the state of glory only.

Though written 88 years after Calvin's 1559 *Institutes*, the Westminster Confession advances the same themes: the will was created good and free, yet through the Fall has lost all ability for self-conversion, or any preparation for conversion. Such conversion is attributed to God alone, in which the will is set free from its "natural bondage under sin" and is enabled "to will and to do that which is spiritually good, though the regenerated will is always mixed until "in the state of glory" in heaven.

The Westminster Shorter Catechism (1647) [PCUSA]

(Intended as a teaching tool for children, the Shorter Catechism is a brief summary of the Confession in a question-and-answer format, featuring one-sentence responses and definitions that can be rapidly memorized.)

In brevity of language, the Shorter Catechism asserts inability.

Q. 82. Is any man able perfectly to keep the commandments of God?
A. No mere man, since the Fall, is able, in this life, perfectly to keep the commandments of God, but doth daily break them, in thought, word, and deed.

The Westminster Larger Catechism (1648) [PCUSA]

(Similar in content to the Shorter Catechism, the Larger Catechism goes into more detail and covers more ground than the Shorter. Because of its greater length, it is also lesser known.)

The Larger Catechism not only asserts human inability, but denies perfectionism in this life as well.

Q. 149. Is any man able perfectly to keep the Commandments of God?
A. No man is able, either of himself, or by any grace received in this life, perfectly to keep the Commandments of God; but doth daily break them in thought, word, and deed.

B. THE MEANS OF GRACE.

The Scots Confession (1560) [PCUSA]

The Scots Confession does not expound any explicit doctrine of preaching as the primary means of grace or of God's using the preaching of the Gospel to create faith in unbelievers. What we do find, however, is a high view of preaching the gospel. Preaching is one of three "notes" or marks of the true kirk (church):

> The notes of the true Kirk, therefore, we believe, confess, and avow to be: first, the true preaching of the Word of God, in which God has revealed himself to us, as the writings of the prophets and apostles declare; secondly, the right administration of the sacraments of Christ Jesus, with which must be associated the Word and promise of God to seal and confirm them in our hearts; and lastly, ecclesiastical discipline uprightly ministered, as God's Word prescribes, whereby vice is repressed and virtue nourished. (XXVIII)

And the Sacraments are to be administered only by "lawful ministers," the only ones whom "God has given the power to preach the gospel."

> Two things are necessary for the right administration of the sacraments. The first is that they should be ministered by lawful ministers, and we declare that these are men appointed to preach the Word, unto whom God has given the power to preach the gospel, and who are lawfully called by some Kirk. The second is that they should be ministered in the elements and manner which God has appointed. Otherwise they cease to be the sacraments of Christ Jesus. (XXII)

The Belgic Confession (1561) (CRC, RCA)

The Belgic Confession says more than the Scots Confession with respect to the necessity of the Gospel as the means God uses to produce faith. Article 24 considers faith to be the combined product of hearing God's Word and the work of the Holy Spirit: "We believe that this true faith, produced in us by the hearing of God's Word and by the work of the Holy Spirit, regenerates us and makes us new creatures, causing us to live a new life and freeing us from the slavery of sin." And Article 33 reminds us that the "Word of the gospel" is the means by which God "enables us to understand." "God has added these (sacraments) to the Word of the gospel to represent better to our external senses both what God enables us to understand by the Word and does inwardly in our hearts, confirming in us the salvation imparted to us."

The Heidelberg Catechism (1563) [PCUSA, CRC, RCA]

The Heidelberg Catechism does make the connection between preaching and the work of the Holy Spirit explicit. Where does faith originate? It is produced in our hearts by the Holy Spirit through the means or instrumentality of the "preaching of the holy gospel."

Q. 65. Since, then, faith alone makes us share in Christ and all his benefits, where does such faith originate?
A. The Holy Spirit creates it in our hearts by the preaching of the holy gospel, and confirms it by the use of the holy Sacraments.

The Second Helvetic Confession (1566) [PCUSA]

Chapter I of the Second Helvetic Confession reveals a remarkably high view of preaching. After asserting the full authority and sufficiency of the Canonical Scriptures, the Confession declares that "the preaching of the Word of God is the Word of God." "Wherefore when this Word of God is now preached in the church by preachers lawfully called, we believe that the very Word of God is proclaimed, and received by the faithful...." And while it is true that the efficacy of the outward preaching of the Gospel depends on the inward illumination of the Holy Spirit, still preaching is to be esteemed because it is God's will that "his Word should be preached outwardly also." The Catechism reminds us that in the case of Cornelius (Acts 10), though he could have been converted directly by the ministry of the Spirit or an angel, "nevertheless, he refers him to Peter, of whom the angel speaking says, 'He shall tell you what you ought to do.'"

The combination of the outward preaching of the gospel and the inward work of the Spirit is seen clearly in Paul's preaching at Philippi, where he "preached the Word outwardly to Lydia, a seller of purple goods; but the Lord inwardly opened the woman's heart (Acts 16:14)," and in Romans 10, where "Paul, after a beautiful development of his thought, in Rom. 10:17 at length comes to the conclusion, 'So faith comes from hearing, and hearing from the Word of God by the preaching of Christ.'"

Though the Confession concedes that God may illumine whom he will with or without the external preaching, yet "we speak of the usual way of instructing men, delivered unto us from God, both by commandment and examples."

THE PREACHING OF THE WORD OF GOD IS THE WORD OF GOD.

Wherefore when this Word of God is now preached in the church by preachers lawfully called, we believe that the very Word of God is proclaimed, and received by the faithful; and that neither any other Word of God is to be invented nor is to be expected from heaven: and that now the Word itself which is preached is to be regarded, not the minister that preaches; for even if he be evil and a sinner, nevertheless the Word of God remains still true and good.

Neither do we think that therefore the outward preaching is to be thought as fruitless because the instruction in true religion depends on the inward illumination of the Spirit, or because it is written "And no longer shall each man teach his neighbor . . ., for they shall all know me" (Jer. 31:34), and "Neither he who plants nor he who waters is anything, but only God who gives the growth" (I Cor. 3:7). For although "no one can come to Christ unless he be drawn by the Father" (John 6:44), and unless the Holy Spirit inwardly illumines him, yet we know that it is surely the will of God that his Word should be preached outwardly also. God could indeed, by his Holy Spirit, or by the ministry of an angel, without the ministry of St. Peter, have taught Cornelius in the Acts; but, nevertheless, he refers him to Peter, of whom the angel speaking says, "He shall tell you what you ought to do."

INWARD ILLUMINATION DOES NOT ELIMINATE EXTERNAL PREACHING.

For he that illuminates inwardly by giving men the Holy Spirit, the same one, by way of commandment, said unto his disciples, "Go into all the world, and preach the Gospel to the whole creation" (Mark 16:15). And so in Philippi, Paul preached the Word outwardly to Lydia, a seller of purple the same Paul, after a beautiful development of his thought, in Rom. 10:17 at length comes to the conclusion, "So faith comes from hearing, and hearing from the Word of God by the preaching of Christ."

At the same time we recognize that God can illuminate whom and when he will, even without the external ministry, for that is in his power; but we speak of the usual way of instructing men, delivered unto us from God, both by commandment and examples.

The Canons of Dort (1619) [CRC, RCA]

The Canons of Dort would go further in insisting upon the indispensability of the outward means of preaching. How does God save snners? God "calls men by the gospel" (3/4, 9). "What, therefore, neither the light of nature nor the law can do, God accomplishes by the power of the Holy Spirit, through the Word or the ministry of reconciliation. This is the gospel about the Messiah, through which it has pleased God to save believers, in both the Old and the New Testament" (3/4, 6). To save the elect, God sees to it that they hear the gospel, to which he adds the saving power of his Spirit.

> Moreover, when God carries out this good pleasure in his chosen ones, or works true conversion in them, he not only sees to it that the gospel is proclaimed to them outwardly, and enlightens their minds powerfully by the Holy Spirit so that they may rightly understand and discern the things of the Spirit of God, but, by the effective operation of the same regenerating Spirit, he also penetrates into the inmost being of man, opens the closed heart, softens the hard heart, and circumcises the heart that is uncircumcised. He infuses new qualities into the will, making the dead will alive, the evil one good, the unwilling one willing, and the stubborn one compliant; he activates and strengthens the will so that, like a good tree, it may be enabled to produce the fruits of good deeds. (3/4, 11)

Thus the necessary means for saving faith is the preaching of the gospel. And this means must not be neglected. Even though it is God who sustains our bodies through the means of physical food, we do not despise the means and neglect eating. So preaching the gospel is God's means of spiritual nourishment, and we should not despise that means.

> Just as the almighty work of God by which he brings forth and sustains our natural life does not rule out but requires the use of means, by which God, according to his infinite wisdom and goodness, has wished to exercise his power, so also the aforementioned supernatural work of God by which he regenerates us in no way rules out or cancels the use of the gospel, which God in his great wisdom has appointed to be the seed of regeneration and the food of the soul. For this reason, the apostles and the teachers who followed them taught the people in a godly manner about this grace of God, to give him the glory and to humble all pride, and yet did not neglect meanwhile to keep the people, by means of the holy admonitions of the gospel, under the administration of the Word, the sacraments, and discipline. So even today it is out of the question that the teachers or

those taught in the church should presume to test God by separating what he in his good pleasure has wished to be closely joined together. For grace is bestowed through admonitions, and the more readily we perform our duty, the more lustrous the benefit of God working in us usually is and the better his work advances. To him alone, both for the means and for their saving fruit and effectiveness, all glory is owed forever. Amen. (3/4, 17)

But what about means other than preaching the gospel? What about techniques designed to bring about a "complete disorientation" and then to reform that person into a new way of thinking and living. Can not these techniques "'prepar(e) the way of the Lord,' making the trenches ready to receive the Grace which will flow into man as a result of prayer and to ease his journey toward Grace" as they "awaken and animate desire"?[435] Where is the place for creating the "right atmosphere and surroundings"? Is it not true that "Everyone knows that words penetrate effectively only when the doors of our souls are open to them and these doors are opened only under favorable circumstances."[436] Can not these "favorable circumstances" be planned by "managing the group" through "merited respect" employed by "someone who has learned to understand people, to know their reactions and preferences; someone who knows how to adapt this authority or prestige to the situations in which men will yield freely, but which they will not tolerate if force is applied"?[437]

Not according to the Canons of Dort. The Canons categorically condemn and reject those

> *Who teach that the grace by which we are converted to God is nothing but a gentle persuasion, or (as others explain it) that the way of God's acting in man's conversion that is most noble and suited to human nature is that which happens by persuasion, and that nothing prevents this grace of moral suasion even by itself from making natural men spiritual; indeed, that God does not produce the assent of the will except in this manner of moral suasion, and that the effectiveness of God's work by which it surpasses the work of Satan consists in the fact that God promises eternal benefits while Satan promises temporal ones.*

For this teaching is entirely Pelagian and contrary to the whole of Scripture, which recognizes besides this persuasion also another, far more effective and divine way in which the Holy Spirit acts in man's conversion. As Ezekiel 36:26 puts it: *I will give you a new heart and put a new spirit in you; and I will remove your heart of stone and give you a heart of*

---

[435] Bonnin, *The How and the Why*, 34.
[436] Ibid.
[437] Ibid., 36.

flesh.... (3/4, Rej. VII)

Here is, perhaps, the clearest condemnation of the Cursillo technique by a Reformed document. It flatly declares that the Cursillo technique cannot do what it claims. No amount of methods, techniques, persuasion, psychological tricks and manipulation or high-pressure indoctrination under controlled circumstances can genuinely make a dead heart new and living. This the Canons condemn as heretical "Pelagianism."

The Westminster Confession (1647) [PCUSA]

The Westminster Confession considers the proclamation of the gospel to be the "divinely established and ordinary method of grace." God offers salvation "to all men in the gospel" and in the proclaiming of the gospel "by his Spirit accompanying the Word, (God) pleads with men to accept his gracious invitation." For this reason, the gospel is to be foremost in the ministry of the church:

> Since there is no other way of salvation than that revealed in the gospel, and since in the divinely established and ordinary method of grace faith cometh by hearing the Word of God, Christ hath commissioned his Church to go into all the world and to make disciples of all nations. All believers are, therefore, under obligation to sustain the ordinances of the Christian religion where they are already established, and to contribute by their prayers, gifts, and personal efforts to the extension of the Kingdom of Christ throughout the whole earth. (Chapter X)

The Westminster Shorter Catechism (1647) [PCUSA]

The Shorter Catechism recognizes three ordinances of the church, "especially the Word, sacraments, and prayer," as "the outward means whereby Christ communicateth to us the benefits of redemption" (Q. 88). Yet it gives first place to the preaching of the Word: "The Spirit of God maketh the reading, but especially the preaching, of the Word an effectual means of convincing and converting sinners, (1) and of building them up in holiness and comfort, through faith unto salvation" (Q. 89).

The Westminster Larger Catechism (1648) [PCUSA]

The Larger Catechism expands on the Shorter by delineating more clearly the effect of the preached word:

> The Spirit of God maketh the reading, but especially the preaching of the Word, an effectual means of enlightening, convincing, and humbling sinners, of driving them out of themselves, and drawing them unto Christ, of conforming them to his image, and subduing them to his will; of strengthening them against temptations and corruptions; of building them up in grace, and establishing their hearts in holiness and comfort through faith unto salvation. (Q. 155)

But the Larger Catechism also gives guidelines for how the Word is to be preached, among which is "not in the enticing word of man's wisdom" (quoting 1 Cor. 1:17).

> They that are called to labor in the ministry of the Word are to preach sound doctrine, diligently, in season, and out of season, plainly, not in the enticing word of man's wisdom, but in demonstration of the Spirit, and of power; faithfully, making known the whole counsel of God; wisely, applying themselves to the necessities and capacities of the hearers; zealously, with fervent love to God, and the souls of his people; sincerely, aiming at his glory, and their conversion, edification, and salvation. (Q. 159)

But the Cursillo technique is designed to present the message in the persuasive technique of man's wisdom, which the catechism (and Scripture!) forbids.

CONCLUSION

Can the external efforts of others (not by the ordinary means of grace of preaching with prayer, but by controlling circumstances, use of persuasive techniques, psychological reactions, etc.) make the unregenerate "more willing" to embrace Christ? We take for granted the fact that through education, propaganda or advertising, the will may be swayed this way or that. But can the will be swayed to believe with saving faith? The Reformed answer is a unanimous, resolute and unyielding, "No." And so, the Cursillo technique should be judged *a priori* unnecessary and completely ineffective. Admittedly education may teach a child geometry or French. Advertising may convince a consumer to buy Pepsi rather than Coke. Propaganda may turn a free-marketer into a socialist. But what effect do education, advertising or propaganda have in convincing a sinner to embrace Christ? None whatsoever. The mind is blind to God, the will is dead to God and the heart is solid rock.

Yet God is pleased to use some human means to apply the grace of salvation to the elect. And the unanimous and emphatic Reformed answer is that God has ordained to use the proclamation of the Gospel alone: Word and Spirit.

Proponents of the Cursillo would undoubtedly insist that the gospel is presented during the Cursillo weekend. This may be granted. What is objectionable about the Cursillo technique is not that the gospel is presented, but that it is considered insufficient, that the proclamation of the gospel must be supplemented by persuasive psychological techniques designed to "'prepar(e) the way of the Lord,' making the trenches ready to receive the Grace which will flow into man as a result of prayer and to ease his journey toward Grace," to "awaken and animate desire" and to create the "right atmosphere and surroundings" because "everyone knows that words penetrate effectively only when the doors of our souls are open to them and these doors are opened only under favorable circumstances."

Use of persuasive techniques, however suggests that the gospel is not enough, a direct contradiction to Paul's declaration that the gospel is "the power of God for salvation to everyone who believes" (Romans 1:16). In the Cursillo, the biblical and Reformed "Word and Spirit" becomes "Word and Spirit AND psychological persuasion." Adding the psychological effects is tantamount to proclaiming the gospel in "words of eloquent wisdom," which the Apostle Paul forbade, "lest the cross of Christ be emptied of its power" (1 Corinthians 1:17). It is a human attempt to make "the word of the cross" less foolish to those who are perishing, when it is God's work alone to make it the "the power of God" to those who are being saved (1 Corinthians 1:18).

Admittedly, the Cursillo technique is effective. At issue is what precisely it effects. Most of the results are largely temporary and wear off in a matter of weeks. This would suggest that the Cursillo creates an emotional event leading to a false sense of conversion or religious experience, and this is, in fact, what mostly happens. For many, then, the Cursillo community comes to be considered the true spiritual home. Cursillo replaces the church, fellow Cursillo participants are counted as true brothers and sisters, and the "us vs. them" / "have's and have not's" mentality prevails. All of these are part of the undeniable reality of the Cursillo technique. And so, as noted before, the Cursillo technique should be discontinued altogether, especially in Reformed and Presbyterian churches whose doctrinal commitments would declare the techniques not only unnecessary, but detrimental to the genuine work of the Gospel.

APPENDIX B: *A History of Confusing Psychology with Religion*

"Is This for Real?"

As stated in chapter one, this simple question ("Is this for real?") turned my thinking in an entirely new direction. Though I honestly seldom used them, I had become quite skilled in the application of manipulative techniques to achieve predictable, emotional results. But three high school students called me on it. They had sensed that what they experienced might not be real, might be a trick. I certainly never intended to trick them. I only used a method that I had been taught and had found successful. The method regularly produced an altered state of consciousness (I would not have called it that at the time) in subjects including a (usually) pleasurable catharsis or cleansing of pent-up emotions and a bonding with others in the group. I had assumed that this catharsis was genuine Christian experience but was suddenly faced with the possibility that it might only be an emotional ruse.

There is an inborn and unquenchable religious impulse in human beings. Ecclesiastes 3:11 states that God "has made everything beautiful in its time. Also, he has put eternity into man's heart, yet so that he cannot find out what God has done from the beginning to the end." We possess a sense of the eternal, yet, unaided by God's special revelation in Scripture, we are unable to discern the divine plan. Hence we seek for religious experience. Paul also affirms our universal religious consciousness, a knowledge which we actively suppress and distort until we worship the creature instead of the Creator (c.f. Romans 1:18ff). This explains in part why Calvin declared that "...man's nature, so to speak, is a perpetual factory of idols."[438] I would suggest that this includes the propensity to create new religions. And one consistent source of new religions stems from the continual re-discovery of various means of achieving altered states of consciousness, including catharsis, and redefining these natural, physiological, and psychological events as encounters with the mystical, the

---

[438] Calvin, *Institutes of the Christian Religion*, 108.

numinous, the eternal-spirit, the divine, or, as University of Zurich Professor of Classical Philology Walter Burkert calls it, "the extraordinary experience."[439]

The Bible clearly describes similar experiences. God met Abraham and made a covenant with him in Genesis 15, and "behold, dreadful and great darkness fell upon him." (15:12) God met Jacob in a dream in the wilderness, and Jacob "was afraid and said, 'How awesome is this place! This is none other than the house of God, and this is the gate of heaven.'" (Genesis 28:17) God met Moses in a burning bush, and Moses said, "I will turn aside to see this great sight." (Exodus 3:3) God met Isaiah in the temple, and Isaiah's response was one of dread: "Woe is me! For I am lost; for I am a man of unclean lips, and I dwell in the midst of a people of unclean lips; for my eyes have seen the King, the LORD of hosts." (Isaiah 6:5). Simon Peter was unnerved by Jesus' fish-producing miracle, and his response was, "Depart from me, for I am a sinful man, O Lord." (Luke 5:8) Saul (later Paul) was struck down by a blinding vision of Christ on the Damascus road (Acts 9) and became a champion of Christ. He was later "caught up to the third heaven—whether in the body or out of the body I do not know, God knows." (2 Corinthians 12:2) John was "in the Spirit on the Lord's day" (Revelation 1:10) when he was granted his astonishing revelation, seeing Christ after which he "fell at his feet as though dead." (Revelation 1:17) These are only a few of the noteworthy encounters God gave to his people in Scripture.

We would expect that counterfeit religion would need to offer some kind of numinous experience if people are to embrace it. As with temptation, which only works when it is enticing, false religion must provide some kind of "extraordinary experience" if it is even temporarily to satisfy the religious impulse. And since there is a host of pharmacological, physiological, and psychological ways of achieving altered states of consciousness, there is a corresponding plethora of "mystical" religions, religions that promise "extraordinary experiences" which are assumed to be encounters with the ultimate.

Baal Worship

An example of this kind of altered-state, mystical religion is most likely preserved in Scripture in the description of Baal worship in 1 Kings 18. The story is familiar. God instructs Elijah to challenge the prophets of Baal to a "showdown" on Mt. Carmel: which god can answer with fire from heaven? The 450 prophets of Baal go first, but it is the description of their worship practice that is to the point. After arranging their sacrifice, they began to call on their god. Following an initial lack of success "they limped around the altar that

---

[439] Walter Burkert, *Ancient Mystery Cults* (Cambridge, MA: Harvard University Press, 1987), 89.

they had made." (18:26) Rhythmic dancing, an apparent feature in Baal worship, is one means of inducing catharsis according to psychologist and physician William Sargant. "Emotions can also be discharged by vigorous dancing....Some primitive tribes use dancing for the same purpose."[440]

Still finding no success and after being taunted by Elijah, the prophets stepped up their efforts. "And they cried aloud and cut themselves after their custom with swords and lances, until the blood gushed out upon them. And as midday passed, they raved on until the time of the offering of the oblation, but there was no voice. No one answered; no one paid attention." (18:28-29) The writer indicates that the common practice of Baal worship included prolonged, rhythmic dancing, self-inflicted blood loss (dehydration), and chanting, all of which can produce trance-like, altered states of consciousness and catharsis. So it is probable that Baalism really consisted of a methodology for inducing an altered state and a concomitant mythology (devotion to Baal) largely intended to explain their extraordinary experience.

Note by contrast the simplicity of Elijah's worship: preparation of the sacrifice according to God's commandment, and prayer. Note that Elijah's worship was not simply subjectively felt but also objectively answered as the fire fell (c.f. 1 Kings 18:30-39). And note that God severely punished Baalism: the 450 prophets of Baal were all put to death.

Many more examples of altered-state religions exist.

Other Forms of Psychologically-Induced Religions

1. Alcohol Religions. Ringo Starr sang McCartney and Lennon's lyric, "I get by (high) with a little help from my friends," in reference to chemical "friends." Others have decided that they can "get *religion* with a little help from" their friends. There are several expressions of drug-induced altered states of consciousness which are interpreted as religious experiences.

According to John Ferguson's *Encyclopedia of Mysticism and Mystery Religions*, alcohol "is the commonest of all drugs" acting "as a depressant on the brain."[441] It is ubiquitous to all cultures dating back to the earliest civilizations. Since it was impossible to keep fruit juices and other liquids containing sugar or starch from fermenting, the resultant alcoholic drink was widely available. Its relaxing and consciousness-altering properties (including the creation of illusions) also gave it apparent religious qualities. Numerous cultures attributed spiritual significance to alcohol (spirits) as in the mystery religion of Dionysius, for example. These properties were heightened by the discovery of the process of distillation. "The Hindu Soma, and Persian Haoma were ritual libations of

---

[440] Sargant, *Battle for the Mind, A Physiology of Conversion and Brain-Washing*, 58-59.
[441] John Ferguson, *Encyclopedia of Mysticism and Mystery Religions* (New York: Crossroad, 1982), 10.

fermented juice. The god Indra drank great quantities of Soma and said, 'I have drunk Soma, I have become immortal.'"[442] In a curious twist of the Alcoholics Anonymous' terminology, alcohol itself is the "higher power."

2. The Oracle of Delphi. Long-thought discredited, the ancient Greek historian Plutarch had spoken of a spring which emitted "fragrance and breeze" into the temple of the Oracle at Delphi, creating a frenzy and trance for the virgin priestesses and resulting in their delivery of supposed prophetic messages from an ecstatic state. Researchers in the 19th and 20th centuries had found no such springs or gases, and so Plutarch was dismissed.

But more recent discoveries have led to a revision of the revision. Archaeologist John Hale and geologist Jelle de Boer discovered two intersecting fault lines at the base of the ancient temple, fault lines which could indeed emit gases from deep in the earth. "De Boer posited that limestone deposits buried deep beneath the ground might have released hydrocarbon gases—specifically, methane, ethane, and ethylene—into the air."[443] Ethylene was of greater interest since it bears a sweet aroma (it makes fruits smell sweet), according with Plutarch's observation of "fragrance." Ethylene also produces mental confusion and in low doses can create trance-like symptoms. According to Hale, "Early-20th-century researchers found that ethylene could produce an anesthetic state twice as fast as nitrous oxide" (so-called "laughing gas"). Water samples from natural springs discovered at the faults indeed detected low levels of ethylene along with other gases.

> Though scholars continue to debate the precise nature of the gas—an Italian team published a paper last year arguing that methane-induced oxygen deprivation was the culprit—Hale says the bigger point is that the debate is happening at all. "People were responding to a very specific phenomena in the Earth's surface," he says. "Modern science confirms the validity of those ancient observations, and this is a great way of looking at ancient religion."[444]

Once more we find an example of a drug-induced altered state of consciousness confused with a religious or mystical experience.

3. Peyotism. A more telling and evident example of pharmacological mysticism is found in Peyotism, called "the most widespread

---

[442] Ibid.
[443] Kent Garber, "Explaining the Oracle's Visions," *U.S. News & World Report*, November 26/December 3, 2007, 46.
[444] Ibid.

contemporary religion among (native Americans) in the United States."[445] Peyotism is a syncretic blend of Christian teachings, ethics, and eschatology with Native American culture. Originating about 1885, it has spread to many tribes and boasts a congregation of some 300,000. In this religious practice, an all-night ceremony of symbolic ritualism centers on consuming the peyote buttons, which come from a spineless cactus and contain the active hallucinogenic agent mescaline. The resulting trance-like state is thought to convey healing powers and spiritual wisdom through heightened awareness, visions, and mystical experiences. Proponents claim that while others only talk *about* Jesus, they talk *to* Jesus. "And its resources are inexhaustible: 'You can use the Peyote all your life, but you never get to the end of what there is to be known from Peyote. Peyote is always teaching you something new."[446]

4. Psilocybin and the Magic Mushrooms of Marsh Chapel.

Another hallucinogenic drug found in a natural source became famous for its purported religion-enhancing properties in a well-known "experiment" on Good Friday 1963, in the basement of Marsh Chapel at Harvard Divinity School. A few years earlier, a New York banker and his Russian wife, Richard and Valentina Wasson, with a special interest in mushrooms, traveled to Mexico to track down the fabled mystical mushroom that had been the source of legends in the journals of Spanish conquistadors. Richard consumed some of the mushrooms, had what he described as a profound mystical experience, and presented his findings at Harvard University. This happened to coincide with the hippie movement, and the press covered the event widely. Psilocybin mushrooms were readily available in grassy areas of North America. The Wassons' discovery heralded the beginning of the recreational/spiritual hallucinogen movement in the United States.

By 1963 many youth were leaving formal churches in search of spiritual reality through hallucinogens. A noted religious philosopher, Huston Smith, sought to discover if psilocybin alone could produce a religious experience. Together with interested staff from Harvard, including the junior lecturer, Timothy ("Tune in. Turn on. Drop out.") Leary, Smith devised an experiment in which Harvard Divinity School students with no previous drug use were invited to volunteer. In a blind study, half of the group was given a placebo of nicotinic acid which merely produces a tingling sensation. The other half was given psilocybin. The experiment took place on Good Friday in the basement of Marsh Chapel as chapel services were being held above. It later became known as "The Good Friday Experiment" or "The Miracle of Marsh Chapel." Their findings were that the half which were given the placebo experienced

---

[445] Ferguson, *Encyclopedia of Mysticism and Mystery Religions*, 135.
[446] Ibid.

boredom while many in the other half reported the most profound religious experience of their lives, a claim which they reaffirmed when interviewed some 25 years later.

Did these intoxicated divinity school students truly encounter "the ultimate?" Most Christians would dismiss this claim.

5. LSD. The man who discovered LSD also assumed that its use was true religion. *The Week* magazine summarizes his conclusion:

> Albert Hofmann believes he gave the world a spiritual gift, says Craig Smith in The New York Times. On a Friday afternoon in April 1943, the Swiss chemist accidentally synthesized some poisonous ergot rye fungus into lysergic acid diethylamide—LSD. Hofmann, who just turned 100, is certain the discovery is no accident. "LSD spoke to me," he says. "He came to me and said, 'You must find me.'" Testing the drug on himself, Hofmann was flooded by technicolor memories of a long-forgotten mystical experience he had had as a child in a Swiss forest. He was soon convinced that LSD could show people "a miraculous, powerful, unfathomable reality." The drug, he says, should not be trifled with. But properly used, it opens a doorway into human perception, so that it's possible to see one's connection to nature and to the entire universe. "It's medicine for the soul," he says. "It's very, very dangerous to lose contact with living nature. In the big cities, there are people who have never seen living nature, all things are products of humans." Hofmann has used LSD dozens of times, but his mysticism no longer needs an artificial boost. "I know LSD; I don't need to take it anymore." On second thought, he might take it one more time: "Maybe when I die."[447]

The celebrated author Aldous (*Brave New World*) Huxley began experimenting with mescaline in the 1950s, later with LSD, resulting in the account of his experiences in his book *The Doors of Perception*. Anticipating Hofmann's final move, Huxley on his deathbed received a final injection of LSD and died under its influence. The point is that pharmacological mysticism is receiving serious attention as true spirituality. If getting high or turned on can be seen as true religion, so can the artificial, psychological catharsis of the Cursillo movement.

6. The Whirling Dervish. But there are other ways of getting high and turning on which do not involve ingesting illicit substances. The

---

[447] *The Week*, January 27, 2006, 10.

physiological effects of spinning, bouncing, hyperventilating, dietary changes, and protracted, rhythmic dancing can all create altered states of consciousness and a heightened state of awareness which have been variously interpreted as religious experiences.

The word "dervish" can refer to a poor man, religious fervor, or a mystic. Though there are various sects of dervishism, the most well-known is probably the "Whirling Dervishes" or Mevlevi, a version of Sufism, which is still practiced in Turkey, Syria, and Egypt. Their distinguishing whirling motion is said to reflect the rotation of the universe, but it also allows them to achieve the altered state of ecstasy, and this state is said to lead to "a full awareness of the divine presence."[448]

The children's game of turning round and round and becoming dizzy is known universally. Spinning is an obvious physiological means to an altered-state of consciousness, which, in the case of dervishism had been supplied with a mythology (replicating the rotation of the universe and becoming aware of the divine presence), and, as a result, has spawned a religion.[449]

7. Chanting and Repetitive Singing. Hyperventilation, the common result of vigorous chanting and repetitive singing, has been discussed in chapter three. Clinical psychologist Margaret Singer relates the demonstration of a "Hoo meditation" by a former follower of Rajneesh:

> He stood with his feet wide apart, his arms above his head, and began to bow at the waist, rapidly with stiff arms, blowing out air as sharply, forcefully, and as fast as he could, turning the heavy puffs into the sound "hoo" while bowing. This was done, he said, until most members fell to the mats on the floor.[450]

The light-headedness experienced during hyperventilation is called "respiratory alkalosis."

> Respiratory alkalosis also causes fainting. People often drop to the floor and are briefly unconscious. While they are unconscious, underbreathing occurs to compensate for the period of overbreathing and to restore the normal acid-base balance of the blood. People awaken limp, exhausted, and aware that they have been through a dramatic and frightening experience.

---

[448] Ferguson, *Encyclopedia of Mysticism and Mystery Religions*, 47.
[449] Some present-day cults also employ spin dancing according to Margaret Singer. Singer, *Cults in Our Midst*, 95-96, 131.
[450] Ibid., 128-129.

Cults, quacks, and manipulators have become aware of the predictable outcomes of hyperventilation—the giddiness, the out-of-control feeling, the possible loss of consciousness, the tingling, and the clenching of fingers and toes. Similarly, they have recognized the impact of immediately reframing the experience. By consciously reframing, or relabeling, the effects, thus confounding individuals' gut-level reactions that something unpleasant has happened, leaders turn a frightening state into a supposedly positive one, telling neophytes, for example, that they are "becoming blissed out,...getting or receiving the spirit,...on the path."[451]

8. Bodily Manipulations. Remarkably, something as common as pressing on the eyes can be interpreted as mystical experience. Margaret Singer cites reports from members of the Divine Light Mission. In dim lighting, the guru would grant "divine light" to individual members by pressing on their eyes until they saw flashes of light. Medically speaking, these flashes were caused by pressure on the optic nerve. But this purely physiological phenomenon was re-cast as a religious experience. She reports that the same members told of being instructed to place their fingers into their ears, pushing in until they heard a buzzing sound. This noise was explained as the sound of Divine Harmony.[452]

9. Hypnosis and Trance. And sometimes the mystical experience can be achieved without any chemical aid or with minimal physical manipulations. Psychological factors alone can produce an altered state of consciousness: euphoria, ecstasy, or catharsis. The altered state of consciousness which is often reinterpreted as mystical religious experience can be achieved through hypnosis or through a trance-like state. Margaret Singer explains:

> Hypnosis is classed as a psychological rather than a physiological method because it is essentially a form of highly focused mental concentration in which one person allows another to structure the object of concentration and simultaneously suspends critical judgment and peripheral awareness. When this method is used in a cultic environment, it becomes a form of psychological manipulation and coercion because the cult leader implants suggestions aimed at his own agenda while the person is in a vulnerable state.

---

[451] Ibid., 129-130.
[452] Ibid., 136.

A trance is a phenomenon in which our consciousness or awareness is modified. Our awareness seems to split as our active critical-evaluative thinking dims, and we slip from an active into a passive-receptive mode of mental processing. We listen or look without reflection or evaluation. We suspend rational analysis, independent judgment, and conscious decision making about what we are hearing or taking in. We lose the boundaries between what we wish were true and what is factual. Imagination and reality intertwine, and our self and the selves of others seem more like one self. Our mental gears shift into receptivity, leaving active mental processing in neutral.[453]

Activities which contribute to stopping thought and escaping reality tend to create the trance-like state. Some religions achieve this through the repetitive chanting of a mantra, rocking, swaying, etc.

10. Zen. Zen is a form of meditation associated with Mahayana Buddhism introduced into China about 1500 years ago. It utilizes the techniques of zazen, a meditation posture, and koan, paradoxical questions and answers which attack rational thinking. Zazen is sometimes called the process of non-thinking.

'If you wish to attain enlightenment, begin at once to practice *zazen*. For this meditation a quiet chamber is necessary, while food and drink must be taken in moderation. Free yourself from all attachments, and bring to rest the ten thousand things. Think of neither good nor evil and judge not right or wrong. Maintain the flow of mind, of will, and of consciousness; bring to an end all desires, all concepts, all judgments. Do not think about how to become a Buddha.'[454]

The koan consist of: "startling verbal methods almost to shock the listener into fresh thought. Paradox for instance...."

Empty-handed I go and yet the spade is in my hands.

I walk on foot, yet am riding on an ox's back.
When I pass over the bridge, look, the water is not flowing, the bridge is flowing.

---

[453] Ibid., 151.
[454] Ferguson, *Encyclopedia of Mysticism and Mystery Religions*, 214.

This is one way of directing attention to the unity of all being. One famous Zen sermon is reminiscent of some words of Jesus: 'If you have a staff I will give you one; if you have not, I will take it away from you.' This is in a sense a denial of the law of non-contradiction. A thing *can* be both A and not A, and the Zen masters are liable to answer Yes or No impartially to the same question.[455]

The psychological techniques of contradictory thoughts are combined with a "process of non-thinking" to create an altered state of consciousness which is interpreted in religious terms.

11. Yoga. Yoga is defined as "a method of discipline and linking oneself to the spirit world."[456] This is accomplished through developing the skill of concentration to the point that one can control or censor all distractions. This skill is only achieved through difficult discipline and rigorous practice, grouped under eight categories:

> First, 'restraints' (*yama*). These are five moral restrictions on actions tolerated by the rest of society: *ahimsa* (not to kill or do violence), *satya* (not to lie or deceive), *asteya* (not to steal), *brahmacarya* (to abstain from sex), *aparigraha* (to avoid avarice). Second, 'disciplines' (*nijama*). These include cleanness of the body, tranquility of mind, asceticism, religious study and the dedication of all actions to God. Third, 'postures' (*asana*). The body must be in a stable and comfortable position. There must be relaxation and the avoidance of physical effort and fatigue: 'Posture becomes perfect when the effort to attain it disappears....' Fourth, 'respiration' (*pranayama*). Breathing should be disciplined, first by prolonging inhalation and exhalation: the irregular breathing of the average man produces a dangerous psychic fluidity. Fifth, withdrawal of sensory activity from external objects (*pratyahara*). Sixth, 'concentration' (*dharana*), fixing the attention on a single point of thought. Seventh, 'meditation' (*dhyana*), 'a current of unified thought, a kind of extension of the concentration on a single point of thought'. Finally, 'union' (*samadhi*).

It hardly needs pointing out that diligent practice of the third through the seventh sets of disciplines described ('posture' or deep relaxation, 'respiration' or hyperventilation, 'withdrawal from sensory activity' or sensory deprivation, and 'concentration' and 'meditation') would be sufficient to cause

---

[455] Ibid., 214-215.
[456] Ibid., 212.

virtually anyone to slip into an altered state of consciousness, with or without the religious context. Once again we find that natural means of achieving an altered state, the extraordinary experience, is combined with a mythology, and the result is another expression of mystical religion.

12. The Mystery Religions. The mystery religions were secret sects of ancient Greece and Rome. They offered a pathway to spiritual experiences not available in the officially-sanctioned religions. Originating in primitive, tribal ceremonies from various parts of the world, these practices and initiation rites were widely available to individuals on a voluntary basis. Though their origins are much older, the mystery religions were most popular in the first three centuries after Christ.

Walter Burkhert, a foremost historian of the Greek religion, describes these mystery religions even while recognizing that their secrecy has left many of their mysteries unrevealed. The resemblance of the expected effect of this mystery religions to the goals of the Cursillo is remarkable: "'something is bound to happen to the soul,' so that initial bewilderment is changed into wonder, and acceptance into sense. In religious terms, mysteries provide an immediate encounter with the divine....In psychological terms, there must have been an experience of the 'other' in a change of consciousness, moving far beyond what could be found in everyday life."[457]

The mystery religions sought to create great emotional upheaval. "The experience is patterned by antithesis, by moving between the extremes of terror and happiness, darkness and light."[458] Those undergoing initiation should "bear up to the first purifications and unsettling events and hope for something sweet and bright to come out of the present anxiety and confusion."[459] Like the Cursillo clausura (or closing ceremonies) "one of the main characteristics of the mysteries is the makarismos, the praise of the blessed status of those who have 'seen' the mysteries. As the initiate is accepted and hailed by a chorus of those who have gone through the same peripeties of experience, his feelings of relief will rise to the heights of exultation."[460]

What techniques were used to create the sense of "something sweet and bright" and "the blessed status of those who have 'seen' the mysteries"? The methods varied, and again, since they were secret, some information is unavailable. But the various initiations included shocking, nighttime practices of candidates being smeared with clay, confronted by priestesses dressed as demons, poisonous snakes, rhythmic dance, shrieks and cries, or being lowered into a pit only to be drenched in the warm blood of a bull agonizing and dying

---

[457] Burkert, Ancient Mystery Cults, 90.
[458] Ibid., 93.
[459] Ibid.
[460] Ibid.

just above. Emerging from the pit, the candidate would be "'adored' by the others, as one who had risen to a superior state, and feelings of liberation and a new life would have been overwhelming by contrast, just because of the horrifying procedure undergone before."[461] "The basic idea of an initiation ritual is generally taken to be that of death and rebirth."[462]

Another possible avenue to enlightenment in the mystery religions was torture. There remains some evidence of mutilation and human sacrifice, though this charge of torture was largely raised by the contemporary opponents of the mystery religions. "Psychological terror, however, is well-attested: 'all those terrible things, panic and shivering and sweat,' to quote Plutarch once more."[463]

Sexuality was another means to achieve the end. Mystery initiations we often filled with sexual symbolism and ritualism, and were often preceded by periods of sexual abstinence. "This would stimulate expectations and attentiveness to certain signals. Sexuality becomes a means for breaking through to some uncommon experience, rather than an end in itself."[464] And drugs likely played their part with suggestions ranging from hallucinogenic drinks, to mushrooms, to a natural form of LSD, and opium. And, of course, wine.

Some ancient witnesses offered their observations regarding the source of these experiences, including:

> a clinical description of ecstasy in the cult of Meter, as seen by a doctor: the *galloi* "are turned on by flute music and gladness of heart [thymedie], or by drunkenness, or by the instigation of those present"—an interesting observation of the interdependence of performers and onlookers. "This madness is divine possession. When they end the state of madness, they are in good spirits, free of sorrow, as if consecrated by initiation to the god." More simple is the account that Aristides Quintilianus, the musicologist, gives of Bacchic initiation; he follows to some extent Aristotle's concept of *katharsis*: "This is the purpose of Bacchic initiation, that the depressive anxiety [*ptoiesis*] of less educated people, produced by their state of life, or some misfortune, be cleared away through the melodies and dances of the ritual in a joyful and playful way." This, then, is a form of psychotherapy that would be compatible even with the latest trends of today....Still more deprecating and purportedly realistic is the explanation given by Livy for the ecstasy and miracles experienced at

---

[461] Ibid., 98.
[462] Ibid., 99.
[463] Ibid., 103.
[464] Ibid., 108.

the Bacchanalia: it was just lack of sleep, he writes, and the wine and the musical sounds and cries throughout the night that stunned people.[465]

Burkhert acknowledges that these means were widely employed, yet he maintains that the mysteries were something more: "This is a collection of stimuli that every rationalist may endorse. But this interpretation closes the door of the secret rather than revealing it."[466]

He concludes that the mystery religions offered an extraordinary experience, the hope of something beyond a drab life:

> It was enough to know that there were doors to a secret that might open up for those who earnestly sought it. This meant that there was a chance to break out of the enclosed and barren ways of predictable existence. Such hopes were attempts to create a context of sense in a banal, depressing, and often absurd world, providing the experience of a great rhythm in which the resonances of the individual psyche could be integrated through an amazing event of *sympatheia*.[467]

Yet what we discover once again is that the employment of psychological and physiological methods produce a predictable breakthrough response which is then supplied with a mythology and reinterpreted as a religion.

13. Contemporary Christian *"Praise and Worship."*

We conclude our survey of mystical religions, that is, altered states of consciousness reinterpreted as religion, with one that is commonly practiced among professing, evangelical Christians, namely the "praise and worship" portion of many church services. Barry Liesch, Professor of Music at Biola University, both describes and defends the "praise and worship" style in his book, *The New Worship*.[468] The model Liesch cites is the five-phased pattern developed by John Wimber and Eddie Espinosa. Espinosa likens this sustained period of singing to "a physical workout. Just as sustained periods of exercise are good for the cardiovascular system, so sustained singing for fifteen to forty minutes is good for worshipers' spiritual systems,"[469] a questionable analogy.

The five phases sound innocuous enough: invitation, engagement, exaltation, adoration, and intimacy. Most troubling, though, is the close

---

[465] Ibid., 113.
[466] Ibid.
[467] Ibid., 114.
[468] Barry Liesch, *The New Worship: Straight Talk on Music and the Church*, Expanded ed. (Grand Rapids: Baker Books, 2001).
[469] Ibid., 54.

attention paid to the psychological impact each of the five phases has upon the worshiper. Liesch offers a chart called "Five-Phase Worship Curve Respects Psychological Dimension," which graphs the rising and falling emotional state of the participants. The invitation phase is an extended call to worship, seeking to draw people into worship with lyrics that are directed mostly to the people. The key is to attain the psychological response from those gathered, "Leaders continue the *invitation phase* until they have made contact with the people and everyone is focused. 'The skillful leader woos the congregation into worship like the patient lover draws the beloved.'"[470]

The engagement phase follows the invitation "as the people begin to draw near to God."[471] It is likened to the "engagement period before marriage, for now we are attentive, serious."[472] The exaltation phase is next in which "the people sing out to the Lord with power." The intent is a rising tide of emotional fervor. Note the careful attention to the part the music plays in shaping the emotional response: "The pitch spans are greater than in the other phases because high notes help bring out a dynamic response and project a sense of God's greatness. If the people stand throughout the invitation, engagement, and exaltation phases, *response will be stronger.*"[473]

After the climax of emotional fervor has been reached, it's time to slow things down and move into the adoration phase. "In the adoration phase the people can be seated, the dynamics subside, the melodic range may reduce to five or six notes, and the key words may be *you* and *Jesus*....Transitions and modulations can be longer and more expressive in the adoration phase. Don't rush it!"[474] Then Liesch makes an astonishing statement: "In the exaltation and adoration phases, two sides of God's character receive expression: his transcendence (majestic greatness) and his immanence (closeness to us). *The expression of both together tends to allay contrived emotion.*"[475] Up to this point the focus of the five-phase pattern is almost exclusively devoted to "contriving" the emotions of the gathered. The whole purpose of the five-phase pattern from beginning to end is to control and shape the emotional response of those assembled.

The last phase is the intimacy phase, "the quietest and most personal of all."[476] And how are the gathered maneuvered into this intimacy? Chiefly by shifting the personal pronouns from "we" to "I" and "me." Of course, the instrumentation must be likewise modified to create the new mood: "The

---

[470] Ibid., 56. It should be noted that *drawing* is a work that is explicitly attributed to God, cf. John 6:44, 12:32.
[471] Ibid.
[472] Ibid.
[473] Ibid., 57, emphasis added.
[474] Ibid., emphasis original.
[475] Ibid., emphasis added.
[476] Ibid.

acoustic guitar could be used to project intimacy. Brushes or no percussion sounds may be most appropriate."[477] The conclusion of this "worship" is to have people stand for a closeout chorus or hymn. The purpose of this song is that it "leads out of intimacy and helps everyone *adjust* to the next event in the service."[478] Once again the main focus is on shifting the emotional state of those in attendance.

To his credit, Liesch does note that some object to this mood music:

> Some critics believe contemporary worship is guilty of promoting manipulative, self-indulgent worship experiences. They object to the use of music to induce, urge, cause, or empower a worship experience—to push people's "worship buzzer"—like a conditioned reflex. Some even object to the concept that music can be used to aid, facilitate, or enhance a worship experience.[479]

One such critic he cites is Harold Best, former dean of Wheaton College's Conservatory of Music, who declares: "'Depending on music to aid, induce, or enhance worship is idolatry dressed up in psycho-aesthetic finery. It confuses the power of music with the presence of God.'"[480] It also places the "worshiper" in the difficult position of experiencing "contrived emotion" and yet falsely thinking it to be a genuine experience of the Divine.

Some time ago I attended a large gathering of evangelicals. The worship leaders distributed a song sheet. One of the songs on the sheet contained the lyrics: "Celebrate Jesus, celebrate." This phrase was repeated several times along with affirmations of Christ's resurrection. But what amazed me was the note at the bottom of this chorus. It read, "Repeat until euphoric" (that is until you are in a happy, giddy mood). I guess I've never seen it stated that obviously before. Here was an instance where large group "praise" music was clearly used to achieve an altered state of consciousness, euphoria, an elevated mood, while at the same time interpreting it as true religion, an encounter with the ultimate. This startling, candid admission demonstrates that much contemporary, evangelical "praise and worship" is simply another expression of one of the three false religions, mysticism.[481]

---

[477] Ibid., 58.
[478] Ibid., emphasis added.
[479] Ibid., 65.
[480] Ibid.
[481] For the proper use of music in worship, see this author's book on worship music selection, *Sing to the Lord a New (Covenant) Song; Thinking about the Songs We Sing to God* (Eugene, OR: Resource Publications, 2009).

The Three False Religions

There are really only three false religions: mysticism, moralism, and magic. Each of these false religions seeks to fulfill a human need. It diagnoses a specific human problem that either creates the need or inhibits its fulfillment. And each religion attempts to contact, influence, or control God (or the Ultimate) in an attempt to satisfy this need.

For *mysticism*, the perceived need is a lack of fulfillment or happiness. The key desire is PLEASURE. The supposed problem is that God is distant and unreachable, so true religion involves experiencing God directly or immediately. God is in a different dimension, and so we must attain an altered state of consciousness through some special, secret knowledge or esoteric insight in order to experience the divine in sustained ecstasy.[482]

For *moralism*, the perceived need is a lack of moral or intellectual completeness. The key desire is a sense of superiority or PRIDE. The apparent problem is that God is righteous and offended by our failures, inadequacies or false beliefs. True religion consists of proper behavior or correct beliefs, those which God approves. God must be placated, appeased, or won over by our better behavior or superior beliefs.

For *magical religion*, the perceived need is a lack of the ability to control our environment, ultimately to control God. The key desire is for POWER. The problem is that God is aloof, unwilling, unable, or unpredictable. God (or our circumstances) must be manipulated, controlled, or co-opted by formulas, rituals, incantations, and/or mind-over-matter/positive thinking.[483]

1. Organized religions (Islam, Buddhism, Hinduism, distorted Christianity, etc.) may contain elements of each of the three religions. And organized religions may have factions within them which are really devoted to one of the three religions (mystics, moralists, or magicians). That's why Christian, Hindu, and Islamic mystics find more in common with each other than with members of their own organized religion, for example, or why the mystics "Diadochus of Photice in the middle of the fifth century AD, and John Climacus in the early seventh century" could recommend "the continual repetition of the name Jesus in prayer"[484] rather than the syllable om as in eastern meditation. It explains why translated episodes of *Veggie Tales* (moralism) are so well received in parts of the Arabic-speaking (moralistic Islam) world. It also explains why the Cursillo method can be adapted to Catholicism, Lutheranism, Anglicanism, Methodism, and Reformed theology.

---

[482] For a critique of evangelicalism as mysticism, see Michael Scott Horton, *In the Face of God* (Nashville: Thomas Nelson, 1997).

[483] For a critique of religion as power in evangelicalism, see Michael Scott Horton, ed., *Power Religion: The Selling Out of the Evangelical Church* (Chicago: Moody Press, 1997).

[484] John Ferguson, *Encyclopedia of Mysticism and Mystery Religions* (New York: Crossroad, 1982), 92.

Cursillo is really an expression of mysticism.[485] In truth, mysticism is its own religion which spans all religions. E. G. Browne writes of the unity of mystical experience, whatever its formal expression:

> There is hardly any soil, be it ever so barren, where Mysticism will not strike root; hardly any creed, however formal, round which it will not twine itself....Wonderfully uniform, too, is its tenor: in all ages, in all countries, in all creeds, whether it comes from the Brahmin sage, the Persian poet, or the Christian quietist, it is in essence an enunciation more or less clear, more or less eloquent, of the aspiration of the soul to cease altogether from self and to be at one with God.[486]

2. Scripture condemns all three of these false religions. Magic, sorcery, divination, and necromancy are all explicitly and universally condemned by God's Word.[487] Moralism is revealed as a sham (Galatians), and Jesus roundly condemned the self-righteous Pharisees. Mysticism is condemned in the rejection of false prophecy: those who erroneously claim to have encountered God and to speak for him.[488]

3. Each of the three false religions is a corruption of some aspect of the biblical faith. Mystics seek experiences similar to those reported in Scripture, though in an unmediated (unapproved) manner. Moralists rightly observe that God is righteous and commands obedience, but make our obedience the means of placating God. Magicians note the presence of biblical rituals (signs and seals), but turn them into means of manipulating God.

4. Biblical Christianity can degenerate into any of these three false religions. Mysticism takes many forms including quietism, Keswick higher-life teaching, and some forms of revivalism and Pentecostalism which stress direct, ecstatic encounters with God. This would, of course, include the subject of this book, the Cursillo method. Examples of Christianity reduced to moralistic religion abound, including theological liberalism, moralistic fundamentalism, and the legalism-lite of evangelicalism's ubiquitous "principles for living." And Christianity as magical religion is found in the Word of Faith movement's "name it-claim it" practice of "positive confession," as well as the various forms of "mind-over-matter" teaching, most notably Norman Vincent Peale's "power of positive thinking" and Robert H. Schuller's "possibility thinking."[489]

---

[485] One could almost imagine the future development of a Jewish or an Islamic Cursillo.
[486] Quoted in Ferguson, *Encyclopedia of Mysticism and Mystery Religions*, 126-127.
[487] Cf. 2 Chronicles 33:6, Galatians 5:20, Revelation 21:8, 15.
[488] Cf. Deuteronomy 18:20.
[489] Robert Schuller reportedly declared the following in a taped message for the Amway Corporation entitled *Possibility Thinking: Goals*, "You don't know what power you have within you!... You make the world into anything you choose. Yes, you can make your world into whatever you want it to be." For a more complete treatment of Robert Schuller, see Henry

5. And it should be noted that, most seriously, in each of these false religions, God becomes the means to a more desirable end, i.e. pleasure, pride, or power (read "idols"). Such blasphemy is a violation of the first commandment and should be exposed as contemptible irreligion. God will not be mocked.

But is This For Real?

How can one determine whether mystical experience is genuine or contrived? Few Christians would accept the legitimacy of LSD religion or the trance of the whirling Dervish. But what about claims of extraordinary experiences among Christian groups like Pentecostals and the Cursillo? Is it possible to distinguish between Christian mysticism and that claimed by other religions? Can one develop criteria to differentiate genuine from merely imagined or contrived extraordinary experiences? Here is where proponents of Christian mysticism run the risk of becoming inextricably lost in one of Calvin's labyrinths, since Scripture provides no such "guidelines." So where do we turn for guidance?

The problem quickly becomes intractable. Who might possess the authority to make such a determination? John Ferguson demonstrates the difficulty:

> How is 'genuine' mystical experience to be identified as opposed to experience that is consciously or unconsciously stimulated?
> Elmer O'Brien has suggested three criteria. First, the experience should be contrary to the subject's fundamental world-view. (Here O'Brien surely underestimates the power of the unconscious in throwing up those things which we have suppressed or repressed precisely because they are contrary to our world-view.) Second, the mystic should be reluctant, so that the experience is not mere wish-fulfillment. (But again the wish may be repressed; and it would be hard to deny the genuineness of some experiences willingly entered into; in other words if reluctance is a test of genuineness, still willingness should not be taken as a test of falsity.) Third, the experience alone gives meaning and consistency to the mystic's doctrines. (This would seem to suggest that only systematic thinkers can have genuine mystical experience.) Many others, including some of the greater mystics, have claimed that true experience is distinguishable from false by its fruits. *In truth there is no infallible test.*

Krabbendam, "Scripture Twisting," in *The Agony of Deceit*, ed. Michael Horton (Chicago: Moody Press, 1990).

Appendix B: Confusing Psychology with Religion

But it is important to see that if all mystical experience is in fact illusory, there are different levels of illusion, and Catherine of Genoa and Teresa de Jesus knew perfectly well the difference between mere hysteria and other sorts of experience.[490]

Apparently *they* can tell the difference; they just cannot tell *us* the difference, which forces us to ask *whether there is any difference.*

Conversions True and Spurious

British evangelical leader and statesman D. Martyn Lloyd-Jones offers helpful counsel in his short book: *Conversions: Psychological and Spiritual.*[491] The monograph is an extended critique of the thesis of William Sargant in his *Battle for the Mind*, namely that all "sudden conversions," political, social, and religious, are the result of physiological and psychological processes. Sargant seeks to demonstrate "how beliefs, whether good or bad, false or true, can be forcibly implanted in the human brain; and how people can be switched to arbitrary beliefs altogether opposed to those previously held."[492]

Though Lloyd-Jones obviously denies (and disproves) that biblical conversions such as on the day of Pentecost in Acts 2 or the conversion of St. Paul are merely psychological events, he does grant that many "conversions" can be created through purely psychological processes:

> Let me begin by saying that, within his own sphere, and speaking purely medically [Lloyd-Jones was formerly a physician], it seems to me that we must grant what Dr. Sargant is saying. The findings from his own cases and those of other similar workers in this field are substantiated facts and we do not dispute them.[493]

The main problem with Sargant's thesis, according to Lloyd-Jones, is that he ignores the supernatural aspect of Christianity:

> To sum up, then, the fallacy which seems to run right through the book, *Battle for the Mind*, is that the Person and work of the Holy Spirit are entirely overlooked. It is assumed throughout that the history of the Church can be explained solely in terms of human activity. As we

---

[490] John Ferguson, *Encyclopedia of Mysticism and Mystery Religions* (New York: Crossroad, 1982), 126, emphasis added.
[491] D. Martyn Lloyd-Jones, *Conversions: Psychological and Spiritual* (London: Inter-Varsity Fellowship, 1959).
[492] Ibid., 9.
[493] Ibid., 12.

have seen, the very facts of Church history utterly disprove this assertion.[494]

Lloyd-Jones then turns to the positive value of Sargant's study, a caution for Christians to avoid the use of the questionable, emotionally-manipulative techniques which Sargant highlights. Lloyd-Jones grants that various methods and means can influence the human mind and that primitive religions abound with such emotional techniques such as dancing, drumming, and rhythmic singing or chanting. But he also grants that sometimes well-intended evangelicals have been guilty of something similar.

> As I see the situation, we have to admit that wrong tendencies *can* develop and spread even amongst those who are sincerely desirous to spread the true gospel. I think that in sheer honesty we must take note that some of these tendencies have crept into evangelical circles in the past. Let us examine some examples.
>
> I am second to no-one in my admiration of the great Jonathan Edwards and his preaching; yet it does seem to me that Edwards in his preaching concerning hell went at times well beyond what he was warranted to do and to say by Holy Scripture. He allowed his imagination to run riot. Thereby he began to do something closely akin, to put it mildly, to that which is described by Dr. Sargant in his book. Again, we have the facts concerning George Whitefield, who probably was one of the greatest preachers the Church has ever known since the apostles. Yet I would have to admit that even Whitefield occasionally exceeded his warrant. I mean that he allowed his own eloquence and his own imagination to run away with him. He reached a point at which he was not so much presenting the message of the gospel as producing an oratorical, not to say a psychological, effect upon his congregation.[495]

Lloyd-Jones then relates the account of a contemporary spell-binding preacher who created an immediate emotional affect on his congregation.

> What could we say about an occurrence such as that? I would unhesitatingly condemn *that* kind of preaching. None can deny, surely, that at that point the influence was almost purely *psychological*, that the congregation had ceased to be aware of the truth, and that their minds had been so gripped by this graphic picture that they were

---

[494] Ibid., 31-32.
[495] Ibid., 33-34, emphasis original.

acting almost automatically. At this point it is the 'flesh' that is operating rather than the 'Spirit.'

We must therefore start with this admission, that though our doctrine may be right and true, we may very well transgress and expose ourselves to the kind of criticism offered by Dr. Sargant by adopting—even with good intentions—wrong and false methods.[496]

Lloyd-Jones raises the concern of seemingly spurious conversions, and the tendency of the psychological approach to create them.

Another question, I think, which forces us to examine ourselves in the light of Dr. Sargant's thesis, is the so-called 'temporary results' of evangelistic campaigns. We must note the discrepancy between the large numbers that go forward at the appeal and the comparatively small numbers that really join and remain in the Church. Now that, again, is a fact—a phenomenon—which we must investigate. It is not enough simply to say, 'Ah, but look at those who did stick.' That is all right; but what has happened to the others? What at the outset *did* happen to them? It is something which we must explain....

I feel that we must be concerned about this for three main reasons. The first is that, if our methods are wrong at these points, we open the door to the very kind of criticism that is being offered by Dr. Sargant. That of itself would be a very serious thing. But that is not my only reason. To me it is not even the most pressing one. Much more important is that fact that such wrong methods are un-scriptural, that they bring the gospel into disrepute, and that they allow the man who is outside the Church to scoff. He comments, 'This is all psychology; you can see it happening at the time; and look at what happens afterwards!' In such a manner the gospel is discredited. The most serious reason, however, which should impel us to examine ourselves is that such tendencies and use of techniques imply a lack of faith. Over-attention to techniques and methods, I would say, is indicative always of a lack of faith in the work of the Holy Spirit.[497]

Lloyd-Jones then offers three helpful guidelines to avoid these dangers of bringing discredit upon the gospel and creating false (purely psychological) conversions.

---

[496] Ibid., 35, emphasis original.
[497] Ibid., 36-37, emphasis original.

> The first consideration is that there must be no divorce between the message we give and the methods we use. Surely, all must agree that our methods as well as our message are to be controlled by the New Testament and its teaching?[498]

He cites 1 Corinthians 2:1-5:

> And I, brethren, when I came to you, came not with excellency of speech or of wisdom, declaring unto you the testimony of God. For I determined not to know any thing among you, save Jesus Christ, and him crucified. And I was with you in weakness, and in fear, and in much trembling. And my speech and my preaching was not with enticing words of man's wisdom, but in demonstration of the Spirit and of power: That your faith should not stand in the wisdom of men, but in the power of God. (KJV)

To which Lloyd-Jones observes:

> Here the great apostle goes out of his way to explain to us that he deliberately rejected certain methods, and he did so in order that it might be clear to everybody that the results were not of man but of God. He did everything 'in demonstration of the Spirit and of power'. He deliberately did not use 'enticing words of man's wisdom'. In other words, the apostle deliberately avoided what he knew would appeal to the congregation, what they liked and what they were accustomed to. He carefully avoided the method of the Greek rhetoricians and philosophers. He became a 'fool', he tells us, and he did it of set purpose. In this statement we have the apostolic pattern and the apostolic authority for saying that our methods must be controlled in a similar manner, and that always it must be 'in demonstration of the Spirit and of power'. Is it not true to say that some have been guilty of giving a message which is controlled by Holy Scripture, while at the same time arguing that any method that the world finds to be successful may be employed, whether or not it is in keeping with New Testament principles? Thereby, I say, we open the door widely to the kind of criticism that we have in the book *Battle for the Mind*. In reply to such a warning, people often will ask: 'But why should not the Holy Spirit make use of these modern techniques? Why set them in opposition to one another?' The answer is that the apostle Paul would never have argued like that, but

---

[498] Ibid., 37.

Appendix B: Confusing Psychology with Religion 261

deliberately avoided all that can be subsumed under the heading 'man's wisdom'. He *could* have argued in that manner about the use of philosophy and rhetoric, but deliberately did not do so.[499]

Lloyd-Jones's second guideline to avoid the dangers of confusing merely psychological conversions with the genuine work of the Holy Spirit is to steer clear of the use of *any* psychological techniques.

> In the second place I think we must avoid anything that leads to a suspicion that in evangelistic activities we are 'conditioning' people in a psychological manner. We must exclude anything which opens the door to criticism of the type we have been considering. It is, of course, not the criticism which is important to avoid, but the use of any method which God cannot approve. This again suggests that we must avoid any deliberate use of 'techniques' as aids to the gospel.[500]

He cites the frequency of the use of the word "technique" in Sargant's book, and notes:

> Naturally, if what you desire is to produce *psychological* results then, of necessity, you will have to employ the proper psychological techniques. But I am arguing that we are not to do so if we really believe in the work of the Holy Spirit. We are to present the truth, trusting to the Holy Spirit to apply it. I would urge, therefore, that on scriptural grounds we must not of set purpose decide to employ techniques. That is to go over to the side of, and to the use of, psychology.[501]

Lloyd-Jones emphasizes that the gospel must be primarily directed to the mind.

---

[499] Ibid., 37-38, emphasis original.
[500] Ibid., 38-39.
[501] Ibid., 39, emphasis original. It should be noted that the Cursillo is purely technique. In the words of American Cursillo leader, Al Blatnik, "It may have seemed to you something that was just thrown together and just happened to 'jell' because a group of good fellows were [sic] there and because the Holy Spirit made his presence felt. There were [sic] a group of good fellows there, and the Holy Spirit certainly made His presence felt. But something thrown together, it was not! The weekend is the result of long years of work, experience and prayer. The psychology involved, the schedule, order of talks and events, and the content are carefully planned. Nothing is left to chance." (Blatnik, *Your Fourth Day*, 25) Likewise Reformed Cursillo leader Roderick Jackson stated, "Everything that is humanly possible, from the best insights of psychology, pedagogy and group dynamics to the clearest understanding of Scripture is put together in an orderly sequence to achieve the aims of the Cursillo." (Jackson, "A Handbook for Leaders in the Cursillo Movement for the Reformed Church in America," 6.)

> Another important principle is that in presenting the Christian gospel we must never, in the first place, make a *direct* approach either to the emotions or to the will. The emotions and the will should always be influenced through the mind. Truth is intended to come to the *mind*. The normal course is for the emotions and the will to be affected by the truth after it has first entered and gripped the mind. It seems to me that this is a principle of Holy Scripture. The approach to the emotions and the will should be *indirect*. Still less should we ever bring any *pressure* to bear upon either the emotions or the will. We are to 'plead' with men but never to bring pressure. We are to 'beseech', but we are never to browbeat. This, it seems to me, is a vital distinction which every preacher and missioner must always bear in mind.[502]

The reason for all of this is apparent:

> I would affirm that much of the modern approach to evangelism, with its techniques and methods, is unnecessary if we *really* believe in the doctrine of the Holy Spirit and His application of God's message. I suggest that our 'techniques' and our 'mechanics' actually divert the attention of people from *the truth of the message* to some lower, particular, immediate and practical action which may have the opposite effect from what is intended. The point I am making is that it is surely our business to avoid anything which produces a merely *psychological* condition rather than a *spiritual* condition.[503]

The following statement is directly applicable to those who promote the Cursillo method:

> In other words, I am suggesting that this book by Dr. Sargant, which has focused attention on the psychological element which exists in religious work as well as in politics, does bring us face to face with the questionable nature of the methods used by some well-meaning people and warns of the danger which is inherent in the increasing tendency to employ various planned 'techniques.'[504]

Lloyd-Jones concludes with a final challenge, a question that much of the evangelical church should be asking today.

---

[502] Ibid, 39, emphasis original.
[503] Ibid., 39-40, emphasis original.
[504] Ibid., 40.

Finally, we must face a radical question. Are we to be primarily and almost exclusively concerned with evangelistic campaigns and with the attempt to make them more efficient by new methods and techniques? Or should we not concentrate more, as the Church has done throughout the centuries, upon praying for, and laying the basis of Christian instruction for, revival as it is described in the Bible? Should we not pray with the greatest earnestness for a visitation of God's Holy Spirit both upon the Church and upon ourselves as individuals? The biblical rule has not been abrogated even in 'this twentieth century' and still is 'Not by might, nor by power, but by my Spirit, saith the Lord of hosts.'[505]

---

[505] Ibid.

BIBLIOGRAPHY

Araneta, Antonio S. *Inside the Cursillo.* S.l.: s.n., 1970.
Ayella, Marybeth F. *Insane Therapy: Portrait of a Psychotherapy Cult.* Philadelphia: Temple University Press, 1998.
Azurdia, Arturo G. III. *Spirit Empowered Preaching: Involving the Holy Spirit in Your Ministry.* Fearn, Ross-Shire, Great Britain: Mentor/Christian Focus Publications, 1998.
Blatnik, Al. *Your Fourth Day: For the New Cursillista.* Dallas: National Ultreya Publications, 1973.
Bonnin, Eduardo. *Cursillos in Christianity: The How and the Why.* Dallas: National Ultreya Publications, 1981.
Bonnín, Eduardo, Bernardo Vadell, and Francisco Forteza. *Structure of Ideas: (Vertebration).* Dallas: Ultreya Press.
Boyd, Kevin R. "Decently De Colores: A Reformed Evaluation of the Cursillo Movement in the Presbyterian Church" D.Min. diss., Austin Presbyterian Theological Seminary, 1998.
Burkert, Walter. *Ancient Mystery Cults.* Cambridge, MA: Harvard University Press, 1987.
Calvin, John, *The Bondage and Liberation of the Will: A Defense of the Orthodox Doctrine of Human Choice against Pighius.* Texts and Studies in Reformation and Post-Reformation Thought, vol. 2. Edited by A. N. S. Lane, translated by Graham I. Davies. Grand Rapids, MI: Baker Books, 1996.
_____. *Institutes of the Christian Religion.* The Library of Christian Classics, vol. 20-21. Edited by John Thomas McNeill, translated by Ford Lewis Battles. Philadelphia: Westminster Press, 1960.
Capõ Bosch, Juan. *Lower Your Nets.* S.l.: s.n., 1965.
Capo, Juan. *The Group Reunion: Theory and Practice.* Dallas: National Cursillo Center United States National Secretariat, 1982.
Capo, Juan, and National Seminar for Diocesan Priest Directors. *The Cursillo, Yesterday and Today.* Dallas: National Cursillo Center, 1974.
Clark, Stephen B., and Ralph C. Martin. *The Cursillo Method: The Purpose of the Movement.* Dallas: The National Cursillo Center, 1969.
Cursillos in Christianity in the United States of America. *Pilgrim's Guide.* Dallas: National Cursillo Movement, 1994.
DeTar, John Hensley, and Thomas M. Manion. *To Deceive...The Elect.* Reno, NV: Athanasius Press, 1966.
Dragostin, Sigmund. "All That Glistens Isn't: A Look at the Cursillo Exercise." *Una sancta* 23 (1966): 44-53.
_____. "The Cursillo as a Social Movement." In *Catholics/U.S.A.; Perspectives on Social Change,* ed. William Thomas Liu and Nathaniel J. Pallone, 479-489. New York: John Wiley & Sons, Inc., 1970.

Eby, David. *Power Preaching for Church Growth*. Fearn, Ross-Shire, Great Britain: Mentor/Christian Focus Publications, 1996.
Edwards, Jonathan. *A Treatise Concerning Religious Affections in Three Parts*. Edited by John E. Smith. Vol. 2 of *The Works of Jonathan Edwards*, edited by Perry Miller. New Haven: Yale University Press, 1959.
Enroth, Ronald M. *Churches That Abuse*. Grand Rapids: Zondervan, 1992.
Ferguson, John. *Encyclopedia of Mysticism and Mystical Religion*. New York: Crossroad, 1982.
Garber, Kent. "Explaining the Oracle's Visions." *US News & World Report*. November 26/December 3, 2007.
Gilmore, Richard, and Janine R. Gilmore. *Sponsorship: The Emmaus Library*. Nashville: Upper Room Books, 1999.
Groothuis, Douglas R. *Unmasking the New Age*. Downer's Grove, IL: InterVarsity Press, 1986.
Hassan, Steven. *Combating Cult Mind Control*. Rochester, VT: Park Street Press, 1988.
Hervás, Juan. *Questions and Problems Concerning Cursillos in Christianity*. Tucson, AZ: Ultreya Publication for Euramerica S.A. - Madrid Spain, 1963.
_____. *Cursillos in Christianity, Instrument of Christian Renewal*. 2nd ed. Madrid: Ultreya Publications for Euramerica, 1967.
_____. *Leaders' Manual for Cursillos in Christianity*. 3rd ed. English trans. of the Fourth Spanish Edition by Collice H. Portnoff and Maria J. Escudero. Dallas: National Ultreya Publications of the United States National Secretariat, 1967.
Hoekema, Anthony A. *The Four Major Cults*. Grand Rapids: William B. Eerdmans Publishing Co., 1963.
Horton, Michael Scott. *In the Face of God*. Nashville: Thomas Nelson, 1997.
Horton, Michael Scott, ed. *The Agony of Deceit*. Chicago: Moody Press, 1990.
_____. *Power Religion: The Selling Out of the Evangelical Church* Chicago: Moody Press, 1997.
Hughes, Gerry, ed. *Our Fourth Day for the New Cursillista*. Dallas: National Ultreya Publications, 1985.
Jackson, Roderic Douglas. "A Handbook for Leaders in the Cursillo Movement for the Reformed Church in America." D-Min. Diss., North American Baptist Seminary, 1981.
Janov, Arthur. *The Primal Scream: Primal Therapy: The Cure for Neurosis.*. New York: Dell Publishing Co., 1970, Laurel Edition, 1972.
Jones, Robert D. *Forgiveness: "I Just Can't Forgive Myself!"* Phillipsburg, NJ: P & R Publishing, 2000.
Lackner, Paul. M. *The Theology of the Laity in the Cursillo Movement and Its Comparison with Vatican II and the Theology of John Paul II*. Pittsburgh: Typecraft Press, Inc., 1995.

Langone, Michael, D., ed. *Recovery from Cults: Help for Victims of Psychological and Spiritual Abuse*. New York: W.W. Norton & Co., 1993.

Lieberman, Morton A., Irvin D. Yalom, and Matthew B. Miles. *Encounter Groups: First Facts*. New York: Basic Books, 1973.

Liesch, Barry. *The New Worship: Straight Talk on Music and the Church*, Expanded ed., Grand Rapids: Baker Books, 2001.

Lifton, Robert Jay. *Thought Control and the Psychology of Totalism: The Study of Brainwashing in China*. New York: W.W. Norton & Co., 1961. Reprint, Chapel Hill, NC: University of North Carolina Press, 1989.

Lloyd-Jones, D. Martyn, *Conversions: Psychological and Spiritual*, London: Inter-Varsity Fellowship, 1959.

Luther, Martin. *The Bondage of the Will. A New Translation of De Servo Arbitrio (1525), Martin Luther's Reply to Erasmus of Rotterdam*. Translated by J. I. Packer and O. R. Johnston. Westwood, NJ: Fleming H. Revell, 1957.

Main, Robert L. *Encountering Christ: Lay Witness, One Key to Renewal*. Nashville: Tidings, 1970.

Marcoux, Marcene. *Cursillo, Anatomy of a Movement: The Experience of Spiritual Renewal*. New York: Lambeth Press, 1982.

Martin, Walter R. *The Kingdom of the Cults*. Minneapolis: Bethany House, 1982.

McDowell, Virginia H. *Re-Creating: The Experience of Life-Change and Religion*. Boston: Beacon Press, 1978.

Murray, Iain Hamish. *The Invitation System*. Edinburgh: The Banner of Truth Trust, 1973.

_____. *Revival and Revivalism: The Making and Marring of American Evangelicalism 1750-1858*. Edinburgh: Banner of Truth Trust, 1994.

The National Cursillo Center. *The Fundamental Ideas of the Cursillo Movement*. Dallas: National Ultreya Publications, 1974.

The National Secretariat of the Cursillo Movement in the United States. *The Cursillo Movement: What is It?* Dallas: The National Cursillo Center, 1995.

_____. *The Three Days: A General Commentary on the Lay Talks of the Cursillo Weekend*. Dallas: National Ultreya Publications, 1984.

The National Secretariat of the Cursillo Movement in the United States, and Gerald P. Hughes. *The Cursillo Movement's Leaders' Manual*. Dallas: Office of the National Secretariat, 1985.

Nichols, Michael P., and Melvin Zax. *Catharsis in Psychotherapy*. New York: Gardiner Press, 1977.

O'Sullivan, Ralph G. "Structure, Function, and Cognitive Development in Cursillo: An Interactionist Analysis." *Sociological Spectrum* 8, no. 3 (1988): 257-275.

_____. "Climbing Jacob's Ladder: Symbolic Renunciation, Reference-Group Identification, and Status Mobility in Cursillo." *Sociological Spectrum* 9, no. 3 (1989): 329-342.

_____. "Cursillo in Social Movement Literature." *Free Inquiry in Sociology* 25, no. 2 (1997): 131-135.

_____. "Bill W. Meets the Spanish Armada: Sinners' and Saints' Retold Epiphanies from A.A. to Cursillo" *Free Inquiry in Sociology* 27, no. 1 (1999): 27-33.

Packard, Vance. *The Hidden Persuaders.* Brooklyn: Ig Publishing, 2007.

Powlison, David. *God's Love: Better Than Unconditional.* Phillipsburg, NJ: P & R Publishing, 2001.

Prochaska, James O. *Systems of Psychotherapy: A Transtheoretical Analysis.* Homewood, IL: The Dorsey Press, 1979.

Reilly, Ralph T. "Is the Cursillo Movement Winding Down?" *U.S. Catholic.* January, 1980, 25-30.

Rogers, Carl R. *Carl Rogers on Encounter Groups.* New York: Harrow Books/Harper & Row, 1970.

Rohloff, Ivan J. *The Origins and Development of Cursillo (1939-1973).* Dallas: National Ultreya Publications of the United States National Secretariat, 1976.

Rydholm, Daniel C. "Theology and Methodology in the American Episcopal Cursillo Movement." Unpublished manuscript. Berkeley, CA: Spiritual Counterfeits Project, 1987.

Sargant, William. *Battle for the Mind: A Physiology of Conversion and Brain-Washing.* New York: Doubleday, 1957. Reprint, Cambridge, MA: Malor Books, 1997.

Schein, Edgar H. *Coercive Persuasion.* New York: W.W. Norton, 1971.

Singer, Margaret Thaler, and Lalich, Janja. *"Crazy" Therapies: What are They? Do They Work?* San Francisco: Jossey-Bass Publishers, 1996.

Singer, Margaret Thayler, with Janja Lalich. *Cults in Our Midst: The Hidden Menace in Our Everyday Lives.* San Francisco: Jossey-Bass Publishers, 1995.

Sproul, R. C. *Willing to Believe: The Controversy over Free Will.* Grand Rapids, MI: Baker Books, 1997.

Vitz, Paul C. *Psychology as Religion: The Cult of Self-Worship.* 2nd ed. Grand Rapids, MI: William B. Eerdmans Publishing Co., 1977.

Wells, David F. *The Search for Salvation: Issues in Contemporary Theology.* Downers Grove, IL: InterVarsity Press, 1978.

_____. *Turning to God: Biblical Conversion in the Modern World.* Grand Rapids, MI: Baker Book House, 1989.

_____. *No Place for Truth, or, Whatever Happened to Evangelical Theology?* Grand Rapids, MI: W.B. Eerdmans Pub. Co., 1993.

_____. *God in the Wasteland: The Reality of Truth in a World of Fading Dreams.* Grand Rapids, MI: W.B. Eerdmans Pub. Co., 1994.

_____. *The Bleeding of the Evangelical Church.* Edinburgh: Banner of Truth Trust, 1995.

Wood, Robert. *The Early History of the Walk to Emmaus.* Nashville: Upper Room Books, 2001.

Wood, Robert and Marie Livingston Roy. *Day Four: The Pilgrim's Continued Journey.* Nashville: The Upper Room, 1986.

Zablocki, Benjamin D., and Thomas Robbins, eds. *Misunderstanding Cults: Searching for Objectivity in a Controversial Field.* Toronto: University of Toronto Press Inc., 2001.

Brian V. Janssen has been pastor of the First Presbyterian (PCA) Church of Hospers, Iowa since 1986. A graduate of Wheaton College and Trinity Evangelical Divinity School, Brian received the Doctor of Ministry degree in 2007 from Covenant Theological Seminary in St. Louis. The focus of his dissertation was on the long-term effects of the Dutch Reformed Cursillo in Northwest Iowa. He has been married to Susanne for over 25 years, and together they have three children: David, Kristin and Jonathan. You can contact him at pastorbvj@gmail.com.

Also by Brian Janssen:

Sing to the Lord a New (Covenant) Song: Thinking about the Songs We Sing to God

[Forthcoming]

ChurchIsFun.com? Renewing Our Vision for the Church
Christ More Excellent: The Better Signs of Jesus

www.ingramcontent.com/pod-product-compliance
Lightning Source LLC
Chambersburg PA
CBHW050434240426
43661CB00055B/2376